Introducing English for Sp
Purposes

Introducing English for Specific Purposes presents the key concepts and practices of ESP in a modern, balanced, and comprehensive way. This book defines ESP and shows how the approach plays a crucial role in the world of English language teaching. Explaining how needs analysis, language and learning objectives, materials and methods, and evaluation combine to form the four main pillars of ESP, the book includes:

- practical examples that illustrate how the core theories and practices of ESP can be applied in real-world academic and occupational settings;
- discussion of some of the most hotly debated issues in ESP;
- insights into how ESP courses can be organized and integrated to form a complete program;
- reflection boxes, practical tasks, extension research questions, and resources for further reading in each chapter.

Introducing English for Specific Purposes serves as an ideal textbook for graduate and advanced undergraduate students studying courses on English for Specific Purposes or English for Academic Purposes, as part of degrees in English for Specific Purposes, Education, ELT, Applied Linguistics, TESOL or TEFL. This comprehensive publication is also an invaluable reference resource for pre-service and in-service teachers of ESP, and for English program managers and administrators.

Laurence Anthony is Professor of Applied Linguistics at the Faculty of Science and Engineering, Waseda University, Japan. He has served as Director of the Center for English Language Education in Science and Engineering (CELESE), and has created large-scale ESP programs in academia and industry for over 25 years.

Routledge Introductions to English for Specific Purposes

Series Editors: Brian Paltridge and Sue Starfield

Routledge Introductions to English for Specific Purposes provide a comprehensive and contemporary overview of various topics within the area of English for specific purposes, written by leading academics in the field. Aimed at postgraduate students in applied linguistics, English language teaching and TESOL, as well as pre- and in-service teachers, these books outline the issues that are central to understanding and teaching English for specific purposes, and provide examples of innovative classroom tasks and techniques for teachers to draw on in their professional practice.

Brian Paltridge is Professor of TESOL at the University of Sydney. He has taught English as a second language in Australia, New Zealand and Italy and has published extensively in the areas of academic writing, discourse analysis and research methods. He is editor emeritus for the journal *English for Specific Purposes* and co-edited the *Handbook of English for Specific Purposes* (Wiley, 2013).

Sue Starfield is a Professor in the School of Education and Director of The Learning Centre at the University of New South Wales. Her research and publications include tertiary academic literacies, doctoral writing, writing for publication, identity in academic writing and ethnographic research methods. She is a former editor of the journal *English for Specific Purposes* and co-editor of the *Handbook of English for Specific Purposes* (Wiley, 2013).

Titles in this series

Introducing Genre and English for Specific Purposes
Sunny Hyon

Introducing Course Design and English for Specific Purposes
Lindy Woodrow

Introducing English for Specific Purposes
Laurence Anthony

For more information on this series visit www.routledge.com/series/RIESP

Introducing English for Specific Purposes

Laurence Anthony

Routledge
Taylor & Francis Group
LONDON AND NEW YORK

First published 2018
by Routledge
2 Park Square, Milton Park, Abingdon, Oxon OX14 4RN

and by Routledge
711 Third Avenue, New York, NY 10017

Routledge is an imprint of the Taylor & Francis Group, an informa business

British Library Cataloguing-in-Publication Data
A catalogue record for this book is available from the British Library

Library of Congress Cataloging-in-Publication Data
Names: Anthony, Laurence, author.
Title: Introducing English for specific purposes / Laurence Anthony.
Description: London ; New York : Routledge, [2018] | Series: Routledge introductions to English for specific purposes | Includes bibliographical references and index.
Identifiers: LCCN 2017056550 | ISBN 9781138936645 (hardcover : alk. paper) | ISBN 9781138936652 (softcover : alk. paper) | ISBN 9781351031189 (ebook)
Subjects: LCSH: English language—Study and teaching—Foreign speakers. | English language—Business English—Study and teaching. | English language—Technical English—Study and teaching. | Curriculum planning.
Classification: LCC PE1128.A2 A56 2018 | DDC 420.1/47—dc23
LC record available at https://lccn.loc.gov/2017056550

ISBN: 978-1-138-93664-5 (hbk)
ISBN: 978-1-138-93665-2 (pbk)
ISBN: 978-1-351-03118-9 (ebk)

Typeset in Sabon
by Apex CoVantage, LLC

MIX
Paper from responsible sources
FSC® C013056
FSC www.fsc.org

Printed and bound in Great Britain by
TJ International Ltd, Padstow, Cornwall

Contents

Figures

Tables

Acknowledgments

This book could not have been completed without the incredible support of the series editors, Brian Paltridge and Sue Starfield, and the amazing editorial staff at Routledge. From the original drafting of the book proposal, through the writing of the various chapters, to the final editing and revision process, I cannot thank them enough for their help and advice.

I would like to give special thanks to my beautiful wife, Maki, and my two fantastic children, May and Richard. They have not only forgiven me for locking myself away as I wrote this book, but they have been a constant source of support and encouragement from the beginning to the end of this writing endeavor.

Introduction

How to use this book

In this book, I hope to provide you with a contemporary and comprehensive view of English for Specific Purposes (ESP). In simple terms, ESP can be defined as follows:

> English for Specific Purposes (ESP) is an approach to language teaching that targets the current and/or future academic or occupational needs of learners, focuses on the necessary language, genres, and skills to address these needs, and assists learners in meeting these needs through the use of general and/or discipline-specific teaching materials and methods.

Of course, at this point, you may not understand all of these concepts. For example, how might academic needs differ from occupational needs? What are the differences between language, genres, and skills? In what ways might general teaching materials and methods differ from those used in specific field? This book sets out to not only provide you with answers to these questions, but also help you apply that knowledge in your own studies and teaching.

Target readers

If you are currently studying a course in applied linguistics or Teaching English to Speakers of Other Languages (TESOL), this book should provide you with useful information about ESP that will help you later in your career when you will need to decide on course designs, select teaching materials and methods, and evaluate learners in the classroom. If you have already stepped out into the world of language teaching and are currently in pre-service training, the book will not only provide you with a framework for your teaching, but also give you immediate and practical advice as you get ready for your first classes. On the other hand, if you are already a practicing teacher, this book can serve as a useful in-service training guide that introduces you to some innovative materials and methods, and explains how ESP principles can improve your effectiveness both inside and outside the classroom.

Assumptions

When writing this book, I made the following assumptions about the background and experience you might have. If you match these assumptions, you should find the contents are closely aligned with your needs and interests. But, if you don't quite match my intended audience, I think you will still find plenty of useful information that can help you.

First, I assumed that you prefer reading a book that is written in clear, direct, friendly, and accessible language. By writing the book in this way, I hope that it can cater to a mixed audience of native, second language, and foreign language speakers. Second, I assumed that you have little or no prior experience of teaching English, although I suspect that you might have some basic knowledge of language and teaching theory. As a result, I will always try to clarify how the points made in the book relate directly to real learners and classroom settings. If you have had some teaching experience, the material in this book will allow you to reflect on that experience and improve on what you already do well. Third, I assumed that you are likely to use the book either as a part of a course (e.g. Master of Arts in Teaching English as a Foreign Language [MA TEFL]) or for self-study professional development. If you are using the book as a course book, you should probably proceed through it in a linear fashion. But, if you are reading it for professional development, you are welcome to pick and choose the most relevant chapters for your current needs and return to other chapters later. Each chapter has been written to logically follow on from the preceding chapter but is also written to be completely self-contained. Finally, I assumed that you might not necessarily have access to a good university library or a fast Internet connection. As a result, even though some of the tasks and resources in the book might refer to library or online materials, they should be considered optional.

Overview of the contents

In Section 1 of the book, I'll explain the background to ESP. First, I'll describe the history of ESP and discuss how it is situated within English Language Teaching (ELT). Next, I'll describe how ESP addresses many of the challenges that language learners face in our increasingly globalized world. Then, I'll introduce the four key 'pillars' of ESP: needs analysis, learning objectives, materials and methods, and evaluation.

In Section 2 of the book, I'll explain the theories and practices that form the basis of the four key 'pillars' of ESP. First, I'll discuss the importance of needs analysis and explain some of the different ways that a needs analysis can be conducted. Next, I'll show how learning objectives can be expressed through effective course and program design. Then, I'll discuss the design of useful materials and methods for the ESP classroom. Finally, I'll explain the importance of evaluation in ESP. Here, I'll offer some effective ways to evaluate learners, and also discuss how administrators might evaluate the performance of teachers and the ESP course or program as a whole.

In Section 3 of the book, I'll explain how ESP can be applied in real-world settings. First, I'll explain some of the different ways in which ESP can be implemented in different settings frequently encountered by ESP instructors. Next, I'll discuss some of the main challenges that instructors face when teaching ESP in isolation or within an ESP program, and explain how you might address these challenges through actions that lead to change. Finally, I'll conclude the book by giving my thoughts on the future direction of ESP.

Features of the chapters

Each chapter of the book opens with a brief statement describing the importance of the topic, a short review of what will be covered in the chapter, and an explanation of what you should have learned by the end of the chapter. Then, in the body of the chapter, the main topic is discussed with reference to past and present theories and best practices in the field.

Reflections

Each chapter contains an opening and closing "Reflection" task. The opening "Reflection" task is designed to help you relate your current knowledge and/or experience of language teaching to the topic at hand. The closing "Reflection" task, on the other hand, is designed to help you reflect on what you have learned in the chapter and consider how you might apply the material in your current and/or future teaching.

Tasks

In the main body of each chapter, one or more optional tasks are presented that are designed to help you contextualize the material. Sometimes the tasks ask you to apply the ideas in a familiar context, or imagine what you would do in a new teaching situation. Other tasks ask you to carry out a small pilot project based on the material in the chapter, or reflect on how the ideas in the chapter might influence your teaching of learners.

Contentious issues

Researchers in the field of ESP hold many different views that sometimes lead to misunderstandings and controversies. This section looks at a contentious issue related to the topic of the chapter that has caused much discussion in ESP. After considering the different perspectives, you should be in a good position to form your own opinion about the issue and be able to present that to others.

Research ideas

Students are often looking for ideas for mini-projects and final thesis topics. This section presents some suggestions for small- and/or large-scale research projects related to the topic that are likely to be of interest to research scholars, learners, teachers, and ESP program administrators.

Further reading and resources

Each chapter finishes with a list of useful readings, websites, and other resources that can help you expand your understanding of the chapter material.

How best to use the book

Students

I suggest that you read each chapter of the book in a linear fashion, pausing at the reflection boxes, and coming up with answers (perhaps in your head) before proceeding to the next section. These reflections will help you understand and remember the material far better than if you just read the chapters in a passive way. As you study each chapter, try to relate the points to your own target teaching context, thinking what the challenges might be and how you would overcome them. Also, if you have the available resources and if time permits, try to complete some of the optional tasks as they will certainly help you deepen your understanding of the material.

Teachers

If you plan to use the book as an in-class core textbook, I recommend that you use the opening reflection box for initial class or group discussions to help orient the learners to the topic. The "Contentious Issues" section might also serve as a useful platform for discussion, but I suggest this is introduced toward the end of a session or perhaps assigned as a homework activity. The tasks presented throughout the chapters are narrowly scoped and have been designed so that they can be completed either through individual, independent work or as pair/group activities. As a result, they can serve as useful in-class activities or be assigned as homework. The suggestions presented in the "Research Ideas" section, on the other hand, are quite broad in scope and may serve as possible topics for end-of-course assignments or even starting points for thesis projects.

If you plan to use the book as a reference resource, I recommend that you encourage learners to consult the additional resources at the end of each chapter to deepen their knowledge of the material. I would also suggest that you remind learners to not simply skip past the reflections and tasks. You may also consider utilizing the reflections and tasks as in-class activities and leave learners to study the topic in more depth outside of class.

Final notes

Throughout the book, I will attempt to present a balanced view of ESP showing how it is implemented in both academic and workplace contexts. I also hope to show how the principles of ESP can be applied not only by individual teachers in isolated courses, but also by teams of teachers at the program level. In view of these quite different settings, I will use the following generic terms to avoid confusion:

"Course":	a set of integrated sessions (each maybe 45, 60, or 90 minutes in length) focusing on a particular subject of study (e.g. "*Testing 101*")
"Program":	a set of integrated courses leading to a broader understanding of a subject area (e.g. "*MA Program in TEFL*")
"Institution":	a place where ESP might be conducted (e.g. *school, university, office, factory, airport, call-center, workplace*)
"Learner":	somebody studying ESP (e.g. *student, office worker, factory worker, client, nurse, pilot)*
"Instructor":	somebody teaching ESP (e.g. *teacher, lecturer, practitioner, coach, advisor, consultant)*
"Administrator":	somebody managing a course or program but not necessarily involved in day-to-day teaching (e.g. *director, head of department, chief, manager, owner, boss)*
"You":	you – the reader of this book!
"They":	a gender-neutral third person form to replace *s/he, he/she, he or she* or similar expressions

I hope you enjoy reading this book and find it useful in your learning, teaching, and professional development.

Section 1

Contextualizing ESP

Chapter 1

Situating ESP in English language teaching and learning

English for Specific Purposes (ESP) is one of the most established teaching approaches in English Language Teaching (ELT). It has been informed by over 50 years of research and practice and is perhaps the most influential of all language teaching approaches in academic settings (Charles, 2013) and the workplace (Marra, 2013). ESP is an eclectic approach that takes the most useful, successful, and valid ideas from other theories and practices, combining them into a consistent whole. It incorporates elements from Communicative Language Teaching (CLT), Task-Based Language Teaching (TBLT), Project-Based Learning (PBL) (Richards & Rodgers, 2014), and many other teaching approaches, but also has its own unique features, including a commitment to learner-centeredness, a close connection with specialist subjects, and a focus on collaboration in both planning and teaching. In many countries, experts in ESP can be the most highly regarded and sought-after members of staff, serving as coordinators for entire academic English programs and playing key roles in companies that are developing their international strategies.

In this chapter, I'll first present a short, contemporary definition of ESP and introduce the two major branches of ESP that will feature throughout the rest of the book. Next, I'll describe the characteristic features of ESP before comparing and contrasting ESP with other well-known ELT approaches to highlight their similarities and differences. Then, I'll review and critique two well-known and commonly cited definitions of ESP in an attempt to resolve some of the confusion surrounding the approach.

By the end of the chapter, you should be able to define ESP, explain its key characteristics, and point out similarities and differences with other ELT approaches. But, most of all, you should get a sense of why ESP is useful in many ELT contexts where learners have particular needs for English that cannot be satisfied through traditional approaches to language teaching.

Opening reflection

In this chapter, you will learn that ESP is aimed at providing language support for learners so that they can successfully address their specific academic or occupational needs. But, what exactly are those needs?

Think of some of the things you do in academia or work that might have some kind of language component. Now, imagine you were a doctor. What are some of the things a doctor does that might require language knowledge or skills?

Commentary

If you are a student in a tertiary education setting, you might have noted that you use English when you write essays, listen to lectures, discuss topics, or even order lunch, make an appointment, or send a message to a friend on social media. If you are currently teaching at a tertiary institution (e.g. college or university), you might have noted that you use English when you explain points to students, attend meetings, or write research funding applications. Doctors around the world also use English in their work; for example, when they read a research study on a new medicine, meet with a patient to discuss their symptoms, write prescriptions, or attend conferences to present on their work. ESP is about offering language support so that people can successfully accomplish current and perhaps future tasks in their studies or work that have a language component.

But, you should note that not all language needs are *ESP needs*, even though they might be important to achieve a particular language goal. For example, most ESP experts wouldn't consider 'mastering the past tense', 'learning the top 100 most frequent words of English', or 'speaking with good pronunciation' to be ESP needs. ESP needs are in a sense *non-linguistic* needs that have a linguistic component. In order for a student to write a good essay, they probably need to know how to use the past tense, but it is the need to write an essay that governs what is taught in the ESP class. When a teacher starts explaining the past tense to students because it might be useful for some unspecified later goal in their lives, we are in the realm of a traditional general English (GE) class.

A definition of ESP

So, what is ESP? Here is the definition that I used in the introduction to this book:

> English for Specific Purposes (ESP) is an approach to language teaching that targets the current and/or future academic or occupational needs of

> learners, focuses on the necessary language, genres, and skills to address these needs, and assists learners in meeting these needs through the use of general and/or discipline-specific teaching materials and methods.

In this definition, a few of the words and phrases might be new to you. *Academic needs* refers to the needs of learners in a school, university, or other setting where the primary goal is learning. To illustrate what these might be, we need only look at some of the common settings where ESP teaching commonly takes place. In Japanese universities, for example, you can find ESP courses that help science students learn how to listen to and understand content lectures given in English through a process of note taking and discussion. In US universities, there are numerous ESP courses offered to overseas students to help them with their academic writing. Around the world, there is an increasing demand for ESP courses that help non-native speakers of English to improve their communication skills as part of Master of Business Administration (MBA) programs.

Occupational needs, on the other hand, refer to the needs of learners in a workplace setting, such as a factory, restaurant, or hospital. In the manufacturing industry, for example, many companies organize special intensive ESP courses to help sales staff improve their presentation skills. In the aviation industry, pilots receive specialized language training so they can communicate effectively with flight controllers, avoiding communication errors that could lead to injury or death. We can also find ESP courses offered as part of vocational training, such as in the Philippines and India, where workers at call-centers are guided on how to respond appropriately to confused or irate customers.

In many cases, though, things are not so simple. What if you are a teacher at a university? Do your needs count as academic or occupational? Or, what if you are in an industrial research center and part of your job is writing research articles? Does that part of your job count as an academic need or an occupational need? Later in this chapter, you will learn that the divisions in ESP are actually quite fuzzy and need to be treated with care. But, let's stay with these two categories of needs for now.

You may also be unsure how *language* differs from *genre* and *skills*. Here, *language* is used in a quite broad sense to refer to lexis (words and multi-word units), morphology (lexical derivation), syntax (sentence grammar), semantics (lexis and grammar meaning), pragmatics (lexis and grammar use), and phonology (sound systems). *Genre*, on the other hand, refers to a spoken or written product of language, for example, a research presentation, business letter, or prescription, while also capturing the processes, agents, and contexts that govern how that product is created, interpreted, and acted on (Swales, 1990). *Skills* refer not only to traditional abilities like reading, writing, listening, and speaking, but also metacognitive skills such as planning, noticing, problem solving, evaluating, and correcting. Again, don't be too concerned about the different divisions here. Instead, focus more on the fact that ESP addresses many different facets of the communication process that are needed to achieve a particular goal.

Finally, you may be intrigued by the idea that ESP uses both general and/or specialist-field materials and methods to meet the needs of learners. This means that in some cases, the materials and methods used in an ESP classroom will be identical to those used in traditional GE classes. For example, an ESP instructor may ask learners to translate a sentence or passage into their first language, which is a classic grammar-translation method (Larsen-Freeman & Anderson, 2013). They may even drill learners on the pronunciation of a particular vocabulary item, which is one of the core principles of the audio-lingual method (Larsen-Freeman & Anderson, 2013). But, these methods should only be used if they serve the needs of the learners. Clearly, the grammar-translation method would be appropriate if the learners were hoping to become second language (L2) to first language (L1) translators and needed to develop accuracy in their sentence level translation skills. Similarly, drilling learners on the pronunciation of a key vocabulary item might be important if they were hoping to give research presentations at an international conference, where the item had particular importance and needed to be conveyed clearly to the audience. It might also be important if the learners were training to become airline pilots, as comprehensible pronunciation is a crucial factor for maintaining in-flight safety.

On the other hand, ESP instructors will often adopt materials and methods that are quite removed from traditional English classes and more closely match those used in the discipline of the learners. In a business English class, for example, learners may be asked to carry out a case study on the language that they need, following the same principles by which they might conduct a case study of a successful company in their specialist courses. Similarly, in a STEM (Science, Technology, Engineering, and Mathematics) English class, learners may be encouraged to collect word frequency data and analyze it using computers in a similar way to how they might collect and analyze temperature or pressure data in lab experiments.

Branches of ESP

You have now learned that ESP is a broad field that focuses on addressing the specific needs of learners in various academic and occupational contexts. If you want to learn more about the broader issues of ESP that span these two contexts, a good place to start is with one of the many journals devoted to ESP, including the oldest, and perhaps most well-known journal, *English for Specific Purposes*, and newer journals such as the *Asian ESP Journal*, *ESP Today*, *English for Specific Purposes World* (*ESP World*), and the *Taiwan International Journal on English for Specific Purposes*. Not surprisingly, though, many discussions on ESP are focused on issues related to more narrowly defined branches of ESP, which sometimes even have their own special acronyms.

Perhaps the most influential branch of ESP is English for Academic Purposes (EAP), which focuses on ESP in academic settings. Many ESP journals, such as *English for Specific Purposes*, are heavily weighted in favor of EAP topics, and there is even a dedicated journal devoted to EAP work called the *Journal of English for Academic Purposes*. The huge attention that EAP receives in the field of ESP is not surprising when you consider that many ESP researchers are based in academic institutions and many second and foreign language learners have a strong need for EAP skills in order to complete their school and university studies. However, this attention does sometimes lead to confusion, especially when ESP and EAP are presented as a kind of dichotomy through phrasing such as "ESP and EAP" and "ESP/EAP", as we see in many of the works in the field (e.g. Boulton, Carter-Thomas, & Rowley-Jolivet, 2012; Ding & Campion, 2016; Fortanet-Gómez & Räisänen, 2008; Holme, 1996).

The other major branch of ESP is English for Occupational Purposes (EOP). Although there is no major journal dedicated to EOP research, you will find papers related to EOP in a broad range of journals, from *English for Specific Purposes* to the *IEEE Transactions on Professional Communication*. You will also find that many foreign language textbooks marketed as following an ESP approach are in the area of EOP; for example, *Cambridge English for Nursing* (McGerr & Allum, 2010), *Aviation English* (Emery & Roberts, 2008), and *English for International Tourism* (Strutt, 2015). As you will learn in Chapter 2, some of the earliest and most important developments in ESP have emerged out of work in EOP settings. Unfortunately, this has led to some researchers (and publishers) using the term ESP as a synonym for EOP, which again leads to a confusing dichotomy between ESP (= EOP) and EAP (≠ ESP).

The two major branches of ESP can be divided further. EAP can be divided into English for General Academic Purposes (EGAP) and English for Specific Academic Purposes (ESAP), and EOP can be divided into English for Professional Purposes (EPP) and English for Vocational Purposes (EVP). Of course, these sub-branches can be divided even further leading to an increasingly narrow set of sub-sub-branches, including English for Research Publication Purposes (ERPP) (J. Flowerdew, 2013), English for Business Purposes (EBP) (Bargiela-Chiappini & Zhang, 2013), English for Medical Purposes (EMP) (Ferguson, 2013), Nursing English (Bosher, 2013), and Aviation English (Moder, 2013).

Figure 1.1 shows how the branches of ESP might expand out almost indefinitely, with English for Atomic and Nuclear Physics (with a possible acronym of EANP) at one extreme of EAP, and English for Emergency Room Nursing (with a possible acronym of EERN) at one extreme of EOP.

You will notice that none of the neatly boxed categories in Figure 1.1 are really independent of the others. For example, within the EAP categories, students studying atomic and nuclear physics are likely to need general

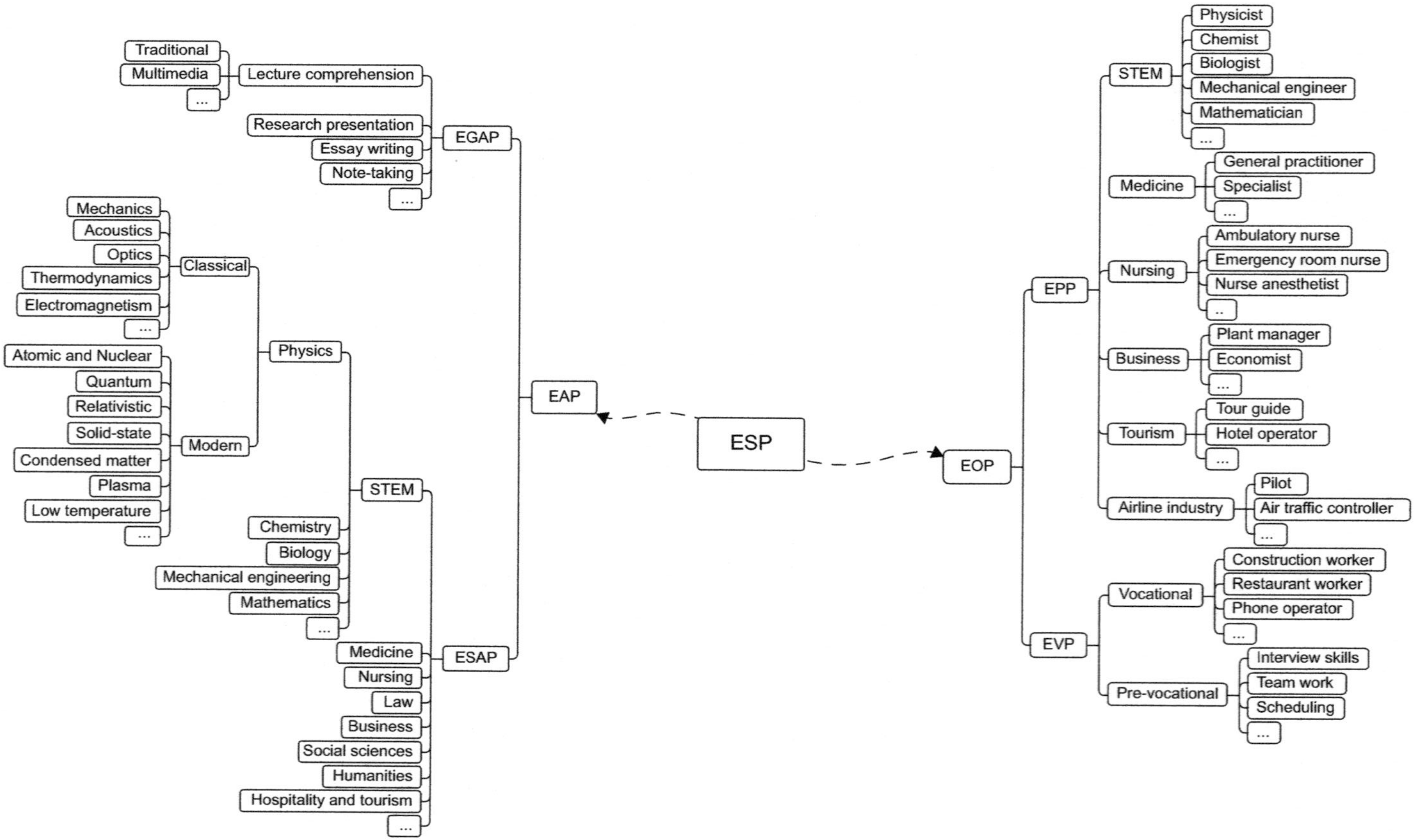

Figure 1.1 Some of the branches and sub-branches of ESP.

academic listening comprehension skills to help them understand lectures, as well as specific language skills from a range of disciplines to explain mathematical theories (English for Mathematics), nuclear reactions (English for Chemistry), and reactor properties (English for Mechanical Engineering). Similarly, within the EOP categories, learners of emergency room nursing are likely to have overlapping needs with ambulance nurses, and they may even need some of the skills of biologists and phone operators, as well as pre-vocational teamwork skills.

It is also clear that even EAP and EOP cannot be separated so easily. In Figure 1.1, we have the EAP category of Physics on the left and the EOP category of Physicist on the right. How different are the two? Clearly, studying physics is not the same as being a physicist, but the language needs are clearly going to be similar in many ways.

What is important to remember is that all categories are abstractions; they are simplifications of reality that help us to explain and communicate complex ideas. In reality, there is no EAP or EOP. Instead, we have a continuum of needs that are weighted more strongly in one area or setting than another, or relate to one group more strongly than another. Similarly, we have language features that appear more prominent or frequently in one context than another, and genres and skills that are more important for one person or group than another.

In practical terms, this blurring of boundaries means that most, if not all, presentations of ESP will be overly simplistic. We know, for example, that mathematics research articles are written in a very different way to mechanical engineering papers, even though they are both STEM subjects (Anthony & Bowen, 2013). This point raises questions about how an EAP instructor can and should talk about the features of research articles in an academic writing class, without ignoring the huge amount of variation that exists within and between academic disciplines. Similarly, we know that different branches of nursing will each have their own specialized vocabulary. If an EOP instructor wants to introduce learners to 'important' nursing vocabulary, they might attempt to focus on the vocabulary used in a particular branch of nursing, but this would naturally lead to vocabulary in other branches being ignored. Alternatively, they might attempt to identify vocabulary that is used frequently across a broad range of nursing disciplines, but this runs the risk of introducing gaps in vocabulary in the branches of interest to learners.

You may be left wondering at this point what teachers can do to better describe the complexities of ESP to learners. Should they present ESP in neat boxes as in Figure 1.1? Or, should they admit that ESP is messy? I'll return to these issues in later chapters, but my recommendation here is that you explain the reality of fuzzy categories in ESP from the outset. Once learners know that they are dealing with continuums and probabilities rather than absolutes, they will be in a much better position to evaluate what they learn and relate it to their own experiences and target goals.

TASK 1.1 Plotting a path to ESP

Pick an academic discipline or career profession that interests you. Try to extend the branches and sub-branches of ESP presented in Figure 1.1 to include the discipline or profession that you chose. What difficulties do you have?

Characteristic features of ESP

Now that you have a good idea about the meaning of ESP, let's look at some of the characteristics of ESP that distinguish it from other approaches to language teaching and learning.

A learner-centered approach

You can see from the definition of ESP that one of its most important characteristics is learner-centeredness. This is an important point that was highlighted by Hutchinson and Waters (1987) in their seminal work on the subject. Many approaches to language teaching and learning claim to be learner-centered in some way, but the priority given to learner-centeredness in ESP means that the course or program administrator, the instructor in the classroom, and even the learners themselves should always be considering how language items, activities, and explanations will ultimately help the learners meet their current and/or future 'non-linguistic' target needs.

A multidisciplinary approach

Dudley-Evans and St. John (1998) describe ESP slightly differently than Hutchinson and Waters (1987) in the title of their seminal work on ESP. Although they recognize the importance of learner-centeredness in ESP, they characterize it instead as a *multidisciplinary* approach, in which the ESP 'practitioner' can draw on insights of researchers in other disciplines and may also engage with researchers in other disciplines through teaching.

In many ESP contexts, specialists in the target areas of the learners are often important stakeholders that can influence policies and funding, and may even serve as judges on the success of the program. Therefore, it is vital that ESP administrators and instructors draw on the insights of target specialists not only within their own institutions, but also through published research on specialist language. On this latter point, you may be surprised how often specialists in a target discipline publish research and opinion pieces on language and communication in their fields. It is quite common (see, for example, Gregory Dawes (2001) and Choi (2005) in nursing). In fact, some fields actively encourage discussions about language and communication through journals dedicated to the topic (see, for example, the *IEEE Transactions on Professional Communication*, which focuses on language and communication in a broad range of engineering fields). Of course, the learners themselves can also provide valuable insights into the language and skills that they need to learn if they are aware of them.

Specialists can support ESP teaching in other ways, too. In the role of a specialist informant, they can directly contribute to the creation and running of a course. For example, they can provide suitable texts that can form the basis for descriptions of target language, genres, and skills. They may also help to analyze and interpret those texts and provide suggestions for course goals. Evaluating success on an ESP course or program can also be a challenge, so having specialist informants provide input on the design of performance tests and interpret the results can be a great help. Finally, Dudley-Evans and St. John (1998) and others suggest that specialist informants may have a role to play inside the classroom, where ESP courses are taught through team-teaching. In an academic setting, this is often difficult to achieve because of timetable clashes and the physical distances between faculty offices that limit interactions. It is also a sad fact that many faculty members have little interest in the goings-on in other research labs, let alone other departments on campus. The situation in EOP settings, on the other hand, is often more suitable for team-teaching. In companies, for example, an 'outsider' ESP expert might be explicitly hired to work with company 'insiders' to develop and teach an ESP course, which is then evaluated by the company and the participants themselves.

An attention to theory and practice

A third characteristic of ESP that leads from the other two is an attention to theory and practice. ESP experts are likely to have to deal with a wide range of different genres in their work. In order to identify the stable characteristics of these genres, find features that are likely to vary the most, and create teaching points of maximum use to the learners, they need to have a strong set of theoretical language and learning principles with which to work. But theory is not always enough when an ESP instructor may face a large group of learners with widely different needs and interests on one day, and a small group of learners with very similar needs on another. To deal with these situations, ESP instructors also need to develop strong pedagogic practices that 'work' in real-world settings. Of course, strong theoretical language and learning principles can facilitate the development of good pedagogic practices, but in ESP, sometimes the direction has been the other way, with pedagogic practices leading to novel innovations in language and learning theory (Swales, 1985).

TASK 1.2 Understanding the characteristic features of ESP

Imagine you are an ESP instructor in an EAP or EOP setting and you are devising a class to teach a particular target goal (e.g. writing a compare/contrast essay). What actions could you take from a learner-centered perspective to help you devise an effective classroom teaching plan? List some of your ideas below (the first is given as an example).

1 Ask students about their experiences writing this type of essay.

How could you improve your teaching plan from a multidisciplinary perspective? List some of your ideas below (the first is given as an example).

1 Ask department faculty members what topics might be suitable to discuss in a compare/contrast format.

In terms of theory and practice, how else could you improve your teaching? List some of your ideas below (the first is given as an example).

1 Read the literature on how to write a good paragraph.

Complementing and competing approaches to ESP

In recent years, many new approaches to language teaching have been proposed that in some cases complement an ESP approach and in other cases compete with it. Let's look at a few of these complementary and competing approaches to gain a clearer understanding of what ESP is and isn't.

One example of the former case is Task-Based Language Teaching (TBLT). This is a learning approach that was popularized in the 1980s by researchers such as Prabhu (1987) and later by researchers such as Willis (1996) and Ellis (2003). As an extension of communicative language teaching, TBLT attempts to connect the language practiced in the classroom with real-life situations in which the learners may find themselves. It achieves this through the use of *tasks*, which Ellis (2003) describes as being primarily meaning-focused, and containing some kind of information, reasoning or opinion gap that must be negotiated by the learners. Tasks should also be designed to have a clearly defined, non-linguistic outcome.

It is clear that TBLT overlaps with ESP in some ways, particularly with its focus on learner-centeredness and connecting what happens in the classroom with what learners might actually experience later in the real world. As a result, it is not surprising that TBLT activities clearly have their place in the ESP classroom. ESP instructors might consider devising TBLT activities that target learner needs, develop the necessary language skills for a particular academic or occupational setting, and help learners to practice these language skills in authentic or near-authentic situations. In workplace ESP settings, TBLT activities are particularly appropriate because the learners will have recognizable tasks that they must complete to be successful in their jobs.

One variation on the concept of TBLT is Problem-Based Learning (PBL), which is a learner-centered approach in which learners work actively and collaboratively in small, often multidisciplinary, groups to solve specific problems (Wilkinson, 2008). TBLT activities can also be linked together and structured into the form of a larger project, which is sometimes termed Project-Based Learning, unfortunately with the same acronym of PBL. Of course, both PBL approaches can be used successfully to compliment an ESP approach.

Two learning approaches that are often seen as direct competitors to ESP are Content-Based Instruction (CBI), which is sometimes termed Content-Based Learning (CBL), and English-Medium Instruction (EMI).

CBI is an approach to language teaching that was derived from Communicative Language Teaching (CLT) and has gained popularity in recent years, especially in Asia. It is based on the idea that learners will acquire language when they are exposed to highly motivating topics that they themselves may choose, and engage in those topics through interactive task- and project-based activities (see Brinton, Snow, & Wesche, 2003). Some teachers of CBI choose topics for classes that target the specialist subject areas of the learners. These cases, unfortunately, have given rise to confusion that CBI is a kind of variant of ESP. CBI courses do not, however, have to be discipline-centered. In fact, topics such as the learners' favorite movies or pop stars are equally valid.

So, why do we need ESP when the CBI approach is available? One of the main problems with CBI is that language, in principle, is not explicitly taught, leading learners to question how well they are improving their language skills. In reality, many CBI teachers do teach language, but, there is still a tendency for CBI teachers in many EFL settings to use the

Figure 1.2 The language-content continuum.

L1 excessively in class (Peachey, 2004). Another criticism of CBI is the lack of suitable materials. Finding good CBI materials is often difficult as the topics of choice may emerge suddenly from in-class discussion, making the time-consuming process of writing materials impossible. In a worst-case scenario, the only available authentic materials on the topic may also be too difficult for the level of the learners. One further criticism is that CBI places emphasis on topics that are motivating to the learners, even when in some cases they may not match the learners' present or future needs.

To understand where English-Medium Instruction (EMI) fits into the picture, it is worth considering the language-content continuum shown in Figure 1.2. In this figure, the Grammar-Translation Method (GTM) is placed on the left side of the continuum, and CLT and CBI are placed toward the middle. This leaves EMI on the far right of the scale.

In the purest form of EMI, teachers simply teach traditional content courses using English as the language of instruction. Content is primary. From an educational and administrative standpoint, EMI courses offer many advantages over traditional English courses. The first is that only the target language is used in class, maximizing a learner's exposure. EMI courses, by definition, also target the immediate needs and often the future needs of learners because they are essentially equivalent to specialist subject courses that the learners would traditionally take in the first language. The materials and even the learning context of an EMI course are, by definition, authentic. This leads to relevant, useful, and hopefully motivationally rich content.

Again, we need to consider why ESP is needed when an approach like EMI is available. In theory, EMI courses do not target the language problems traditionally associated with second and foreign language learners, such as lexical, syntactic, and rhetorical issues. It is on this point that there is a clear divide between EMI and ESP. Whereas EMI is primarily focused on the content needs of learners (i.e. content instruction through the medium of English), ESP is focused on the language used to achieve these content-related goals). In practice, many EMI teachers target ESL/EFL language issues if they are observed in class, but in this case we could argue that they are entering the realm of ESP.

When viewed in its purest form, it is easy to see why there are also many problems associated with EMI. First and foremost, learners who are not already proficient in English will obviously struggle to cope in an EMI course. To consider EMI courses as a way to teach language might be considered equivalent to throwing somebody who cannot swim into the deep end of a pool and hoping they will survive. Some will, but many won't. A second problem is that EMI relies on an institution having a faculty body that is willing and able to teach content courses in English. It is still a sad fact that in many countries this is simply not the case. A third problem, which is related to the second, is that some institutions mistakenly believe that English language faculty can teach EMI courses. This is clearly not the case, unless the English faculty is retrained in some specialist field. Quite surprisingly, in some regions, such as Taiwan, this is exactly what has happened; English faculty members have been encouraged to acquire special certificates and in some cases even Master's degrees in subjects such as tourism and hospitality in order to teach EMI courses. This example shows that EMI is often seen as an alternative to ESP even though it is clear that the two approaches have quite fundamentally different goals. Perhaps a better way to view ESP, and particularly EAP, is as a useful bridge to EMI.

It is important to note that despite the many difficulties associated with EMI, there is a clear move toward EMI courses in many institutions around the world. What's more, the trend is increasing. One of the reasons for this is that universities are hoping that the introduction of EMI courses will encourage a new influx of overseas students. Another reason is to increase the job opportunities of local students, even though in many cases this will appear as wishful thinking. I will return to these issues in Chapter 2, where I will show that a growth in EMI is likely to lead to an even greater importance of ESP.

One final teaching approach that has gained popularity in continental Europe and is sometimes viewed as a rival approach to ESP is Content and Language Integrated Learning (CLIL). Within CLIL, language teachers are encouraged to become more involved with content, and content teachers are encouraged to become more involved with language. In their Universitat Jaume I CLIL program, for example, Ruiz-Garrido and Palmer-Silveira (2008) describe how English language instructors work as language coaches for content teachers, enabling them to gain confidence in teaching content courses in English. Clearly, again, there are overlaps with some of the principles and characteristics of ESP, especially in terms of the multidisciplinary nature of CLIL. However, CLIL should probably be considered more as a language teaching policy than a language teaching and learning approach (Arnó-Macià & Mancho-Barés, 2015). Viewed in this way, again, there is no competition between ESP and CLIL. On the contrary, one might consider that the English teachers in Ruiz-Garrido and Palmer-Silveira's CLIL program are practicing a new form of ESP that addresses the needs of content teachers instead of a traditional student body.

TASK 1.3 Placing courses on the language/content continuum

Review a set of language courses offered at the institution where you study or work or one that you are familiar with. Try to place the courses somewhere on the language/content continuum presented in Figure 1.2. Now, try to place any ESP courses that you are familiar with on the same continuum. Which courses do you find easy to place, and which courses do you find more difficult to place? Why?

Contentious issues in ESP: absolute and variable characteristics

If you look at the definition provided earlier in this chapter, I hope you will agree that ESP is not an impossible concept to understand. Unfortunately, there has been a great deal of confusion surrounding the ESP approach, particularly in regard to its defining characteristics and choices of teaching methodologies. For example, you will often hear supporters of ESP talk about how it differs from general English and how it motivates learners because it is focused on the content of their specialized discipline. You will hear opponents of ESP, on the other hand, claim that ESP is narrowly focused on adult learners in workplace settings, and that you can't be an ESP instructor unless you are an expert in a specialized discipline. You may even hear people say that ESP is just about teaching technical terminology. In this section, let's look at two commonly cited definitions of ESP and see if they explain some of this confusion.

One of most widely cited early definitions of ESP is that of Strevens (1988). He proposed that ESP consisted of both absolute and variable characteristics:

I. Absolute characteristics

ESP consists of English language teaching which is:

- designed to meet specified needs of the learner;
- related in content (i.e. in its themes and topics) to particular disciplines, occupations and activities;
- centered on the language appropriate to those activities in syntax, lexis, discourse, semantics, etc., and analysis of this discourse;
- in contrast with general English.

II. Variable characteristics

ESP may be, but is not necessarily:

- restricted as to the language skills to be learned (e.g. reading only);
- not taught according to any pre-ordained methodology.

Following the earlier discussion, it is clear that the first three of Strevens's absolute characteristics listed in Part I are non-controversial. As for the first point, it could be said that any language course is designed to meet the needs of the learners. In ESP contexts, however, we have seen that these needs are essentially 'non-linguistic' in nature. The second point follows naturally from the first when you consider that ESP contents are situated in either academic or occupational settings. The unique feature of ESP is that it targets the precise needs that these academic and/or occupational settings impress on learners. Similarly, the third point follows naturally from the second. ESP teaching is language teaching, and so the focus of classes will be on the language needed to achieve a particular goal. In the case of ESP, it just so happens that these language needs are often discipline-specific due to the nature of the needs.

The fourth absolute characteristic in Strevens' definition is more problematic. In this case, Strevens is attempting to define something in terms of what it is not, and so without a complete definition of general English to go alongside this, the point has little meaning. It should be remembered, however, that at the time Strevens formulated his definition, ESP was a fledgling teaching approach that was striving to distinguish itself from those around it. Announcing that it was uniquely different from the dominant approach at the time, i.e. general English, allowed ESP to gain a platform from which ESP today has emerged.

From the point of view of a definition, the variable characteristics listed in Part II are also problematic. For example, stating that ESP may be restricted to a specific language skill suggests that it also may not have such restrictions. In addition, stating that ESP "may not necessary be taught accordingly to any pre-ordained methodology" is a rather convoluted way of stating that any methodology can be used. As such, these variable characteristics provide us with few additional insights into the approach. However, they do plant a seed in some people's minds that ESP is in some way narrowly focused on a particular set of language skills and utilizes a unique method of teaching, which is not the case.

Building on the work of Strevens, Dudley-Evans and St. John (1998) created a more elaborate definition of ESP, which is still used by many researchers in the field today. Like Strevens, they divided ESP into absolute and variable characteristics:

Absolute characteristics

- ESP is defined to meet specific needs of the learners;
- ESP makes use of the underlying methodology and activities of the discipline it serves;
- ESP is centered on the language appropriate to these activities in terms of grammar, lexis, register, study skills, discourse, and genre.

Variable characteristics

- ESP may be related to or designed for specific disciplines;
- ESP may use, in specific teaching situations, a different methodology from that of general English;
- ESP is likely to be designed for adult learners, either at a tertiary-level institution or in a professional work situation. It could, however, be for learners at secondary school level;
- ESP is generally designed for intermediate or advanced students;
- Most ESP courses assume some basic knowledge of the language systems.

You will notice that the first and third absolute characteristics are almost identical to those of Strevens, although Dudley-Evans and St. John have added 'genre', which was not such a commonly used term in Strevens's time. The second absolute characteristic, in contrast, is subtly different having been transformed into one that highlights the connection between ESP methodology and the target disciplines it serves, rather than simply a content connection. Another difference is that Strevens's fourth absolute characteristic has been completely removed.

More striking differences can be found when you look at Dudley-Evans and St. John's variable characteristics. Here, the number of characteristics has been increased from two to five. They are also different in nature, with the first emphasizing the importance of discipline specificity, the second repeating the idea that ESP might be different from general English (interestingly hinting that the methodology used might also be different), the third targeting the ages of learners, and the fourth and fifth characteristics targeting the expected proficiency level of learners.

It is striking that many of the concerns voiced by opponents of ESP reflect characteristics that are presented as variable components in Dudley-Evans and St. John's (1998) definition. Clearly, some scholars have read these characteristics and mistakenly considered them to be defining features – a confusion that is perhaps understandable when considering they are presented under the banner of a definition. However, as we found with the variable characteristics in Strevens' definition, describing characteristics using terms like '*may be related*', '*may use*', '*is likely to*', '*is generally*', and '*most*' provide readers with few insights unless they are already familiar with the subject matter. Indeed, ESP can sometimes be related to or designed for specific disciplines (or professions) but other times not. ESP can also use a different methodology from that of general English, but then again, sometimes it doesn't. ESP may also be used successfully with adult learners with an advanced proficiency. But, this doesn't mean that ESP will be unsuccessful with children and less proficient learners. On the other hand, if we only consider the absolute characteristics in this definition, we find ourselves returning to the concepts captured in the definition of ESP presented at the start of this chapter.

Research ideas

Here are some possible ideas for small-scale or large-scale research projects that stem from the topics discussed in this chapter.

Defining ESP

Review all the major definitions of ESP that have been published. Compare and contrast the definitions to find areas of agreement and disagreement. Based on this analysis, do you see any evolution in the concept of ESP? What aspects have remained fixed over time? What aspects have changed?

Understanding ESP

If you are studying in a language-related department or work with English teachers, ask them what they think ESP means. Now, try contacting teachers in a different institution (possibly in a different country). Ask them what they think ESP means. Do the opinions you hear match the description of ESP presented in this chapter? If there are differences, what factors might account for them (e.g. experience, culture, training)?

Classifying ESP

Review the research articles published in a major ESP-focused journal and try to classify them as having either an EAP, EOP, or mixed focus. What do you notice about the balance between EAP and EOP focused papers? What areas of EAP and disciplines in EOP receive the most attention? What factors might explain these tendencies?

Closing reflection

Now that you have come to the end of the chapter, you should be in a good position to define ESP, explain its key characteristics, and point out some of the similarities and differences with other ELT methods.

Here are a few more questions to consider:

1. Which of the points covered in the chapter were new to you? Did you find them interesting and relevant in terms of your own learning goals? Were there any points that you found confusing or that you disagreed with?
2. What points from the chapter do you think you can immediately put to use in your own learning or teaching context?

3 If you were asked to introduce the concept of ESP to a student who was thinking of taking an ESP class, or explain ESP to a General English teacher who was thinking of adopting an ESP approach in their teaching, which of the points would you feel most confident explaining? What examples would you use to expand on the points you explained?

Further resources

Relevant journals

Asian ESP Journal. Retrieved from: http://asian-esp-journal.com/editorial-board/

English for Specific Purposes. Retrieved from: www.journals.elsevier.com/english-for-specific-purposes

English for Specific Purposes World (ESP World). Retrieved from: http://www.esp-world.info/

ESP Today. Retrieved from: www.esptodayjournal.org/

IEEE Transactions on Professional Communication. Retrieved from: http://ieeexplore.ieee.org/xpl/RecentIssue.jsp?reload=true&punumber=47

Journal of English for Academic Purposes. Retrieved from: www.journals.elsevier.com/journal-of-english-for-academic-purposes

Taiwan International ESP Journal. Retrieved from http://tespaj.tespa.org.tw/index.php/TESPJ/index

Chapter 2

Situating ESP in the world at large

In Chapter 1, you learned that ESP is a well-established English Language Teaching (ELT) approach that addresses the needs of learners in academic or occupational settings. What we did not consider, though, is *why* learners around the world need a strong English language ability to succeed in academia or the workplace. If you know the answer to this question, you'll be better able to understand your own role in an ESP course or program and be more ready to meet the expectations that administrators have of you. Also, in the ESP classroom, you'll be able to communicate the reasons why English is needed in academia and the workplace to learners. This will help them to contextualize the material you give them, provide them with both intrinsic and extrinsic motivation to achieve the goals of the course, and suggest possible directions for their studies and careers paths.

In this chapter, I'll begin by describing the current position and status of English in the world. I'll then explain how changing conditions in industry and academia have led to English becoming the de facto language of many company workplaces and in academia as a whole. Next, I'll describe how ESP courses and programs are usually positioned within industry and academia. Finally, I'll discuss some of the issues surrounding the globalization of English and consider if this trend is really a good thing.

By the end of the chapter, you should be able to understand and explain the importance of English in our increasingly globalized world, the contexts in which ESP instructors often have to work, and the advantages and challenges that these contexts introduce. But, most of all, you should start to see how ESP addresses some of the many challenges that people face in a globalized world where English is often the de facto language of academia and the workplace.

Opening reflection

Do you think English is an important language throughout the world? If so, in what areas do you think it exerts the most influence? If not, what other languages do you think hold positions of dominance in the world? In what contexts might they be used?

In the future, do you think that English will grow in importance? Or, do you think another language, such as Mandarin Chinese or Spanish, will become dominant throughout the world? What reasons can you give for your answer?

Commentary

In all likelihood, you will have answered 'yes' to the question of English being an important language throughout the world. English can be seen in popular culture, in literature, on the Internet, in social media interactions, in advertising, in politics, in the news, and of course in many academic and workplace settings. But, English is not the only language in the world, and depending on where you live, English might have only a minor impact on your daily life. For example, if you live in a country where English is a foreign language, you may only interact with English in your academic studies. Learners of English will also experience the impact of English in different ways in their lives. This will have an enormous impact on their motivations to study and succeed in English classes, regardless of whether or not those classes have an ESP focus.

One interesting thing to consider is if and how the impact of English in the world might change in the future. Today, many countries are committed to a globalized economy where English is the de facto language of trade and industry. Also, academic institutions around the world are encouraging increasing numbers of learners from overseas countries to apply, offering them courses and programs taught in English rather than the L1 of the country. It seems that the importance of English is ever increasing. But, this trend presents workers, teachers, administrators, institutions, and even governments with huge challenges and pressures that cannot always be addressed. What is clear is that many stakeholders in industry and academia are thinking about these issues and considering the best solutions.

The growth of English as a world-wide lingua franca

If we ranked the languages of the world by the number of their native speakers today, English would be third in the list. It is spoken by around 375 million native speakers, which is far below the number of native speakers of Mandarin Chinese at 982 million, and Spanish at 420 million (Statista, 2017). However, English is by far the most *used* language in the world when we consider not only native speakers but also those who use it as a second or foreign language. One estimate puts the number of English *users* at almost

1.5 billion, dwarfing the number of speakers of all other languages (Statista, 2017). English is the one true global lingua franca in the world today (see Nickerson, 2013, for further discussion of this).

One of the main reasons why English has developed into a global lingua franca is due to its strong connection with growth in trade and commerce. The link between English and the business world can be traced back to the 16th Century and the use of English to facilitate connections with refugees who had arrived in England at the time. These were artisans, craftsmen, and professionals who had an interest in English for commerce (Starfield, 2013b).

The link between English and business flourished in the 1940s after World War II, which was a time when many countries involved in the fighting had been destroyed both economically and in terms of infrastructure. Immediately after the war, the economies and infrastructure of the USA, Canada, and to a lesser extent the UK, were largely intact. As a result, these countries became central to the rebuilding effort and business opportunities began to emerge, including the export of technology and technical expertise to Europe, Africa, and Asia. New technical manuals and reports began to be published in English to support this new exportation of goods and services. Around the same time, research journals began to publish findings in English, spurred by a growing trend to carry out research in a collaborative, sometimes international, manner, and the growing need for research to be disseminated to the largest possible audience.

Another factor that led to English becoming a dominant language was the growth of the computer industry. As with much of the other technology that emerged after WWII, most of the early work on the creation and use of computers was carried out in the USA (Cromer, 1992). These developments led to the creation of new programming languages based on English, new communications standards written in English, and the use of English as the primary language for radio communications, aviation, and later the Internet. It is currently estimated that at least 80% of the world's information is stored in English (Invernizzi, 2010), and of course, everybody knows that most of the world's largest computer firms are based in English-speaking countries, including Microsoft, Apple, IBM, Intel, and Google.

Today, the position of English as a global lingua franca is largely uncontested. Even as far back as the mid-1990s, we find English described in the following way:

> English is the main language of books, newspapers, airports and air-traffic control, international business and academic conferences, science, technology, diplomacy, sport, international competitions, pop music and advertising.
>
> (Graddol, 1997, p. 181)

Indeed, looking at China today, for example, estimates suggest there are around 400 million learners of English, and this number is increasing (Bolton & Graddol, 2012).

TASK 2.1 Recognizing the growth of English

List any changes in the English language policy at the institution where you study or work. Have these changes given English a greater or lesser importance at the institution? What reasons do you think the management of the institution had for making these changes?

What changes in the English language policy at your institution would you like to see introduced? Why? List some of your ideas.

ESP in today's globalized economy

As you learned in Chapter 1, ESP operates within two realms, one of them being English for Occupational Purposes (EOP). Here, let's consider the place of English in industry as a way to evaluate the relevance and importance of EOP and ESP in general.

English has become one of the key factors in the global success of a company. Friedman (2005) described ten 'flatteners' that led to a leveling of the global industry playing field, including the rise of personal computers, the development of better communications protocols, the growth of the Internet, the increased ability and use of online collaborative projects, the growth of insourcing, outsourcing and offshoring businesses, and the growth of search engines, wireless technologies, and mobile devices. As you learned in the previous section, English has had a central role in all these developments, and companies are now increasingly demanding that their workforce can understand this global lingua franca and operate smoothly with it. As a result, there is a strong need for language instructors who can understand and implement ESP programs in companies.

To illustrate the importance of English in industry, we need only look at the policies of some of the major companies in non-English speaking countries, namely Japan, Korea, and China. In Japan, the car manufacturer Nissan has used English as its official company language since 1999. In the years leading up to 1999, Nissan almost went bankrupt and so to strengthen the company after its collapse, Carlos Ghosn, the Executive Vice President of the French company Renault, was hired as Chief Operating Officer (COO). On his appointment, Ghosn quickly introduced this radical English-only policy and the turnaround for the company was dramatic. Similarly, an English-only policy was introduced in 2010 at the Japanese IT company Rakuten by its founder and CEO, Hiroshi Mikitani, who wanted to grow the company into a global presence. Sony, in contrast, has not changed their official language, although they did for some time have a non-Japanese Chief Executive Officer (CEO). On the other hand, they have in recent years decided to throw away their traditional recruitment procedures and now actively recruit non-Japanese workers into their Tokyo-based head office.

The trend to recruit global talent has been accelerating rapidly in Korea and China, too. Today, Samsung, the largest electronics manufacturer in Korea, encourages non-Korean graduates to apply for positions by stating on their recruitment page that English is the only required language needed to work in the company. Similarly, two of the biggest companies in China, Haier and China National Petroleum Corporation (CNPC), aggressively recruit overseas workers with the globalization of the company becoming part of the company's mission statement.

Not only are Asian companies recruiting more English-speaking workers, they are also increasingly sending their workers overseas to work in subsidiary companies where wages and product manufacturing costs will be lower. Two prime locations for such a subsidiary company are India and Vietnam. Of course, local workers in Vietnam and India cannot be expected to know Japanese, Chinese, or Korean. As a result, English has become the lingua franca of the workplace. Interestingly, many Japanese, Chinese, and Korean employees are reluctant to work overseas due their lack of confidence in English (see, for example, Koike, Takada, Matsui, & Terauchi, 2010). It is no surprise, therefore, that companies in Asia are willing to pay high prices for ESP experts to train their workers before they depart to these foreign destinations.

The situation in Europe is much more complicated. To date, the European Union has operated using 24 official languages, with English, French, and German serving as 'core' languages. In reality, however, much business is conducted only in English, especially when it involves non-European clients (see, for example, Louhiala-Salminen, Charles, & Kankaanranta, 2005). This is reflected in the fact that the Swedish car manufacturer Volvo has English as the primary language of senior management, and that the European aircraft manufacturer Airbus has had English as the workplace lingua franca since its creation in 1969.

Perhaps the best example of an industry in which English plays a central role is the call-center industry. This industry perhaps reflects all the positive and negative aspects of the 'flattening' world of Friedman (2005). In the Philippines and India, the call-center industry has grown at a phenomenal rate since the early 2000s, as a result of cheaper Internet telephony systems, improved wireless networks, and a greater desire by companies in the West to outsource their services. The growth has been so great that the president of the Call Center Association of the Philippines, Benedict Hernandez, described it as 'hypergrowth' (Magkilat, 2014). Call-center workers can expect to receive some of the highest wages in the country provided they have good enough English skills to respond appropriately to the callers routed through to them from places like the UK and USA. The need to train call-center workers has also led to a new industry of ESP training centers in these countries. But, we should not forget that 'hypergrowth' also has its downside. For example, the result of outsourcing jobs to the Philippines and India has led to the loss of many jobs in the home country and a dramatic change in the lifestyles of people in the target countries. Also, callers may now have to explain problems to people working thousands of miles away, who have little understanding of the customer's local situation or dilemma. And, both parties may need to work extra hard to clarify their meanings as a result of their widely different accents.

One final example of an industry that has dramatically changed as a result of globalization and the increased mobility of people is the tourism industry. Today, non-English speaking countries have seen steady rises in the number of English-speaking tourists due to cheaper airline tickets and the increased abundance of English-based information about destination sites via the Internet. This is particularly true of countries in Asia, such as Japan, Korea, and China, but a similar trend is being seen in South-East Asia, North Africa, and Central and Eastern Europe. In response to these changes, many countries have seen rapid growth in the numbers of new ESP courses in tourism and hospitality. These are appearing in both vocational schools and universities and aim to train would-be tourist guides, hotel staff, and other people connected with the industry.

As you can see, the EOP branch of ESP plays a very important role in the society of many countries and has led to many people seeking to develop strong EOP skills before or after they start work. The is especially true in the case of business, which has led to a huge market for English for Business Purposes (EBP), a topic which is fully explored in *Introducing Business English* (Nickerson & Planken, 2016).

ESP in today's globalized world of academia

The other realm in which ESP operates is English for Academic Purposes (EAP). Following a similar trend to that in industry, Friedman's ten 'flatteners' have had a profound effect on academia across the world, and again, this has led to a rapid growth in the importance of EAP.

Since the early 2000s, universities across the world have had to come to terms with a smaller body of local students and an ever-increasing population of overseas students. When the global market share of overseas students is viewed, two features become apparent. The first is that countries that have traditionally attracted the most overseas students, namely the UK and USA, continue to attract the majority of overseas students. In fact, the number of students going to the UK and USA is increasing (OECD, 2014). These students are not, however, native English speakers. Asian students alone account for 53% of all students studying abroad (OECD, 2014), and when you look at individual disciplines the numbers can be even higher. In fact, in 2014, it was estimated that overseas students accounted for 69% of the global population of students studying for Masters in Marketing and Communications degrees and 82% of students studying for Master of Finance degrees (Estrada & Bruggeman, 2014). The majority of these students are coming from Asia. This means that educational institutions increasingly need to provide language instruction to this body of students in the form of pre-sessional courses, writing center guidance, academic writing and presentation courses, graduate thesis support, and so on. Clearly, the development of such courses, programs, and the instruction within them is in the realm of the ESP expert.

Perhaps counterintuitively, the second feature the data reveals is that the *market share* of overseas students in popular destinations like the UK and USA is actually dropping (OECD, 2014). What this means is that other non-English speaking countries around the world are increasing their share of overseas students. In continental Europe, for example, over 6,500 university Masters programs were taught in English in 2013 (Brenn-White & Faethe, 2013, p. 4). In fact, the number of international students in Europe increased by 114% from 2000–2010 (Maslen, 2014). Part of this growth has been spurred by an expansion of the Erasmus program, which has the specific goal of increasing student mobility among neighboring European countries, but another part is due to the increased number of non-European students going to continental Europe to study postgraduate degrees in English. Brenn-White and Faethe (2013) report that the number of Master's degrees offered in English in continental Europe has increased by 42% since 2011.

In Latin America and Africa, an increasing number of universities are also introducing English courses and programs, but here the goal is to improve the job opportunities of their graduates. In Ecuador, for example, students at the Universidad San Francisco de Quito in the capital city of Quito can only graduate if they reach an advanced level of English. In the East African country of Rwanda, university instruction was traditionally carried out in French, but the country switched to English in 2008 so that it could cooperate better with surrounding countries, the majority of which are English-speaking (Green, Fangqing, Cochrane, Dyson, & Paun, 2012).

In Asia, Hong Kong is rapidly becoming the main hub for regional English-based education. The International Consultants for Education and Fairs (ICEF) report that this is the result of two factors. The first is the increased desire of Asian students to seek overseas degrees within their own locality. The second is the result of government initiatives to attract foreign students through improved scholarships, relaxed visa regulations, and a redesign of courses. Since 2007, Hong Kong universities have seen a steady growth in the number of overseas students, but in recent years this trend has accelerated dramatically. For example, in 2012–2013, the University of Hong Kong saw a 42% increase in overseas students over the previous year, the Chinese University of Hong Kong saw a 50% rise, and the Hong Kong University of Science and Technology reported an even larger 55% rise (ICEF Monitor, 2014). This trend can be captured by the fact that 38% of the student body of the University of Hong Kong in 2013 was international students (ICEF Monitor, 2013).

This is not to say that universities in Japan, Korea, and China are unable to attract foreign students, as well. On the contrary, all these countries are seeing strong growths in the number of foreign students. In Korea, for example, the Korean Advanced Institute of Science and Technology (KAIST) has aimed to conduct all classes in English since 2010. This is partially to attract foreign students but also to improve the job prospects of its local graduates, many of whom will end up working in the English environment at Samsung (as previously discussed) (Kang, 2012). In Japan, the Ministry of Education, Culture, Sports, Science and Technology (MEXT) has initiated the "Global 30" program, with the aim of creating all-English programs for overseas students at the country's top institutions. And in China, the government has required universities to offer bilingual lectures to students since 2007, a move that was initially inspired to improve the overall quality of the Chinese students but has subsequently led to a rapid increase in overseas students (Maslen, 2014).

Globalization has also had an impact on academia from the point of view of research. One of the most dramatic effects of globalization on research has been the proliferation of high-impact English-based journals and journal articles, particularly in the areas of science and technology. For example, between 1980 and 2000, the proportion of English publications listed in the Science Citation Index Expanded (SCI Expanded) index of high-impact journals rose from approximately 85% to almost 96% (Bordons & Gómez, 2004). A similar percentage of 96% was given in 2007 for the number of English publications related to public health listed in the Social-Sciences Citation Index (SSCI) of high-impact journals (Larsen & von Ins, 2010). It should be mentioned, though, that counting publications in SCI and SSCI journals can lead to English journals being over-represented. A more conservative estimate of

80% has been given for the proportion of English journals in the Scopus database of high-impact journals (Weijen, 2012). Still, regardless of which estimate is most accurate, the impact on non-English science researchers is clear; they need to publish in English if they hope for a global audience.

An interesting byproduct of globalization has been the introduction of various policies by journal publishers to deal with a growing number of submissions from non-native speakers of English. In order to publish in the Institute of Electrical and Electronics Engineers (IEEE), for example, authors are advised to have their manuscripts checked by a colleague who is fluent in English prior to submission. Similar policies have been adopted both by the American Chemical Society (ACS) and the American Physical Society (APS). In practice, these policies have forced non-native speaker researchers to turn to local ESP experts in their faculties or alternatively send their manuscripts to editing agencies which charge high fees due to the technical nature of the material. In fact, the ACS even provides its own (paid) editing service. The policy of the open-access science and medicine journal PLOS ONE is even more explicit: potential authors must have their manuscripts proofread by a native English speaker or a scientific editing service prior to submission. This situation is unfortunate, of course, because it results in some excellent research ideas never becoming widely known simply due to the language barrier. Indeed, there has been much criticism of the dominance of English in scholarly publication, but it is difficult to see how the trend can be reversed (Lillis & Curry, 2010).

The growing impact of English in the world of academia cannot be overstated. In view of the previously mentioned trends, academic institutions in non-English speaking countries now have a responsibility to not only provide their students with a solid understanding of their chosen discipline, but also the skills needed to take that knowledge, apply it in new and exciting areas of research that involve interdisciplinary, multinational groups of researchers, and eventually publish it in high-ranked journals. This last point is especially important when we remember that journal publications are one of the most important criteria for determining a university's global ranking.

Institutions also need to provide this same quality of education to a growing number of international students whose first language may not be English or even that of the target country. And, to compound the problem further, these same institutions face the challenge of recruiting English faculty and staff that not only understand how to help students develop these skills, but can also train the non-native faculty in different disciplines to deliver English-medium courses that may have both native and non-native students in the classroom. In this environment, it is clear that an instructor with an understanding of ESP becomes an extremely valuable asset to the institution.

As a final example of the impact of English on academia, consider the discovery of the Higgs boson, which was announced on July 4, 2014. The Higgs boson is a high-energy particle that was predicted by Peter Higgs and others in 1964 and formed the central tenet of the Standard Model, a theory that explained electromagnetic, weak, and strong forces in nature. To detect the existence of the particle, scientists had to build a machine that could recreate the environment in the very first microseconds after the formation of the universe. No one person could build such a machine, and so it ended up being created at the European Organization for Nuclear Research (CERN) through the cooperation of 21 European member states, seven observer states, and the collaborative work of over 2500 scientists and engineers. With such a mix of researchers there was obviously a need for a common language of communication and the chosen ones were French and English. However the actual situation at CERN is quite different. As one of the researchers there describes: "all scientists and engineers at CERN communicate professionally only in English. This is the language spoken in all meetings, conferences, seminars and so on, and obviously, the language in which all scientific papers are published" (Shoshany, 2014, n.p.). This comment is revealing in itself, but it is also interesting to note that the actual announcement of the Higgs boson was through a live feed around the world . . . in English.

Positioning of ESP in occupational and academic settings

Now that we have looked at the importance of English in the workplace and academia, let's see how the positioning of ESP in these two areas impacts on the way it is delivered.

Positioning of ESP in occupational settings

In occupational settings, most companies will offer their workers training opportunities that are not specifically limited to language training. In engineering and manufacturing companies, for example, workers will usually undergo training when they first enter the company and learn about the key parts of the company structure, the knowledge and skills needed to complete particular jobs and tasks, and the handling and operation of specialized hardware and software tools. As part of this training, workers may receive a few tens of hours of language skills instruction, the results of which might determine which division or type of work they are assigned. Then, throughout the time that the worker is contracted to the company, they are likely to receive further opportunities to continue their professional development as they move up the career ladder.

Of course, things are different in industries where effective language skills are the primary factors that determine the success of a worker's performance. Returning to the call-center industry, workers are usually required to complete an intensive and sometimes lengthy program of language training before starting work, and their success in transferring what they learn in training to actual practice may be a significant factor in their ability to keep the job (Friginal, 2007; Lockwood, 2012).

ESP courses and programs in workplace settings are often run by in-house training centers. These might be small-scale units organized by individual sites that hire just a few full-time or contract instructors. Or, they may be very-large scale units positioned centrally within the company structure and staffed by tens or even hundreds of training specialists. Depending on the industry, these training centers might be responsible for organizing all training programs within the company and subsequently have carefully prepared course designs, materials, in-class activities, and evaluation procedures. This is an important point to remember because it means that the responsibilities of a successful ESP program do not always fall on a single individual. On the contrary, in many settings, the complex tasks of designing, implementing, and evaluating an ESP course or program will be shared among the members of a team, each person making a contribution based on their own area of ESP expertise.

If a company does not have the resources to run a training center, it may still offer centralized training through the use of in-house training materials made available to workers in the form of handbooks, workflow plans, guidelines, memos, and online learning packages. Workers are free to consult these resources as and when necessary. Alternatively, or in addition to in-house materials, a company may offer workers the opportunity to take off-site courses and programs and may even hire specialist consultants to provide focused training for small groups of its workers. A company may even hire consultants to help it develop a company-wide strategic training program, including all course designs, materials, and teaching plans. Again, this setting is important to understand from an ESP perspective because it means that experts in ESP can have vital roles to play in the success of a company, and subsequently can demand some of the highest salaries in the teaching profession.

Positioning of ESP in academic settings

ESP courses and programs in academia are usually positioned in one of three locations (Charles & Pecorari, 2016). The first is an academic unit such as a department of English, TEFL/TESL, or Applied Linguistics. In this location, the ESP staff may be hired as fully fledged department members, but they might also be hired as part-time or contract workers without the privileges offered to their co-workers, such as their own offices, research grants, and access to the complete range of university facilities and resources. The advantage of positioning ESP in an academic unit is that the department itself can provide the ESP courses and programs with a certain level of respectability and stability within the institution, leaving them less susceptible to sudden changes from the outside; for example, as a result of budget or staff cuts. The disadvantage is that the ESP staff might end up having to do all the tasks associated with designing and running particular courses on their own. Also, they can easily become isolated from the other members of the department as a result of physical distance, differences in academic interests, and even differences in professional and career interests. Clearly, in this setting there is an important role for administrators to provide the ESP staff with opportunities to meet with the other department members and provide them with resources and support for their courses.

As an alternative to positioning ESP courses and programs in academic units, Charles and Pecorari (2016) explain that some institutions position them in independent support centers, or as part of the institution's general support service framework. In this model, the ESP staff are less likely to be isolated from their colleagues, allowing them to work in teams to develop courses and programs. Also, the independence may help the staff to escape from the lengthy meetings and tedious politics that are often associated with working in an academic department. On the other hand, again, the ESP staff may not be afforded the privileges given to full faculty members and may be offered fewer career and promotion opportunities. Independent support centers are also more easily affected by changes in institution policies, such as budget changes, leading to less stability. Again, administrators have an important role to play to ensure that the ESP courses and programs are properly reviewed and supported, and that the ESP staff are provided with a stable and secure place of work with plenty of opportunities for professional development.

The third case that Charles and Pecorari (2016) describe is for ESP to be positioned within a specialist department. This situation may arise when the specialist department identifies particular language needs of their students that are not provided by the general English program offered within the institution. Rather like some companies in occupational settings, the department may seek out specialist ESP experts in the target area and hire them in a position similar to a consultant (although usually with a far lower salary). In this position, the consultant is likely to be given the task of designing custom courses and teaching these to their students in isolation, with administrators of the program playing only a minor role in its development and implementation.

TASK 2.2 Working in EAP and EOP settings

Using the boxes on the next page, summarize the potential benefits and challenges of working as an instructor in different EAP and EOP settings. Suggestions for the first setting are included. Next, add some other benefits and challenges that were not mentioned earlier.

EAP (in an academic department)

Benefits: good admin support

Challenges: isolated from colleagues

EAP (in a learner support center)

Benefits:

Challenges:

EAP (in a specialist department)

Benefits:

Challenges:

EOP (in a training center)

Benefits:

Challenges:

Based on your responses above, if you had a free choice on where to teach ESP, which setting would you choose?

TASK 2.3 Making a case for ESP

Imagine that you are an ESP instructor in a university support center or a workplace training center. The institution regrettably offers no opportunities for professional development or research opportunities to its staff members.

What arguments could you make to the administrators for introducing a professional development scheme?

What arguments could you present to the administrators for allowing ESP instructors some time to carry out research?

Contentious issues in ESP: is the globalization of English a good thing?

Challenges in the workplace

As you have now learned, there are many historical, economical, and political reasons why English has become the leading language of the globalized workplace. The common language of English allows workers from different countries and cultures to communicate with each other to achieve a common goal, be it the safe take-off and landing of an airplane in the aviation industry, or the successful design and manufacture of cars in the automobile industry. It also allows workers to communicate with senior staff, co-workers, and customers, who may only speak English. The common language of English also reduces the need for potentially misleading translations of documentation, such as safety manuals and user guides, preventing accidents and potential litigation.

However, the adoption of English as a globalized language affects workplace practices in ways that are not always so positive. Companies may choose to cut costs by hiring overseas workers who are used to widely different salaries and standards of living than those of local residents. Or, they may simply outsource jobs completely. As an example of this latter policy, in recent years a call to a local bank, smartphone operator, or insurance company in the UK is often rerouted to a call-center operator in the Philippines or India. Such decisions can have a drastic effect on the job opportunities of local people.

English-only policies in the workplace can potentially be discriminatory against some worker groups. For example, in 2012, a medical center in the USA settled a case with the Equal Employment Opportunity Commission (EEOC) after it was found to be using an English-only policy with Filipino-American workers, but not Spanish-speaking workers (Tuschman, 2012). The requirement to use English for workplace activities can also lead to a decrease in work efficiency and high costs related to the language training of staff. Non-native English-speaking workers may also suffer from a loss of self-confidence, regardless of their level of fluency. This can result in them communicating less with their co-workers, and can cause them to simplify or even avoid documenting tasks. They may even resist the need to use English. As Neeley (2012, n.p.) reports, "Using English as a business language can damage employee morale, create unhealthy divides between native and non-native speakers, and decrease the overall productivity of team members."

Challenges in academia

The globalization of English in academia has given rise to many new learning opportunities for students around the world. It has also democratized teaching and research, allowing people from different countries and cultures to work at the world's most prestigious universities and research centers.

On the other hand, similar problems to those found in industry are associated with this dramatic shift. In a non-English speaking country, courses taught within an English-only framework are likely to be discriminatory toward local students, who can be expected to require longer times than their native-speaker counterparts to read the course materials, process the taught information, and produce the required reports. Local students may also suffer from a loss of self-confidence and their weaker language skills may prevent them interacting fully in class with their teachers and cohort. The same might also be said for local teachers.

At the institutional level, there is evidence that English-only courses cover less material and at a shallower level than courses delivered in the students' native language. The courses can also be more expensive as they require either specially hired native English instructors or an English language training scheme for local instructors. An influx of specially hired instructors can also lead to instability in human resource management, which can then affect the quality of courses and teaching in general.

Finally, it should not be forgotten that the growth of English at a company or academic institution almost always goes together with a decrease in the importance of the local language. Local languages are usually learned during childhood, but the mastery of academic language, specialized terminology, industry jargon, business politeness forms, and other idiosyncratic language can only be gained through formal education and use in real-world settings. By adopting English-only policies in study and work, there is a high risk that these more advanced forms of local language use will be lost.

Many of the negative issues associated with the globalization of English can be mitigated to some extent through careful planning, implementation, and monitoring of newly introduced English language policies. Governments can also play a role in deciding to what extent English policies will be advanced, supported, and controlled. Of course, this topic is often beyond the realm of most ESP instructors. But, if you are or hope to be involved in any way with ESP course planning and administration, it is certainly useful to be aware of these important issues.

Research ideas

Here are some possible ideas for small-scale or large-scale research projects that stem from the topics discussed in this chapter.

Understanding the status of ESP

Select a sample of job postings for English teaching positions at academic institutions in an L1 speaking country. What qualifications, experience, and job expectations are described? From this analysis, how many positions have a clear ESP focus? If you find any, are the conditions of the job better, worse, or the same as those for other teaching positions? Now repeat the experiment for English teaching positions in workplace settings. Do you notice any differences? Finally, repeat both the above analyses for a country where English is a second or foreign language. Again, do you notice any differences? What does your analysis of job postings reveal about the status of ESP in the countries you investigated?

Investigating an English-only language policy

Find or carry out a case study on the implementation of an English-only language policy at a company or academic institution that interests you. What were the reasons for the policy change? How was it implemented? How successful was it? What positive and negative effects did the policy have on the people at the institution and the institution as a whole? How might some of the negative effects be mitigated?

Closing reflection

Now that you have come to the end of the chapter, you should be able to summarize events and conditions that have led to English becoming an important factor in the success of academic and industrial institutions around the world. You should also be able to describe some of the different positions that ESP courses and programs have in these institutions, and explain how the growing importance of English in academia and industry can have negative effects on the people and institutions where new language policies are implemented.

Here are a few more questions to consider:

1 Which of the points covered in the chapter were new to you? Did you find them interesting and relevant in terms of your own learning goals? Were there any points that you found confusing or that you disagreed with?
2 What points from the chapter do you think you can immediately put to use in your own learning or teaching context?
3 Based on what you have learned, which stakeholders in ESP do you think would be most interested in hearing about the history and growth of English?
4 In what ways do you think instructors could use the information in this chapter in the classroom when faced with learners who had little motivation to study?
5 If you were asked to make a case for introducing ESP into an already established general English program, what points would you include?

Further resources

Newspaper articles

Anthony, L., (2009). Japan Times Forum on English Education: Engineers must have English skills to succeed. *Japan Times Newspaper* (in English). Published October 5, 2009, pp. 8–9. Retrieved from www.laurenceanthony.net/research/japan_times/japan_times_disc_20091005.pdf

Trends in globalization

OECD Directorate for Education and Skills. Retrieved from www.oecd.org/edu/

General statistics

Statista – The Portal for Statistics. Retrieved from www.statista.com/

Chapter 3

Introducing the four pillars of ESP

In Chapter 2, you learned that globalization has led to English playing an increasingly important role in academia and workplaces around the world. Although globalization presents many challenges, providing learners with the necessary language, genres, and skills of their target academic or workplace settings can help empower them as they navigate through this complex world. So, how do ESP administrators work with ESP instructors to create an effective environment for the learner? This is the focus of Chapter 3.

In this chapter, I'll first introduce the four 'pillars' of the ESP approach: needs analysis, learning objectives, materials and methods, and evaluation. Next, I'll discuss how these pillars support a learning environment in which learners, instructors, and administrators interact and collaborate in sometimes unique ways to meet the aims of ESP courses and programs. Then, I'll discuss the contentious issue of who can and should teach ESP within this framework.

By the end of the chapter, you should be able to describe the main components of an ESP course or program, and understand how these components fit together. You should also start to understand some of the challenges facing instructors in an ESP program, and be able to present a case why English language experts rather than target subject specialists are in the best position to become ESP instructors.

Opening reflection

Imagine that you have been hired by a global banking company that routes its customer inquiries to a call-center in the Philippines. The company management team has asked you to provide a three-day intensive English course to help the call-center staff improve their responses to customer inquiries. You have been given one day to discuss the course with the management team and one week to prepare the course and create a teaching strategy.

> Prior to the start of the course, what kind of information would you try to gather about the call-center staff? How might you go about obtaining a description of call-center English? What materials and teaching strategies might you employ to help the staff improve their language skills? On completion of the course, how would you measure success?

Commentary

As you attempted to answer the reflection questions, you will have probably found that none of them was straightforward. Each question could be answered in multiple ways, and it would it be difficult to evaluate the correctness of the answers without actually meeting the management team and staff, running the course, and looking at the outcomes. But, that does not mean that the exercise was futile. Each question was designed to help you think about one of the four 'pillars' of ESP teaching. The first question relates to the needs of the call-center staff: what can they already do in English? What new language skills will they require? What do they see as strengths and weaknesses in their English ability? The second question relates to learning objectives: what language skills are used in the call-center industry? What are reasonable goals for a three-day course? What sequence should be used to introduce the target language skills? The third question relates to materials and methods in the classroom: is there a readily available textbook that you can use? Will you need to prepare handouts? What individual, pair work, and group activities should you employ? Finally, the last question relates to evaluation: how will you know if the learners have achieved the goals of the course? How can you assess your own performance and the course as a whole?

The four pillars of ESP

Figure 3.1 shows the four pillars of ESP. These four pillars will be considered in depth in later chapters of this book. Here, let us consider them briefly in the context of the call-center example.

Needs analysis

If you look back at the definition of ESP given in Chapter 1, you'll remember that the starting point of any ESP course is an understanding of the learners' needs. In the opening reflection, the needs of the call-center staff were in some sense given to you by the management team when they explained that

Figure 3.1 The four pillars of ESP.

the call-center staff needed to improve their responses to customer inquiries. However, this stated need is not only implicit but also vague. In answer to the first question, therefore, you would want to establish exactly why the management believes that the staff needed to improve their English.

First, you could ask the management team about their expectations of call-center staff in terms of performance measures. For example, you could ask them how long staff should take to understand a call, decide an action plan, or transfer the call to a senior staff member. You could also ask them about the kinds of questions that staff usually receive, and the ways in which customers evaluate staff; for example, in terms of politeness, ease of understanding, or willingness to listen. These questions would allow you to more exactly specify the *necessities* that determine the success in a customer-call situation. Next, you could ask the management team about the educational background of the staff, their previous exposure to English, their ages and experience, and their general English proficiency. This information would help you to understand the potential *lacks* that the staff might have, and also help you predict the likelihood of the course being a success. Finally, you could also ask about the desires of the staff themselves to help you understand their *wants* at the company. For example, you could ask if the staff actually wanted to take a training course, or if they believed that their English needed improving. If these *wants* diverged greatly from the *necessities* and *lacks*, you may have to consider how to motivate the staff to actively participate in the course.

In addition to these questions, you would probably also want to know about the precise environment in which the course would be conducted. How many staff members would attend? How long would the training sessions be? Would there be facilities to play audio materials? Would the room be large enough to allow the participants to move around and form pairs or groups? The answers to all these questions would have an impact on what you could and couldn't do in the classroom.

All ESP courses start out with questions about the *necessities*, *lacks*, and *wants* of the target learners, as well as questions about the environment in which the learning will take place. Sometimes, the answers may only be available after carrying out lengthy and extensive surveys of the learners through collaborative efforts of administrative staff and colleagues. Other times, the answers may only become known on the first day that you walk into class. Nevertheless, it is important to at least consider these questions and attempt to conduct a needs analysis as best you can (see Brown, 2016; L. Flowerdew, 2013 for further discussions of needs analysis).

Learning objectives

When beginning to prepare for a new course or seminar, an ESP instructor will often not be familiar with the specific field of the target learners. It is therefore important that they can learn to quickly establish what language, genres, and skills the learners might be expected to use in a target situation and form a set of learning objectives for the class.

In the opening reflection, there are many resources that you could use to obtain a description of call-center English. Your first resource might be your own experience of calling a company and being routed to a call-center. What sorts of questions did you ask, and what sorts of reply did you receive? What level of politeness would you expect from the call-center staff, and how native-like would you want their pronunciation to be? Another resource is the company itself. If you ask the company management, they may be able to provide you with sample call interactions and assessment guidelines. In this role, the management is serving as specialist informants, filling in the gaps in your knowledge of the target genre. You might also read up on the skills needed by call-centers operators in specialized ESP journals such as *English for Specific Purposes*. If you are lucky, you may also find textbooks on call-center English that could serve as a useful resource. Finally, you may be able to search the Internet and download actual audio samples or transcripts of call-center interactions to read. With these electronic sample texts available to you, a further possibility is to analyze them using freeware text analysis tools, such as *AntConc* (Anthony, 2017a), that can instantly count all the words and phrases in the data and rank them by frequency of occurrence.

However, learning objectives should not be framed only in terms of language, genres, and skills. It is also important to establish a set of learning *strategy* objectives for the class. For example, many learners believe that rote memorization of long lists of 'difficult' vocabulary words is an effective way to improve their English skills, despite mountains of counter evidence (see Nation, 2001). In class, you may want to introduce more effective vocabulary learning approaches, such as the focused learning of high frequency words using word cards.

Once you have decided on a set of learning objectives, you then need to consider how to *sequence* these in a way that is not only clear and logical, but also interesting and enjoyable. The sequencing should also allow for flexibility and provide learners with opportunities for practice and reinforcement.

Materials and methods

As you learned in Chapter 1, ESP instructors are usually not committed to a single learning theory or teaching methodology. They are often much more eclectic in their approaches to classroom teaching. What works for one set of learners with a particular set of needs may prove to be unsuccessful with another group of learners with similar needs, simply due to the group's different ages and experiences. For this reason, the needs analysis discussed earlier can be helpful not only in establishing what to teach the learners, but also which teaching methodologies are likely to be successful with them. In the case of a call-center English course, a needs analysis would hopefully establish how many learners are coming and what sort of people they are. Based on this knowledge, you might be able to determine if pair work, group work, or class work would be most suitable. Some learners may find role-plays to be engaging, whereas others may prefer to practice simulated calls on a computer, with their responses recorded for you to analyze later. If you determine that politeness strategies may be needed, a more traditional teacher-fronted approach may be useful so you can explain the different strategies in the most time-efficient manner, before allowing the participants to practice these strategies in pairs. If you identify pronunciation problems, you may believe that the time is too limited to give the problem the proper attention in class. In this case, you may believe it is worth helping the participants identify and correct their own weaknesses through the use of online audio analysis and playback tools as one example of developing learner autonomy.

The choice of teaching methodology may be determined by or lead to the use of a particular set of teaching materials. If a textbook is readily available for the course, you might decide to use this or adapt it as necessary for the target learners. Unfortunately, in many situations, a textbook is not available and so provisions must be made. One possible source of useful materials may emerge from your analysis of the target language discussed earlier. If you were able to establish the key language features of call-center interactions based on the materials you found, perhaps those same materials could serve as useful 'authentic' teaching materials in the classroom. Another example might be audio samples or transcripts of call-center interactions. Showing these in the classroom and critiquing them may highlight important language points. One danger with this source of material, however, is its level of complexity. Authentic samples may include noises, fillers, pauses, complex language, insults, and threats. You might believe that these features would overwhelm the target learners, especially if they are only just beginners with little experience of the target setting. In this case, it might be necessary to adapt or simplify the materials allowing you to focus on target language points. On the other hand, if the learners are more advanced, these noises, fillers, pauses, and so on may be exactly the types of phenomenon that you should be helping them to deal with.

Evaluation

The final pillar of any ESP course is evaluation. You may immediately associate evaluation with the measurement of learner performance gains on a test: how much have the learners improved as a result of the course? This is clearly an important question. However, in an ESP setting, it is also important to evaluate the success of the ESP course itself, and also the quality of instruction. In the case of a call-center English course, therefore, you might first want to measure how much the call-center staff had overcome the *lacks* that were identified at the needs analysis stage. In other words, you would need to establish to what degree the learners had successfully achieved the goals of the course. One way to do this would be to ask the learners to carry out a real-world task (or a simulation of a real-world task) and evaluate their performance on it. One challenge in doing this, however, is your own ability to judge the success of the learner. This can be particularly problematic when you are asked to teach an ESP course that is very much outside of your experience. In such cases, again, the use of specialist informants can be particularly useful. For example, you could ask a member of the company management team to come in and evaluate the performances of staff members while they answer a real or simulated call.

In order to evaluate the success of the course, you would want to determine how many participants started the course, how many completed it, and what the success rate was. This quantitative data is usually relatively easy to obtain and can be very persuasive for the management. But you should be careful, because companies are often overly interested in these numbers. To prevent any misunderstandings with the management team, it would be advisable to establish from the outset some reasonable attendance rates, completion rates, and success rates. You might also want to obtain qualitative data about the success of the course. For example, you should probably find out how the learners perceived the course: did they find it useful? Did they enjoy the activities and feel motivated to learn more? Did they believe that the course was too short or long? Did they think some important language skills were missing from the course? This kind of information is often more difficult to obtain, but a well-designed survey completed anonymously by the learners can be very revealing.

Finally, you should try to evaluate your own success in leading the course. One way to partially answer this question is by analyzing test results. If the majority of participants made large gains in their language performance and successfully completed the course, part of this success must be attributed to the instructor. However, again, a qualitative survey of learners' impressions of a course can provide important information on an instructor's effectiveness. For example, learners may report that they appreciated the gains that they made but found the teaching method dull and the amount of homework excessive.

TASK 3.1 Understanding the four pillars of ESP

Imagine that you have been assigned to teach a one-semester university first-year course in academic lecture comprehension. The course is held in the faculty of liberal arts and humanities, and is targeted at a wide range of international students who have English as a second or foreign language.

In a one-hour meeting with the course management team prior to the start of the course, what questions would you ask? List your questions and categorize them in terms of needs, learning objectives, materials and methods, and evaluation procedures.

The roles of learners, instructors, and administrators in ESP

So far, we have looked at the four pillars of ESP in isolation. In practice, if we want a successful ESP course or program, we also need to consider how the building of these pillars will be influenced by the experiences and perceptions of learners, instructors, and administrators. In the opening reflection exercise, the discussion focused on how an individual ESP instructor might prepare for a course. Certainly, instructors play an important role in determining the success of ESP through pre-course planning, in-class teaching, and post-course evaluations. However, it should not be forgotten that ESP is essentially a learner-centered approach. Learners also play a very important role in determining the success of an ESP course. Perhaps even more important is the role of administrators. In many ESP contexts, it is the job of the course and program management team to define the learning and teaching goals, choose materials, and decide on how courses are evaluated. With these points in mind, let us now look at the roles of learners, instructors, and administrators in different ESP contexts.

Learners

The role that learners will see themselves having in an ESP course or program will largely depend on their perceptions of the status of that course or program, the perceptions they have of instructors, and the ways they perceive English in their lives. Working backwards, if a learner perceives English to be an important factor that will determine their current and future success, they are likely to play an active role in their own ESP learning. As a result, they are more likely to select English courses that closely match their needs and choose courses regardless of whether or not the courses are required or elective. They are also likely to be more aware of their *needs* and *lacks*, and have stronger views on what they *want* from their courses. During study periods, they are likely to work hard to understand and master the content, and work toward completing their studies with the highest grades and performance. As a result, they are also likely to be more objective and critical in their evaluation of their courses. On the other hand, if learners perceive English to have little impact on their current or future lives, they are likely to have a poorer understanding of their needs, have a lower motivation to study hard in class, and be less inclined to express their opinions on course surveys.

These tendencies can be exaggerated depending on how the learners perceive their instructors. If they perceive their instructors to be ill-qualified to teach the target material, they may quickly begin to lose interest in study, which will adversely affect the quality of learning, their desire to continue studying, and their success in mastering the target English language skills. This can be a common problem in ESP settings, where learners may believe that they are more knowledgeable about the subject content matter than their instructors.

In all cultures, learners are heavily influenced by their perception of the importance of a particular course or program. In many academic settings, program entry and pre-course requirements are stated in terms of general proficiency scores, such as those determined by IELTS, TOEFL, and TOEIC. As a result, EAP courses that are designed to help learners reach the required entry scores on these tests are likely to be treated very seriously by learners, leading them to play active roles in their own learning. On the other hand, many post-entry EAP courses offered at institutions around the world have only an elective status with a minimal reward structure in terms of credit allocation or tuition-fee reduction. These EAP courses are being positioned at the fringes of regular programs, and so it is no surprise that learners are more likely to dismiss them as having little relevance (Anthony, 2009). The snowball effect from this is that the courses themselves may receive poor enrolments, creating an impression at the institutional level that the courses and their associated instructors and organizational units are ineffective in some way.

A similar situation can occur in an EOP setting when a company creates language materials, resources, and courses that are then positioned at the fringes of a worker's job activities. For example, a company will find little success if they place a new set of EOP materials in its online repository but then provide no incentive or time for workers to access those materials. In reality, however, the opposite is often the case. Companies are generally very strategic in their allocation and use of funds, and pay close attention to the management of both human and learning resources. As a result, it is not uncommon to find companies introducing language programs in a combined package with stringent requirements (e.g. all staff under the age of 25 must participate in the course), strong incentives to learn (e.g. increased salaries and promotion opportunities based on performance scores), and more general educational/promotional packages that introduce workers to the importance of English within the company and the ways in which they are likely to use it (see, for example, Neeley, 2011).

Instructors

In academic settings, ESP instructors play an important role for learners, who may look to the instructors for support not only in their current studies, but also in providing them with guidance for their postgraduate studies and careers. ESP instructors in academia may also be given the role of designing and managing the entire English support program, especially if the institution has a strong focus in a particular discipline that requires English. This means that ESP instructors might be responsible for establishing the four pillars of ESP for multiple courses, affecting how English is taught across a whole faculty or the institution as a whole. They may also be the first points of contact for major publishers wanting to develop general materials and courses. In this case, they can play an important role in changing the way English is taught in the broader scope of society.

In occupational settings, ESP instructors are likely to play a vital support role for workers, helping them manage their daily tasks and providing them with opportunities for career advancement. They are also likely to be in a unique bridging position between workers and management. As a result, they can play a vital role in developing new professional development schemes and may even advise the company on how it can better manage its human resources. Again, these roles can have a surprisingly large effect in the broader scope of society, as we saw in the examples of Nissan and Rakuten in Japan, which were discussed in Chapter 2.

In much of the literature, ESP instructors have often been referred to as *practitioners* to reflect the wide range of work that they can be involved in, including examining the needs of learners, researching target language skills, designing courses and materials, collaborating with specialist informants, instructing learners, and evaluating learner performance and the success the course or program itself (Dudley-Evans & St. John, 1998; Swales, 1985). As we observed previously, this picture of ESP instructors matches a particular type of ESP setting where they are working in isolation, perhaps as a contract ESP instructor in a university department or as an ESP consultant for a company. This is a common setup, but not the only one possible.

In many settings, ESP instructors are working as part of a team, with the responsibilities for establishing the four pillars of ESP courses shared among the members, each with their own strengths and weaknesses. So, where might these strengths and weaknesses lie?

ESP instructors usually come from one of two backgrounds. Perhaps the most common type of ESP instructors have backgrounds in the humanities, where they are likely to have gained undergraduate and graduate degrees in literature, education, linguistics, applied linguistics, TEFL/TESL, or one of many related subjects. On completing their studies, they may have joined a school or university department where they taught general English courses and perhaps only later became interested in ESP on exposure to ideas such as those presented in this book. With a strong background in teaching methodology, these instructors are often best positioned to determine the types of materials and activities that will 'work' with learners. They are also in a good position to judge many of the immediate general language needs of the learners. On the other hand, they may not have a clear understanding of the specific target needs of the learners, especially if the learners are in a highly specialized discipline, such as a STEM subject, medicine, or nursing, with which the instructor has little experience.

The second most common type of ESP instructors have backgrounds in specialized disciplines such as STEM fields or medicine. These instructors are likely to have gained undergraduate and perhaps graduate degrees in one of these subjects and perhaps gone on to work in the field for some years. Some will have moved into ESP later in their careers, perhaps due to the job market, their changing interests, or after retirement in industry. Others may have decided after their studies that their value to society was in another area and landed in English language teaching almost by accident. It is a surprising fact that many ESP instructors started their teaching careers in small English conversation schools and gained experience from teaching learners of many different ages and interests. Clearly, ESP instructors in this category have much to offer from the point of view of identifying the needs of learners. If they were graduates of specialist degrees, they can be well placed to determine the specific needs of learners in EAP settings. Similarly, if they have experience working in industry, the can be uniquely positioned to provide insights on the occupational needs of learners. On the other hand, some ESP instructors coming from a specialist discipline background will have little or no experience in teaching. They may also be unaware of the language difficulties faced by target learners. As a result, they might resort to teaching ESP courses in a similar way to how they learned the target discipline themselves, focusing extensively on word forms, encouraging translations into the L1, and providing lengthy explanations of language phenomenon over practice in language use.

In view of these strengths and weaknesses, there is a clear advantage in adopting a team approach to ESP course and program design where a mixed group of instructors is involved. But, of course, this is not always possible. Ultimately, instructors need to be able to identify their weaknesses and seek support where it is needed. This brings us to the role of administrators.

Administrators

Administrators play a key role in determining the success of ESP courses and programs. First, administrators usually decide if and when ESP courses will run, and will often determine the overall aims of courses. In EAP settings, they may decide to run courses to address language learning problems identified by particular specialist departments. For example, a department may identify that its cohort of overseas learners is struggling to complete essays and assignments and recommend EAP support courses for them. Other times, administrators may be encouraged to run EAP courses to attract overseas students, or increase revenue for the institution. In EOP settings, the decision to run courses may result from the identification of specific language problems that affect customer satisfaction, or a new strategy to attract foreign customers, or perhaps to increase revenue through improved training of the salesforce. As you can see, the factors that administrators have to consider in EAP and EOP settings are not so different.

Administrators are also the people who usually decide how the ESP courses will be run and the importance attached to them. For example, will the courses be given an elective or required status? What will the rewards be for learners who successfully complete the courses? Will the ESP courses be given in isolation or will they be integrated together to form an ESP program?

Finally, administrators have important roles to play in the general management of ESP courses and programs. The first task they may face is the management of funding and the longevity of a program. In EAP settings, administrators need to decide if the budget for ESP will come from learner tuition fees, institution special funding, or perhaps external funding schemes and government initiatives. Student tuition fees are usually a guaranteed source of income, but may vary considerably from year to year. Special internal and external funding, on the other hand, might be more stable, but there is no guarantee that it will arrive each year and usually it has a fixed term of use. If funding is not stable, the administrators may have to increase learner numbers or reduce instructor numbers. Alternatively, they might offer fewer course hours for learners, or ask instructors to teach longer. These decisions will impact directly on the possibly teaching materials and methods available to instructors.

Funding may also determine the acceptable quality of both learners and instructors on a program. For example, to maintain or increase the numbers of learners in a tuition-based system, it might be necessary to accept lower entry requirements. Similarly, to cut personnel costs, administrators may choose to accept instructors with fewer qualifications and less experience, or offer fewer opportunities for later professional development. Again, these decisions will affect how the ESP courses are designed in terms of the teaching and learning objectives, and the expectations of instructors teaching the courses.

In EOP settings, funding will almost always be provided by higher management, but it may be a fixed amount each year, or vary depending on the learner outcomes. This leads to questions about the best uses for funds. Should they be spent on general learning programs for the entire workforce, or should the funds be strategically targeted at the workers most likely to get benefit from the training? Similarly, should the funds be spent on hiring one or two very knowledgeable and experienced consultants, or should they be spent on hiring many less knowledgeable and experienced general instructors?

Another important role for administrators is the management of opportunity in the program. For learners, this means providing them with an opportunity to learn the necessary language and skills to meet their target needs. To achieve this, administrators need to provide courses that are founded on well-established language and learning theories, are delivered using effective teaching methods and materials, and are evaluated fairly and accurately. They also need to hire good instructors with the right balance of teaching experience and knowledge of the target setting. For instructors, administrators must provide opportunities for them to interact with others in the development and teaching of courses so that they are not forced to undertake all the work on their own. In addition, they need to provide opportunities for instructors to take part in professional development and career development initiatives, especially if they are positioned in centers where such chances are normally limited.

As you can see, it is not enough to simply construct four well-designed pillars of ESP. A critical factor in the success of an ESP course or program is an understanding of the roles played by learners, instructors, and administrators, and how each group interacts with the others.

TASK 3.2 Positioning yourself in ESP

Think about your own educational background and teaching experiences.

What strengths and weaknesses do you have when it comes to teaching an EAP or EOP course in a subject area that you are not fully familiar with?

If you could work with others to design an effective ESP course, what strengths and experiences would you want them to have?

If you were an administrator of an ESP course or program, who would you hire: a person knowledgeable about English language teaching but with little specialist subject knowledge, or a subject specialist who has never taught in a classroom? Give reasons for your answer.

Contentious issues in ESP: who should teach ESP?

In the field of ESP, there has been long-running debate about if and to what degree an ESP instructor needs discipline-specific knowledge of the target setting. Should a teacher of an EOP course in English for Nursing, for example, have experience of patient care? If you ask subject specialists in the target field, they will inevitably answer "yes" and support their answer by explaining that without a background and experience in the field, the instructor would be unable to explain to the learners what language is appropriate, how it is used, and – perhaps most importantly – why it is used in this way.

Interestingly, many ESP scholars appear to agree, at least partially, with this view. As a result, they often present an argument for team-teaching in ESP, where a regular English teacher (with possible experience in ESP) works together with a field specialist (see Dudley-Evans & St. John, 1998). In this setup, the specialist informant would provide input on course goals and suitable materials, and perhaps even teach together with the ESP instructor in the classroom. But, this introduces a potentially dangerous power difference between the two parties. If the course is being run within a specialist department, the specialist informant may consider themselves to be the expert in the equation and start monopolizing decisions, despite their limited or non-existent knowledge of and experience with language teaching. This danger can increase if the ESP instructor starts believing everything that the specialist informant says (Swales, 1990). What's more, team-teaching in most cases is impractical due to time constraints, scheduling problems, institutional policies and politics, and different expectation of the individual parties (Barron, 1992).

So, can a case be made for a subject specialist to 'go it alone' in an ESP class? In other words, do we really need ESP instructors at all? One argument against subject specialists teaching ESP alone is that they do not have sufficient English skills to lead a class. Certainly, this is the case in many countries, where the poor language skills of subject specialists serve as the main reason for introducing ESP into the curriculum in the first place (Madeleine, 2007). Second, subject specialists are often too busy with their own teaching and research to care much about ESP. Third, they may simply be unwilling to teach ESP classes; for example, if the courses are considered low in status within the institution or offer few financial rewards. Fourth, even if a subject specialist has sufficient English skills and is willing to teach the course, they are still not experienced language experts. In other words, they will probably have rarely considered what language skills they and others use in the target field, have little understanding about which of these may cause difficulties to learners, and have only very limited experience in presenting language concepts to learners, beyond providing them with definitions and L2-L1 translations. What's more, they are likely to have little or no experience in getting learners to practice using language in a controlled or free environment.

If subject specialists will find it difficult to 'go it alone' in an ESP class, what about ESP instructors? Can they be trusted to teach ESP effectively? Clearly, you would expect an ESP instructor to have sufficient English skills to lead a class, be interested in their learners enough to care about what they are teaching, be willing to teach in the classroom, and have a strong background in language pedagogy. But, what exactly would they introduce to learners if they don't know the 'what', 'why', and 'how' of the target setting? The regrettable reality is that ESP instructors around the world struggle greatly with this problem. Sometimes, they might be lucky and find that a commercial publisher has created a textbook that at least partially meets their learners' needs. Hence, we see many ESP-focused books with titles like *English for Nursing*, *English for Science and Engineering*, and *Business English*. But, what happens when no such textbooks exist? Should the instructor choose to use a more general textbook and effectively move away from the basic premises of ESP? Or, should they begin the time-consuming task of learning about the target setting as a step toward creating their own materials?

I will return to all these questions in later chapters of this book, but perhaps the simple answer is to not consider ESP as an endeavor that should be carried out by individuals at all. Rather, as we saw in some of the ESP settings earlier, it should be considered as a team project, where each individual's expertise is respected and utilized. Some members of the team with a strong understanding and connection with the target setting can establish the basic needs of the learners. Then, members of the team with a strong background in language theory and learning can devise an appropriate set of teaching and learning objectives for the classroom. Other members may have strengths in materials design and others again may be exceptional at presenting material and motivating learners in the classroom. Combining the strengths of team members in this way can result in a stable and effective

ESP program. This does not mean, however, that ESP courses created by individuals working alone are doomed to failure. On the contrary, many successful ESP instructors work in such environments. We will look at what they do in later chapters of this book.

Research ideas

Here are some possible ideas for small-scale or large-scale research projects that stem from the topics discussed in this chapter.

Finding the four pillars

Review the course description or syllabus for an English course given in an EAP or EOP setting (for examples, see Woodrow, 2018). Discuss if and how the four pillars of ESP are detailed in the description. What additional information would you want added to the description if you were taking on the course for the first time?

Crossing the boundaries

If you study or work in an academic context where language support classes are offered to second and foreign language learners of specialist subjects, ask the specialist subject teachers about their impressions of the language support teachers and the courses they manage. Do they believe that the teachers are effective? Do they think the courses are useful? Do they see areas for improvement? Are they interested in working with English teachers to improve the English education of their students? What reasons do they give for their opinions?

If you study or work in an EOP setting that includes some kind of language support program, ask the administrators and learners of that program on their opinions of the instructors, the courses, and the effectiveness of the program.

What conclusions can you draw about the views of ESP instructors from these observations?

Closing reflection

Now that you have come to the end of the chapter, you should have a basic understanding of the four main 'pillars' of ESP. Each of these will be expanded on in subsequent chapters, but even now, you should understand how they stand together and some of the ways in which you can get information about them. You should understand how the roles and perceptions of learners, instructors, and administrators affect the ways in which ESP courses and programs are run, and be able to argue why subject specialists are not always the best people to teach ESP.

Here are a few more questions to consider:

1 Which of the points covered in the chapter were new to you? Did you find them interesting and relevant in terms of your own learning goals? Were there any points that you found confusing or that you disagreed with?
2 What points from the chapter do you think you can immediately put to use in your own learning or teaching context?
3 If you had to make a case for hiring an ESP instructor with no specialist subject knowledge, what points would you make?
4 If you were a learner in an ESP program, would you want the instructor to reveal to you the extent of their specialist subject knowledge? Why/Why not?

Further resources

Research articles on call-center English

Friginal, E. (2007). Outsourced call centers and English in the Philippines. *World Englishes*, *26*(3), 331–345.
Lockwood, J. (2012). Developing an English for specific purpose curriculum for Asian call centres: How theory can inform practice. *English for Specific Purposes*, *31*(1), 14–24.

Software for text analysis

Anthony, L. (2017). *AntConc* (Version 3.5.0) [Computer Software]. Tokyo, Japan: Waseda University. Retrieved from www.laurenceanthony.net/software/antconc

Section 2

Understanding the four pillars of ESP

Chapter 4

Identifying needs in the design of ESP courses and programs

In Chapter 3, you learned that ESP is founded on the four pillars of needs analysis, learning objectives, materials and methods, and evaluation. Of course, it is necessary to understand not only what these pillars are, but also how to construct them, and where to look for possible cracks and problems. So, over the next four chapters, we will focus on the specifics of these four pillars of ESP.

In this chapter, you'll learn all about needs analysis. First, I'll explain the different ways to view needs and the insights that these perspectives can give you. Next, I'll introduce some of the data collection methods that you can use as part of a large-scale, detailed needs analysis that you might conduct before starting to teach a completely new ESP course or when developing an ESP program. Then, I'll discuss how you might conduct a smaller-scale needs analysis that is carried out 'just in time' for the first lesson or maybe even after a course has started. At the end of the chapter, I'll briefly touch on ways that you can evaluate a needs analysis, before discussing a common misunderstanding about needs analysis that is centered on the belief that needs can be identified using just a survey or an interview of learners.

By the end of the chapter, you should be able to work in a team or on your own to design and run a needs analysis that is appropriate for your target ESP setting. You should also be in a position to critique previously conducted needs analyses and be able to make positive suggestions for improving them.

Opening reflection

If you have taught an ESP class before, did you make an attempt to establish the needs of the learners attending the course? What strategies did you employ? What other strategies might you have used to gain a better understanding about what the learners needed to learn, wanted to learn, and had already learned about the topic?

> If you have not taught an ESP class before, what strategies do you think you could easily and quickly employ to gain an understanding of the learners' needs? What other strategies might be effective but require more preparation time?

Commentary

There are many possible ways to get an insight into learner needs. One option you may have considered is talking to other instructors of the course about their experiences. You might have also considered observing some classes and taking notes on what teaching points were made and the learners' reactions to them. In addition, you might have thought of conducting some kind of diagnostic test of the learners' proficiency levels. You may have also considered carrying out an in-class survey asking learners about what they believed they needed to study. These are just some of the many ways that instructors can attempt to establish needs in an ESP class.

However, you may be surprised to hear that many experienced ESP instructors spend little time conducting needs analyses before a course starts. Rather, they rely on established 'assumptions' about their learners that have been developed and tweaked over time. ESP instructors in a well-established program can be confident that the courses they teach have been constructed based on an extensive analysis of learner needs carried out at the section, department, or institutional level over many years. These needs analyses are likely to have been based on most – if not all – the methods mentioned previously. They will also have been informed by not only the learners and other instructors of the course, but also by other stakeholders, such as people in management and external informants, including workplace human resources managers and discipline experts. In this environment, course outlines, syllabuses, materials, and evaluation procedures are likely to have been tailored to the specific needs of learners. It should be noted, though, that instructors in these contexts are still likely to carry out in-class observations and short pre- and post-course surveys of learners to confirm if things are going to plan. When they do notice that adjustments are necessary they can either apply them immediately, or perhaps take their notes to a meeting where program-wide adjustments are considered.

Experienced ESP instructors operating independently of others are also likely to have developed over time an implicit understanding of the types of learners who come to class and their inherent strengths, weaknesses, and desires. Again, they may begin a course with a quick exercise to confirm that their assumptions are accurate for the particular learner group in front of them, but it is unlikely that they need to radically alter the bank of materials and activities they have used successfully in the past.

But, what about the times when you are working with others to carry out a large-scale needs analysis that is to be used to inform the creation of a new ESP program? Or, what if you have to teach learners in a completely new and unfamiliar course? In these cases, it is important to understand the basic concepts of needs analyses and know how to conduct and evaluate them.

Basic concepts in needs analysis

As you learned back in Chapter 1, the starting point of ESP is an understanding of the current and/or future academic or occupational needs of learners. It is the defining of clear and specific needs that perhaps distinguishes ESP most strongly from general English language teaching (Flowerdew & Peacock, 2001). Unfortunately, needs analysis is an often confused concept within the ESP community and the ELT field in general. This is because scholars like to give the principle different names in order to highlight a particular aspect. So, you will read about objective needs analysis, subjective needs analysis, target situation analysis, learning situation analysis, and means analysis among many other similar concepts (Hutchinson & Waters, 1987; Munby, 1978; Richards, 2001; West, 1997).

Brown (2016, p. 4) attempts to resolve the confusion by defining needs analysis as "the systematic collection and analysis of all information used for defining and validating a defensible curriculum". Here, a 'defensible' curriculum means one that can be successfully explained to and accepted by all stakeholders, including learners, instructors, and administrators, and even present and future employers. But, what exactly is the information that is used in this defense? To answer this question, we need to consider the sorts of *needs* that ESP experts consider useful when designing and teaching an ESP course or program.

The meaning of 'needs'

The word *needs* takes on different meanings depending on the stakeholder and the context they are in. For example, learners in an EAP class may consider that they *need* to improve their academic listening skills, whereas the instructor may consider that the learners *need* to improve their reading strategies. Administrators of the course, on the other hand, may consider that the most important *need* for the learners is to improve their general English proficiency scores so that they can find a job after graduating and provide quantitative evidence for stakeholders who fund the course that it is successful. Viewed in this way, we can see why the term *needs* can serve as a synonym for *wants*, *desires*, *necessities*, *lacks*, *gaps*, *expectations*, *motivations*, *deficiencies*, *requirements*, *requests*, *prerequisites*, *essentials*, *next step*, and '*x + 1*', where *x* is the current state and + *1* is the next step, depending on who you ask (Brown, 2016).

A diagnostic view of needs

Brown (2016) explains that there are at least four different views of needs. The first one discussed here is a 'diagnostic' view, where needs correspond to language, genres, and skills that are considered *necessities*, *essentials*, or *prerequisites* for success in the target setting. You may have noticed that I have used Hutchinson and Waters' (1987) term *necessities* to refer to this concept in the chapters up to this point. All stakeholders can provide valuable input on what is *necessary*, but more weight should probably be given to those stakeholders who have direct knowledge and experience of the target setting. In EAP contexts, these can include experienced ESP instructors, course coordinators, heads of department, and subject specialists, as well as future employers and graduate alumni now working in the target field. In EOP contexts, again, experienced ESP instructors can provide valuable input, but the learners themselves are also likely to be very knowledgeable about their own target settings.

A 'diagnostic' view of needs naturally leads to a ranking of learning objectives with those that must be achieved at the top, those that are desirable but less important in the middle, and those that are irrelevant and can be ignored at the bottom. In short-term, intensive ESP courses, such a ranking allows ESP instructors to quickly prioritize objectives. The ranking can also serve as a general guide for the sequencing of classroom materials and the creation of syllabuses and curricula (Nation & Macalister, 2010). For example, in an EAP course on academic presentation skills for researchers about to attend an overseas conference, you might want to prioritize fluency and pronunciation development. Similarly, in an EOP course for hotel staff about to transfer to the reception desk, you might want to prioritize telephone listening skills and politeness strategies.

A discrepancy view of needs

The second view discussed here is a 'discrepancy' view, where needs correspond to the *lacks*, *discrepancies*, or *gaps* between what the learners can currently do in the language and what they will need to do in the target setting. In previous chapters, I have used Hutchinson and Waters' (1987) term *lacks* for this concept. Again, all stakeholders need to be consulted but those with direct knowledge and experience of the target learners and the ways in which they are likely to progress in their language learning will probably offer the most useful insights. In EAP settings, experienced ESP instructors are almost certainly the most useful stakeholders to consult in this case. In EOP settings, on the other hand, line managers and senior staff may have the most accurate understanding of this aspect. Importantly, in both EAP and EOP settings, a discrepancy view of needs often leads to the introduction of placement tests that can be used to determine the current levels of learners and assign them to different streams or ability groupings, and in the case of EOP settings, even different work sections.

A democratic view of needs

The third view discussed here is a 'democratic' view, where needs correspond to what the different stakeholders *want*, *desire*, *expect*, or *request* from the ESP course. In previous chapters, I have used Hutchinson and Waters' (1987) term *wants* to describe this concept. The most important stakeholders here, of course, are the learners themselves. Learners almost universally *want* their courses to be interesting, enjoyable, manageable, and relevant to their future goals. If a course does not satisfy these basic needs, the learners are likely to have poor motivation and will devote little time to meeting the goals. But, you need to remember that learners often lack the knowledge and/or experience needed to accurately judge what, where, when, and how they will use English in the target academic or occupational setting. So, other stakeholders also need to be consulted. In an EAP setting, these stakeholders will include experienced ESP instructors and administrators, and also members of the learner's specialist departments. In EOP settings, again, ESP instructors and administrators need to be consulted, but also floor and office managers, training department teams, and perhaps even the head of human resources.

It is also important to remember that the *wants* of other stakeholders must also be taken into consideration when designing an ESP course or program. Instructors will often want to teach small classes with talented, highly motivated learners. If a course does not match this description, they may ignore the course goals and teaching materials and start 'doing their own thing'. Institution administrators, on the other hand, might want classes to be large and cater for a wide range of ability levels. They may also want the classes to be taught in traditional classrooms, with standard teaching equipment, at fixed dates in the academic or work calendar. Again, if a course does not match this description, it may end up being too costly, impractical, or poorly fitting within the wider perspective of education at the institution. Unfortunately, it is usually impossible to design a course or program that meets all the *wants* of different stakeholders. What you can do, though, is attempt to gain an understanding of these different preferences and institutional constraints and then negotiate with all stakeholders to align their needs and hopefully find a working solution (Anthony, 2009). We will return to this topic later in the book.

An analytic view of needs

The fourth view discussed here is an 'analytic' view, where needs correspond to elements that Second Language Acquisition (SLA) theory and ELT research and practice have shown to be the necessary next step in the learning process (see, for example, Pienemann & Kessler, 2012). To follow this view of needs, ESP course designers need to review the literature on SLA and ELT and consult with teachers who are familiar with learning theory and practice. Brown (2016) considers an analytic view of needs to be problematic as we are still a long way from having a comprehensive understanding of these learning steps. However, it is clear that many instructors adopt some aspects of this view, for example, when they pre-teach isolated vocabulary items before presenting them in the context of a reading passage. This view of needs also leads to the idea of course prerequisites and can help guide the development of a linked set of courses that make up an ESP program.

Clearly, all four views of needs analysis provide insights that can guide ESP experts in the design and teaching of a course or program. On the other hand, you should remember that capturing a comprehensive list of needs from different stakeholders using even one of these perspectives is a difficult if not impossible task. So, if you are going to conduct a needs analysis, you should perhaps aim for what Brown (2016) calls a *Current Best Shot* (CBS). That is one that captures the most useful information for planning a course but makes no claim of being the complete picture.

TASK 4.1 Identifying *necessities*, *lacks*, and *wants*

1. If you have experience teaching, list the procedures that you have used to assess the *necessities*, *lacks*, and *wants* of the different stakeholders in a course you have taught. If you have no experience of teaching yet, ask one of your course instructors what procedures they use to determine needs.
2. Based on your answer to Question 1, what other procedures could easily be employed to more accurately determine the *necessities*, *lacks*, and *wants* of the different stakeholders.
3. What are some of the common mismatches that you have experienced between the *wants* of instructors and administrators and those of learners? How could these differences have been resolved?

Conducting a large-scale, detailed needs analysis

What you are trying to do in a need analysis is establish the diagnostic, discrepancy, democratic, and analytic views on needs from as many of the different stakeholders as possible. Some of these needs will be objective (e.g. *necessities* determined from observations of target writing) and others subjective (e.g. *wants* determined from a survey of learners in the first class). Some needs will be related to the target situation (e.g. *lacks* determined from an analysis of customer complaints about hotel receptionists) and others related to the learners' current situation (e.g. *lacks* determined from a pre-workshop English proficiency test.). Other needs will be related to learning processes and the products of learning (e.g. vocabulary learning techniques in order to master the English names of menu items at a restaurant). Finally, some needs will be related to the ways or means of learning (e.g. the class size, number of hours of study, and so on).

A full-scale, detailed needs analysis is usually very broad in scope and involves many different data collection methods and resources. Some of the most common include:

- reviews of research literature and best practices
- reviews of current learning materials and textbooks
- questionnaires/surveys of learners, instructors, administrators, specialists, and employers
- (structured) interviews/discussions with learners, instructors, administrators, specialists, and employers
- observations of learners and professionals in the target context
- storage and analysis of learner language and target language
- testing of learner performance before, during, and after the course

Using these procedures, you should be able to get answers to most of the questions that will help you design a successful course or program. Some of these questions are listed in Table 4.1 (based on Dubin & Olshtain, 1986, pp. 6–18; Dudley-Evans & St. John, 1998, pp. 145–154; Hutchinson & Waters, 1987, pp. 59–63; Nation & Macalister, 2010, pp. 14–18). You should notice that Table 4.1 lists not only the *necessities*, *lacks*, and *wants* of

Table 4.1 Questions to be answered in a needs analysis

Learners	What is their first language? What is their age, gender, nationality? What is their level of English? How do they prefer to study? Why are they taking the course? What do they want from the course? What is necessary for them to be successful? What knowledge and skills do they currently lack?
Instructors	How confident are they in English? How much training do they have? How much time do they have to prepare and grade? How many (different) classes do they have to teach? What are their preferred teaching methods? What do they want from the course? What is necessary for them to be successful? What knowledge and skills do they currently lack?

(Continued)

Table 4.1 (Continued)

Administrators	What is the organizational structure? Who is in charge? What are their general views of English? What are their views on current instructors, materials, and courses? What are their views of ESP? How enthusiastic are they for change (if change is necessary)? What do they want from the course? What do they consider necessary for the course to be successful? What knowledge about the course do they currently lack?
Setting	What is the target setting? How will language be used in the target setting? How long do learners have to study to reach the goals of the course? What kind of course will be offered (intensive vs. extensive)? How important is the course (credited vs. non-credited)? When is the course run (before, parallel to, or after specialist courses)? Where will the classes be held (e.g. in class, online)? What facilities are available to run the course?

learners, but also those of instructors and administrators. You should also note that questions related to the educational setting and the target language setting are also included.

If you want further information on how to conduct a needs analysis, Brown (2016) provides a refreshingly clear and detailed account. In addition to explaining how to use the various data collection methods listed previously, he shows how the results obtained from these methods can be analyzed, interpreted, and used to inform course syllabus and curriculum design decisions.

Conducting a small-scale 'just in time' needs analysis

Sometimes, you might be put in a situation where you need to teach a course for completely new and unfamiliar learners with only a few days or even hours to prepare and carry out a needs analysis. In these 'just-in-time' cases, the following actions can help you quickly establish the *necessities*, *lacks*, and *wants* of the learners, and perhaps equally importantly, the expectations or *wants* of the administrative team:

- On agreeing to teach the course, discuss briefly with the course coordinators their views of learners and what they expect learners to study in class. Use these views as an initial guide for understanding learner *necessities* and *lacks*, as well as administrative *wants*.

- If the course is already established but has a vague or generic title (e.g. *English I*), work with administrators to reach a consensus on the goals of the course and your freedom to interpret these after meeting the learners. Use these discussions to improve your understanding of the different stakeholders' *necessities*, *lacks*, and *wants*.
- Briefly review any provided materials for the course. Again, use these as an initial guide to the different stakeholders' *necessities*, *lacks*, and *wants*.
- Before entering the classroom, make every effort to obtain samples of learners' outputs from previous iterations of the class. Analyze these samples with the aim of establishing a more detailed and accurate set of *necessities* and *lacks* of learners. If there is an obvious mismatch between the *wants* of the administrators and the *necessities* and *lacks* of previous learners, raise the issue with the management team and reach a consensus on how the course should proceed.
- At the start of the first class, provide learners with a brief overview of what you see as their *necessities*, *lacks*, and *wants* and explain how you arrived at your decision. Monitor their reactions to see if they agree with your opinions. If they appear to disagree with you, give them an opportunity to express what their needs are.
- If you are unsure that the course correctly addresses the learners' *necessities*, *lacks*, and *wants*, in the first class, ask the learners to complete a short survey on what they hope to learn in class. Alternatively, or in addition to a survey, ask them to produce a sample of their intended language output and quickly diagnose to what extent they can already achieve this goal.
- In each class, continue to monitor the learners' performances and expressions of motivation. If a new *necessity*, *lack*, or *want* becomes apparent, be willing and flexible to adjust your teaching accordingly.

Evaluating a needs analysis

Nation and Macalister (2010) make the point that a needs analysis must ultimately be useful in terms of the insights it provides on curriculum design. If the results from a needs analysis have no application, the endeavor is effectively worthless. To ensure the value of a needs analysis, it should be designed in a similar way to a test, making sure that it is reliable, valid, and practical (Brown, 1989).

For a needs analysis to be reliable, it should produce the same results if repeated (adjusting, of course, for time). To be valid, the needs analysis should reveal the individuals' different perspectives on needs, and not some unrelated other factor. In contrast, to be practical, a needs analysis should be designed in a way that allows it to be carried out within a reasonable time and cost.

Full-scale needs analyses that include all the data collection methods listed earlier are likely to be both reliable and valid. However, there is a danger that they can become overly complex and time-consuming, reducing their practical value. Short, 'just-in-time' needs analyses, on the other hand, are likely to be less reliable and valid, but certainly more practical. What type of needs analysis should you use then? Perhaps a good way to answer this question is by matching the characteristics of the needs analysis with those of the ESP course itself. For example, if the course is a short, intensive, one-off course, the needs analysis can probably also be conducted in a short, intensive, one-off manner. On the other hand, if the course is a long, extensive, repeated course, you are likely to have more time to conduct a longer, detailed needs analysis. In this case, you can consult with more of the stakeholders, and you will also have opportunities to repeat the analysis offering even more detailed insights.

TASK 4.2 Evaluating data collection methods and resources in needs analysis

Consider the following data collection methods and resources. What are the advantages and disadvantages of each in terms of the quality of information they provide about needs? One suggested answer is included for the first procedure.

Reviews of research literature

advantages	disadvantages
• Insights can be gained from specialist informants about a potentially unfamiliar subject.	• The context of the study might be quite different to that of target learners.

Learner surveys and questionnaires

advantages	disadvantages

Interviews with subject specialists

advantages	disadvantages

Observations of people in the target context

advantages	disadvantages

Analysis of target language samples

advantages	disadvantages

Testing of learner performance

advantages	disadvantages

Contentious issues in ESP: isn't a learner survey enough?

Many novice ESP instructors and even some experienced ESP administrators appear to believe that the goals of an ESP course can be formulated based simply on the results of a learner survey. In the literature on ESP course design, for example, you can find numerous studies where learners have been asked what they think they need to study and the ESP course was created accordingly.

In some cases, this rather simplistic understanding of needs analysis emerges from a poor understanding of what ESP means. Instructors and administrators read that ESP is a learner-centered approach, they learn that it is characterized by needs analyses, and they naturally conclude that ESP courses can be solely informed by learner surveys. The problem is compounded by the belief among some instructors and administrators that when we talk about needs in ESP, it refers only to the *current* needs of learners and not those that will be relevant later in their lives. Again, this misunderstanding naturally leads to the idea that asking learners what they need is a good basis for an ESP course.

In other cases, the problem relates to the instructors' working environment and their resulting lack of knowledge and experience of the target field. As discussed in Chapter 2, many ESP instructors work in isolated settings within traditional university departments. These settings offer them little opportunity to interact with experienced ESP instructors and administrators or subject specialists in a target discipline. Their chances to meet with industry employers and discuss the language needs of workers are even more remote. It is not surprising, therefore, that these ESP instructors rely heavily on the learners to help guide them in their course planning.

Learner surveys are certainly an important component of any needs analysis. They will help inform an instructor about the learners' *necessities*, *lacks*, and particularly their *wants*. But, as discussed earlier, novice learners in an EAP environment might have a poor understanding of what their current needs are, and they certainly cannot be expected to know what their future language needs will be. Even workers in an EOP setting can misunderstand what their language weaknesses are. In an aviation English course, for example, learners may think that they need to know a greater number of technical terms, whereas in reality it might be their poor pronunciation of already known technical terms that needs attention.

An effective needs analysis will inevitably extend beyond learner surveys to cover the diagnostic, discrepancy, democratic, and analytic views of a wide range of stakeholders. This point holds true not only for large-scale, detailed analyses but also for those carried out 'just-in-time' for the first class.

Research ideas

Here are some possible ideas for small-scale or large-scale research projects that stem from the topics discussed in this chapter.

Visualizing the terminology of needs analysis

As with many other aspects of ESP, the terminology used to describe the different facets of needs analysis can be confusing. Review the different terms used by ESP experts and try to summarize your findings in a clear and simple diagram or other visualization.

Reviewing a needs analysis

Review a published account of needs analysis in a journal such as *English for Specific Purposes*, *ESP Today*, or the *Journal of English for Academic Purposes*. Evaluate its strengths and weaknesses in terms of the information it is able to obtain on the *necessities*, *lacks*, and *wants* of different stakeholders and its reliability, validity, and practicality.

Conducting a needs analysis

Brown (2016, p. 33) provides a detailed table of published needs analysis studies carried out in various EAP and EOP settings. However, it is a surprising fact that there are still many EAP and EOP settings where the needs of learners and other stakeholders are largely undocumented.

Review the literature on needs analysis, target an important EAP or EOP setting that is still undocumented, and carry out a preliminary analysis of the *necessities*, *lacks*, and *wants* of the different stakeholders.

Closing reflection

Now that you have come to the end of the chapter, you should have a good understanding of the different types of needs that ESP instructors and administrators need to know. You should also understand how you might conduct a needs analysis as part of a long-term, team-based project or just before the start of your own classes. Finally, you should now have some ideas on what makes a good needs analysis and be able to critique those that you see in published reports or in real-world settings.

Here are a few more questions to consider:

1. Which of the points covered in the chapter were new to you? Did you find them interesting and relevant in terms of your own learning goals? Were there any points that you found confusing or that you disagreed with?
2. What points from the chapter do you think you can immediately put to use in your own learning or teaching context?

3 Which of the different views of needs was the simplest to understand? Were any of them confusing or less clearly defined?
4 If you had to rank the *necessities*, *lacks*, and *wants* of learners in order of importance, which would you place first and last? Why?
5 If you were hired to teach on an ESP program that appeared to be based on weak assumptions about the *necessities*, *lacks*, and *wants* of learners, what could you do to mitigate the potential problems you might face in class?
6 If you were an administrator of an ESP program, whose *wants* would you give priority to: those of learners or those of instructors? Explain your answer.

Further resources

Books and chapters

Brown, J. D. (2016). *Introducing needs analysis and English specific purposes.* Abingdon, UK: Routledge.
Flowerdew, L. (2013). Needs analysis and curriculum development in ESP. In B. Paltridge & S. Starfield (Eds.), *The handbook of English for specific purposes* (pp. 325–346). Walden, MA: Wiley Blackwell.

Research articles

Serafini, E. J., Lake, J. B., & Long, M. H. (2015). Needs analysis for specialized learner populations: Essential methodological improvements. *English for Specific Purposes*, *40*, 11–26.
Spence, P., & Liu, G. Z. (2013). Engineering English and the high-tech industry: A case study of an English needs analysis of process integration engineers at a semiconductor manufacturing company in Taiwan. *English for Specific Purposes*, *32*(2), 97–109.
Wozniak, S. (2010). Language needs analysis from a perspective of international professional mobility: The case of French mountain guides. *English for Specific Purposes*, *29*(4), 243–252.

Chapter 5

Deciding learning objectives for ESP courses and programs

In Chapter 4, you learned about the many different facets of needs analysis that form the first pillar of ESP. Once you know these needs, you are in a position to start translating the *necessities*, *lacks*, and *wants* of different stakeholders into specific learning objectives for the classroom. These form the second pillar of ESP.

In many real-world settings, learning objectives are decided at the administrative level by ESP course and program designers. But, in other settings, ESP administrators might only give instructors a very general or vague course title and expect them to formulate their own class objectives based on a small-scale, 'just-in-time' needs analysis. Either way, once the learning objectives of a course or program are decided, the ESP administrators or instructors will need to sequence them in some way and explain that ordering to learners. Normally, this is done in the form of a syllabus.

In this chapter, all the different aspects of deciding and sequencing learning objectives will be discussed. First, I'll introduce some important features of language that characterize different types of spoken and written ESP texts. Next, I'll discuss some aspects of learning theory you might also want to target in the classroom. Then, I'll explain some course design approaches that are commonly used to sequence learning objectives. Finally, I'll look at the subject knowledge problem that exists in many ESP classrooms and show you how it might be overcome.

By the end of the chapter, you should be able to turn the results of an ESP needs analysis into a clear and well-structured syllabus that explains the learning objectives to learners and other stakeholders. You should also be in a position to evaluate and give constructive feedback on course syllabuses and even program designs given to you by ESP administrators. Most importantly, by the end of this chapter, you should be ready to start thinking about the actual teaching of your classes.

Opening reflection

Imagine you had to teach an EAP course in scientific reading and writing. In one of the classes, you were scheduled to teach learners how to read and write a research article abstract using the following abstract (taken from applied chemistry) as an example. What language (e.g. vocabulary, grammar, organizational patterns) and skills (e.g. how to read for gist, how to write concisely) might you target in the class? Where would you position the lesson in the course as a whole (e.g. early in the course, at the end of the course)? Are there any aspects of the text that you would struggle explaining to learners?

Synthesis and Surface Modification of Highly Monodispersed, Spherical Gold Nanoparticles of 50–200 nm

*Steven D. Perrault and Warren C. W. Chan**
Institute of Biomaterials and Biomedical Engineering, Terrence Donnelly Centre for Cellular and Biomolecular Research, University of Toronto, 160 College Street, Toronto, Ontario, Canada M5S 3E1
J. Am. Chem. Soc., 2009, 131 (47), pp 17042–17043
DOI: 10.1021/ja907069u
Publication Date (Web): November 5, 2009
Copyright © 2009 American Chemical Society
http://pubs.acs.org/doi/abs/10.1021/ja907069u

Elucidating the impact of nanoparticle size and shape on biological systems is of fundamental importance to nanotoxicology and biomedicine. Currently, the ability to determine this is limited by the lack of a model nanoparticle system having a narrow size and shape distribution over the relevant size range (2–200 nm). Hydroquinone can be used to produce 50–200 nm gold nanoparticles that are relatively monodispersed in size with nearly spherical shapes.

Commentary

The model abstract here is a fairly typical abstract in applied chemistry: it uses a situation-problem-response organization, linked together with the logical connector *currently*; it makes use of both active and passive voices; it is written solely in the present tense; and it contains technical terms, scientific abbreviations, and long noun phrases. If a learner hoped to read and write similar texts quickly and accurately, they would need to know about the different types of vocabulary that scientists use, the grammar forms and organizational patterns that appear frequently in scientific texts, various reading and writing strategies, and a host of other language and learning points. Clearly, as an ESP instructor, you may not be familiar with everything that an experienced and well-published chemist knows about the language of applied chemistry. But, as you'll see in this chapter, you don't need to worry. Your knowledge of ESP will allow you to assist learners in achieving important learning objectives that will ultimately allow them to meet their needs.

Foundations for deciding learning objectives

In many general English (GE) programs, learning objectives are expressed in terms of the traditional categories of grammar and vocabulary. Lesson and course goals are built on concepts such as mastering the past, present, and future tenses; using main, modal, and auxiliary verbs correctly; constructing simple, complex, and compound sentence patterns; expressing ideas in the active and passive voice; learning the rules of article usage; linking ideas with logical connectors; forming nominalizations; and asking questions. Learners in a GE classroom are often encouraged to explain and practice the rules of grammar, and learn longs lists of vocabulary items that appear in the reading and speaking passages of their textbooks. Of course, much of this might have little to do with the language that they need in real-world target settings.

ESP courses and programs, in contrast, are rarely built on grammar rules and vocabulary lists in this abstract way. Instead, the learning objectives of ESP are expressed in ways that are directly linked with the results of a needs analysis and are built on a number of important, theoretical-grounded principles. Let's look at each of these in turn.

Register analysis

Registers are a characteristic set of language elements, including grammar forms and vocabulary items that people will associate with a particular situation, purpose, or social context (see Halliday, 1978, 1989). Registers are often referred to as 'styles,' so you might hear about *formal*, *academic*, and *public* styles contrasted with *informal*, *casual*, *conversational*, *private* and *neutral* styles, among others.

Since the early days of ESP in the 1960s, the study of registers has played an important role in determining what should be taught to learners in the ESP classroom. In fact, early ESP research was almost solely dedicated to identifying the characteristic features of grammar and vocabulary in particular settings. For example, the first major work on ESP according to Swales

(1985) was Barber's (1962) study of sentence structure, verb forms, and vocabulary in a university textbook on engineering electronics, an extract from a university textbook on astronomy, and a research article in the field of biochemistry. Without access to a computer, Barber painstakingly analyzed these three texts to establish sentence lengths, the number of clauses per text, the frequency of clause types, the ratio of passive to non-passive verbs, tense patterns, word frequency patterns, and a whole range of other linguistic features. While Barber's findings might have limited applicability today, being based on only three niche texts, the 'bottom-up' approach that he adopted is still very influential in the field of ESP.

Register analysis provides ESP course designers and instructors with a solid foundation for targeting and teaching ESP-focused grammar. In an EAP setting, for example, it allows them to identify and teach language features that characterize the formal academic writing style. These include complex, compound, and complex/compound sentence structures; the conversion of phrasal verb forms into single verb forms; the use of long, complex noun, verb, and prepositional phrases; the nominalization of verb forms; the frequent occurrence of logical connections; the using of hedging and stance expressions; and various other features that are discussed in the ESP literature. In an EOP setting, register analysis can highlight less common grammar forms that are uniquely characteristic of particular target language settings, such as hotel service encounters (Blue & Harun, 2003), airline flight controller directions (Farris, Trofimovich, Segalowitz, & Gatbonton, 2008), and nurse-patient interactions (Finch, 2014; Staples, 2015).

Register analysis also provides ESP course designers and instructors with an understanding of how vocabulary is distributed in and across texts. One result of this work is the now common practice of targeting vocabulary that belongs to general, semi-technical, and technical categories (Nation, 2001). Many EAP courses present vocabulary to learners in this way, with the *Academic Word List* of Coxhead (2000) used in textbooks around the world. If you suddenly find yourself teaching an unfamiliar discipline, this body of work can be an excellent source of information at the planning stages.

Interestingly, register analysis has seen a renaissance in recent years under the banner of corpus analysis. Today, the availability of large bodies of text data (corpora) and easy-to-use software tools such as *AntConc* (Anthony, 2017a) allows ESP experts to complete detailed studies on the grammar and vocabulary of target texts in a matter of seconds. What we get from such analyses is a more accurate description of language in both narrow disciplines and broad fields of work, leading to greater confidence in what should or should not be taught in the classroom. In fact, the ability to perform a corpus analysis can itself become a goal for learners in the ESP classroom. Instructors can guide learners on how to find or collect language data and then show them how to use software to analyze that data to find characteristic grammar and vocabulary features of their target language. This Data-Driven Learning (DDL) approach has proved successful in many ESP settings (Anthony, 2016). We will return to the topic of DDL in the next chapter of this book.

Rhetorical (discourse) analysis

Rhetorical analysis (or discourse analysis) is another area of research that has greatly informed ESP course and program design. Pioneering work by Lackstrom, Selinker, and Trimble (1973) led many researchers to move beyond the 'bottom-up' study of registers to start looking at *why* particularly language features were more or less frequent than others, and *how* language users combined sentences and paragraphs to construct complete spoken or written texts. This 'top-down' perspective links language form to language use and provides ESP course designers and instructors with a more informed basis for deciding what to include and highlight in ESP courses and programs. In an EAP classroom, for example, instructors can use insights from rhetorical analyses of academic texts to focus on and explain why certain logical connectors appear more commonly than others. Similarly, EOP instructors can use rhetorical analyses to focus on and explain why an increased use of modal verbs appear in the language of telephone operators that need to respond to customer inquiries in a polite and respectful way. What is important is that learners not only understand why the target language is used as it is, but that they begin to develop their own 'rhetorical awareness' that they can apply later in the understanding and creation of as yet unseen spoken and written texts.

Genre analysis

Genre analysis emerged from the work in register and rhetorical studies to become one of most important principles used in ESP today. In his seminal work on the subject, John Swales (1990, p. 58) describes a genre in the following way:

> A genre comprises a class of communicative events, the members of which share some set of communicative purposes. These purposes are recognized by the expert members of the parent discourse community, and thereby constitute a rationale for the genre. This rationale shapes the schematic structure of the discourse and influences and constrains the choice of content and style.

You can see that the 'bottom-up' and 'top-down' perspectives provided by register and rhetorical analyses are included in Swales' definition of genre. He also introduces the important concept of *discourse community*, which positions the people involved in the target communication as a network of interrelated individuals with a shared set of goals, purposes, and understandings of the way in which language works.

Genre analysis is an extremely powerful analytical approach in ESP that allows course designers and instructors to identify the communicative purpose, structure, style, content, and intended audience of target texts. Using this knowledge, they can then formulate course and program objectives that will ensure that learners will be able to recognize genre features and use them in their own language output, helping the learners conform to the practices of their discourse community (see Paltridge, 2013, for a discussion of genre and ESP).

Learners in workplace contexts can immediately put knowledge of genre to use in the creation of successful business letters, reports, speeches, and other language outputs that they need to produce in their jobs. Learners in academic contexts, on the other hand, can use a genre analysis of written and spoken texts to improve their reading and writing of research articles and grant proposals, as well as their understanding and delivery of academic presentations. They can also use knowledge of genre to understand and eventually produce the language outputs of their target discourse community, even though they may not yet be fully fledged members.

It is important to remember that the scope of genre analysis goes beyond just the analysis of static written and spoken texts. Some ESP researchers are interested in how the texts of a genre evolve over time and become blended with those of other genres (see, for example, Bhatia, 2008). Another group of genre analysts, often called the *rhetorical genre studies* group (see Artemeva & Freedman, 2008; Bawarshi & Reiff, 2010; Miller, 1984) focus their work on the context and community in which texts exist, providing us with more detailed insights on *why* genres are created and *how* they facilitate communication (see, for example, Freedman & Medway, 1994).

Learning and metacognitive skills

Beyond language itself, many ESP practices have been influenced by research on learning theory and metacognitive skills development (e.g. planning, selecting appropriate learning strategies, self-correcting). Research on learning theory dates back to the early behaviorist models of Pavlov (1897), Thorndike (1898), Watson (1913), and Skinner (1957), the rule-governed mentalist models of Chomsky (1957), the cognitivist models of Ausubel (1968), and others that focus on thinking, problem solving, and concept-forming, and more recent constructivist models of learning, which emphasize meaning creation over meaning acquisition (e.g. Ertmer & Newby, 1993). There is also the work of Hutchinson and Waters (1987) and more recently Henter (2014) and others that reminds us that learning is an affective process, where the learners' feelings will have a dramatic impact on the success or failure of learning. The main features of these different models are shown in Figure 5.1.

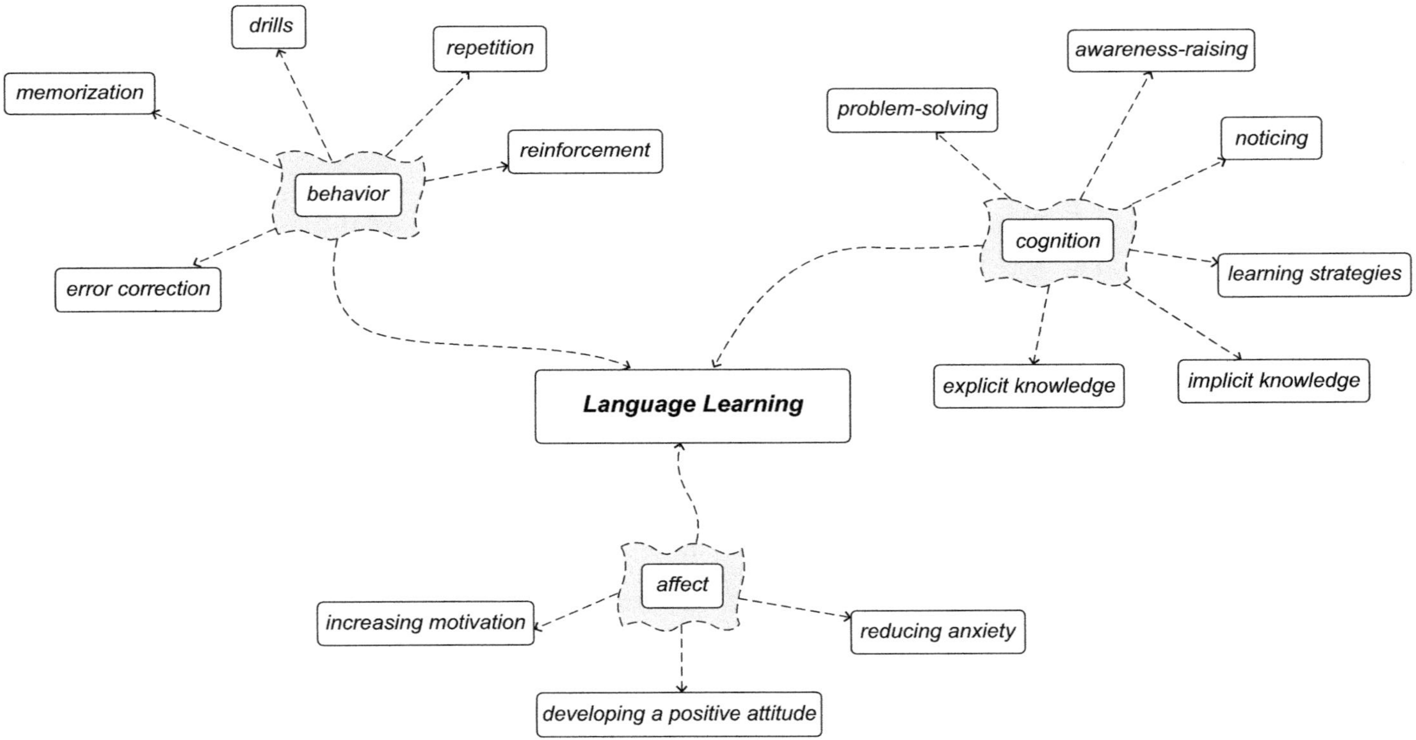

Figure 5.1 A model of language learning.

Most ESP instructors have an eclectic view of language learning and aim to develop and apply different learning approaches depending on the needs of different stakeholders, the learning objectives of the course or program, the backgrounds and expectations of the learners, and the time constraints they are given. In an EAP presentation course, for example, instructors might use a behaviorist approach to help learners improve their pronunciation and signal transitions between slides using a few memorized phrases, such as "Here is the outline" and "Let me now give you the conclusion." But, they are more likely to use a cognitive approach to help learners create the language in the presentation slides, explaining, for example, how bullet points are usually listed as a set of noun or verb phrases starting with the same part of speech. On the other hand, the instructors might focus on affective factors to help learners deliver a successful presentation, giving them motivation to stand up in front of others, helping them to develop and project a positive attitude, and showing them ways to reduce their anxiety about making mistakes so they can perform at their highest level.

Even though each ESP setting will necessitate the use of different learning principles, there are some general principles that apply in almost all settings. These are listed in Table 5.1 (see also Hutchinson & Waters, 1987, pp. 128–130):

Learning theory in ESP addresses not only behavior, cognition, and affect, but also specific sub-skills that will facilitate reading, writing, speaking and listening. Some of these are listed in Table 5.2.

Table 5.1 General principles of language learning

- learning is a decision-making process
  - learners ultimately decide for themselves what, why, how, when, and where to learn
- learning is a building process
  - learners apply what they already know about the world and their experience of learning their first language to the task at hand
- learning is an active process
  - learners use biological and cognitive processes in the understanding, creation, and application of new knowledge
- learning is a monitoring process
  - learners perform better if they notice their strengths and weaknesses, recognize their progress and improvement, and seek help and advice when they are struggling
- learning is an emotional process
  - learners perform better when they see the value of the learning, enjoy the learning, feel relaxed, and have a positive attitude toward the material, the instructor, and the class in general
- learning is often an incidental process
  - learners learn much more than what is presented to them explicitly if they are given opportunities to reflect on and use that material in their own unique ways

Table 5.2 Sub-skills of reading, writing, listening, and speaking

Sub-skills of reading

- building a receptive knowledge of written general, academic, and technical vocabulary
- identifying and understanding cohesive and discourse markers
- identifying main ideas, supporting ideas, and examples
- identifying rhetorical patterns
- identifying the writer's assumptions
- predicting, inferring, and guessing from context
- processing and evaluating information
- scanning for specific information
- selecting what information is relevant
- skimming for content and meaning
- transferring or using the information obtained while or after reading
- understand relations within and between sentences
- utilizing surface-levels features (e.g. layout, color, font types, font styles)

Sub-skills of writing

- adopting and adapting commonly used written genres
- building a productive knowledge of written general, academic, and technical vocabulary
- citing and paraphrasing information obtained from external sources
- crafting surface-levels features (e.g. layout, color, font types, font styles)
- deciding the target reader
- deciding what information is relevant
- employing hedging and persuasive devices
- organizing ideas using rhetorical patterns
- planning the message through brainstorming and outlining
- presenting main ideas, supporting ideas, and examples
- refining the message through drafting and revising
- signaling relations within and between sentences, paragraphs, and sections using cohesive and discourse markers
- understanding the target discourse community
- using models and templates
- utilizing machine translation

Sub-skills of listening

- building a receptive knowledge of spoken general, academic, and technical vocabulary
- deducing the speaker's attitude (e.g. via politeness strategies, volume, and stress)
- identifying and understanding cohesive and discourse markers
- identifying main ideas, supporting ideas, and examples
- identifying redundancy in speech
- identifying rhetorical patterns
- identifying the speaker's assumptions
- identifying unit boundaries
- identifying what information is relevant
- listening for specific information
- participating through active listening (e.g. giving non-verbal and verbal encouragements, making gestures, providing back channels and feedback)
- predicting, inferring, and guessing from context
- processing and evaluating information
- recognizing phonological signals of main points and digressions (e.g. asides, jokes)
- recognizing the communicative functions of volume, speed, stress and intonation

(Continued)

Table 5.2 (Continued)

- transferring or using the information obtained while or after listening (e.g. through note taking)
- understanding relations within and between utterances
- using models and templates
- utilizing machine translation

Sub-skills of speaking

- adjusting the message through volume, speed, stress, intonation, and silence
- adopting and adapting commonly used spoken genres
- asking questions to get information, clarify points, and manage interactions
- building a productive knowledge of spoken general, academic, and technical vocabulary
- deciding what information is relevant
- developing a good pronunciation
- developing fluency
- employing hedging and persuasive devices
- explaining main ideas, supporting ideas, and examples
- finding ways to enter into a conversation
- organizing ideas using rhetorical patterns
- planning and refining the delivery through mental rehearsal
- recognizing the stance and attitude of the audience
- reporting and summarizing information
- signaling relations using cohesive and discourse markers
- understanding and utilizing turn-taking strategies
- understanding the target audience

In order to develop effective learning objectives for the classroom, ESP course designers and instructors can analyze the learners' target language context and identify specific skills and sub-skills that members of the discourse community use. These can then be introduced and developed in class through direct instruction, in-class activities, and learner-centered tasks. At a more general level, an understanding of learning and metacognitive skills can also help an ESP instructor identify and help learners who might find it difficult to interact with others in the class, or who are struggling with the class materials. We will return to this point in the next chapter that looks at classroom materials and methods.

TASK 5.1 Formulating learning objectives in EAP and EOP settings

1 Look again at the abstract that appeared in the reflection exercise at the beginning of this chapter. Using ideas from register analysis, rhetorical analysis, genre analysis, and learning and metacognitive skills, what learning objectives would you include in an EAP

lesson that was designed to help learners be able to write abstracts that summarize their own research findings? List your thoughts.

2 Now, imagine that you are an instructor in an EOP program for air traffic controllers. Again, using ideas from register analysis, rhetorical analysis, genre analysis, and learning and metacognitive skills, list the learning objectives you would include in a lesson on *pilot directives*. Use the following examples as a guide on what *pilot directives* are like.

Northwest eleven seventy-eight, turn left heading three six zero
Continental twelve thirty-four, turn right heading one niner zero
Three twenty-nine, reduce and maintain a hundred and seventy knots
U S Air fifteen eighty-eight, descend and maintain three thousand

Extract from: Air Traffic Control Complete Corpus (Godfrey, 1994)

Sequencing of learning objectives

Deciding the learning objectives of an ESP lesson, course, or program is clearly important. However, it is also necessary to consider what steps will be taken to achieve these goals, how long each step will be, and what order the steps will follow. These decisions are usually stated in the form of lesson plans, course syllabuses, and overall program curriculums. Here, let's focus on how you might sequence the learning objectives of an ESP course and turn that into a course syllabus. Then, let's briefly look at the topic of curriculum design.

General principles of sequencing

Ideally, the sequencing of learning objectives should be based on some kind of theoretical principles or objective measures. But, it is also important that the lesson plans and the overall course structure motivate learners to study, help them develop a positive attitude about the course content, and reduce their anxiety about meeting the goals and passing the course.

Nation and Macalister (2010: 38) suggest several general principles that can guide you in the sequencing of learning objectives.

- progressively cover useful language items, skills, and strategies rather than attempt to teach everything at once
- sequence items to give learners increasingly spaced, repeated opportunities to retrieve and give attention to target items in a variety of contexts

- if items are learned together, ensure that the combination contributes to the learning process and interference effects are avoided
- help learners make the most effective use of previous knowledge
- train learners how to monitor their learning gains so that they can become independent language learners

They go on to explain that learners should be exposed to an equal balance (amount of time) of *four strands* of learning: meaning-focused input (MFI), meaning-focused output (MFO), language-focused learning (LFL), and fluency development (FD) (Nation & Macalister, 2010). In practice, not all needs in ESP are equally balanced in terms of receptive (MFI) and productive (MFO) skills. But, the point here is that you should not be designing courses and programs in which the bulk of the time is spent *teaching* learners what they should be doing in the target setting (LFL). Rather, you need to give them opportunities to actually try for themselves the task at hand. Also, it is important that sufficient time is spent on letting learners develop fluency in the language skills that they have already met (FD).

Sequencing in syllabus and curriculum specifications

Syllabus design

A syllabus specifies the content and sequencing of language, genres, and skills for an individual course (in addition to information about materials and evaluation procedures). Table 5.3 shows six traditional English syllabus types that have been popular for ESP courses at some point in time, and Table 5.4 lists various sequencing patterns that could be used to order the individual items in one of these syllabuses.

Table 5.3 Syllabus types used in ESP course designs

Syllabus type	*Description*
Content-based	focuses on the content of a specific subject and sequenced according to discipline traditions of theory and practice
Genre-based	focuses on the construction of written and spoken texts through building knowledge of the field, analyzing target texts, and constructing target texts either collaboratively or individually, with sequencing determined by the relative importance of the target genres or the logical timing of the text creation process

Syllabus type	*Description*
Notional-functional	focuses on notions (e.g. shopping) and functions (e.g. asking for prices, negotiating a price reduction) and are usually sequenced based on importance or learner interest
Situational	focuses on situations in which the learner might find themselves (e.g. doctor/patient interaction, meeting with an international businessperson) and are usually sequenced based on importance, learner interest, or timing of need
Skill-based	focuses on target skills (e.g. giving a presentation, taking notes, arguing a point) that are usually sequenced based on importance or timing of need
Structural	focuses on grammar and vocabulary items that are usually sequenced according to a difficulty measure
Task-based	focuses on using (any) language to achieve specific, meaningful, real-world objectives that are usually sequenced based on importance, learner interest, or a difficulty measure

Table 5.4 Sequencing patterns used in ESP course designs

Sequencing pattern	*Visual representation*
Linear	A ⇨ B ⇨ C ⇨ D ⇨ E ⇨ F
Linear + revision units	A ⇨ B ⇨ C ⇨ (A, B, C) ⇨ D ⇨ E ⇨ F ⇨ (D, E, F)
Spiral	A_1 ⇨ B_1 ⇨ A_2 ⇨ B_2 ⇨ C_1 ⇨ D_1 ⇨ E_1 ⇨ A_3 ⇨ B_3 ⇨ C_2 ⇨ D_2 ⇨ E_2 ⇨ F_1
Matrix	A_1 ⇨ B_1 ⇨ C_1 ⇨ D_1 ⇨ E_1 ⇨ F_1 ⇨ A_2 ⇨ B_2 ⇨ C_2 ⇨ D_2 ⇨ E_2 ⇨ F_2 ⇨ A_3 ⇨ B_3 ⇨ C_3 ⇨ D_3 ⇨ E_3 ⇨ F_3
Thread	A (G_1) ⇨ B (G_2) ⇨ C (G_3) ⇨ D (G_4) ⇨ E (G_5)⇨ F (G_6)

Letters indicate language item types and subscript numbers indicate the *n*th time the item type features in the syllabus

Many early ESP courses of the 1960s and 1970s followed a structural syllabus, but these were later replaced with courses that followed a notional-functional syllabus. If you look at some of the ESP textbooks of the 1980s and 1990s, you should find many examples of these. Around the mid-1980s, however, the communication language approach began to grow in popularity around the world, and this resulted in a new wave of general English and ESP courses that followed a situational syllabus. In fact, still today, we can find a huge number of conversational textbooks and a few EOP textbooks that follow this structure.

Today, most ESP courses follow a genre-based, skill-based, or task-based syllabus. All of these syllabus types allow for flexibility in presentation and practice of material, and they all place importance on needs over explicit knowledge of language items. However, as mentioned in the opening chapter of this book, in some EAP contexts there has been a recent trend toward English-mediated instruction (EMI) and this has led to a growing use of content-based syllabuses. In some way, a content-based syllabus can be considered to be a unique type of task-based syllabus, where the objective is to master a particular content-oriented goal. But, in practice, you'll find that the ordering of a content-based syllabus often has more in common with structural and notional-functional syllabuses.

Curriculum design

A curriculum specifies the goals for an entire language program and the general sequencing, timing, and duration of courses created to meet those goals. In both EAP and EOP settings, overall program goals can be formulated in terms of learner needs as well as the institution's vision or mission statement. For example, in the ESP program at the Faculty of Science and Engineering, Waseda University, Japan, the goals of the program are expressed as follows (Anthony, 2009):

- develop world-class, international researchers with an ability to study, discuss, and present specialist subject knowledge in English
- develop responsible citizens who can discuss and resolve global issues
- develop valuable members of a dynamically changing and evolving workforce

The overall design of an EAP program often ensures some kind of baseline level competency in target English for all learners in the system. Individual courses within a program are usually sequenced so that they progress from general/basic courses to more specific/advanced courses. General/basic courses are likely to have a required status (with exemptions) and be scheduled in the freshman and sophomore years. The length of these courses can vary from a few weeks to an entire year. Later courses, on the other hand, will commonly have an elective status and be scheduled in junior and senior years, or perhaps even at the graduate school level. The length of these courses can also vary considerably, but you are more likely to find short, intensive three-day and one-week courses at this level than you will earlier in a program.

In EOP settings, programs are usually aimed at specific workers and there is less need to achieve a baseline level of competency. In these settings, courses at all levels may have an elective or required status depending on the position and role of the employee and the company's overall global strategy. Often, new recruits are required to take short, intensive, basic language courses that last from a few days to a few weeks. But, later, they will be expected to continue their language learning through the elective use of additional training programs and online courses that offer some kind of career-long learning possibilities. Employees that have been recently promoted to new positions that require specialized English will also be expected to attend short, intensive courses that focus on more advanced aspects of the language. It should be mentioned that many companies around the world have policies that require workers to have a minimum general English proficiency and they will need to reach a higher level of general English proficiency before they can be promoted to senior levels of management.

TASK 5.2 Sequencing learning objectives in EAP and EOP

Find a description of an EAP or EOP course on the Internet or using the table of contents of a published textbook. Based on information presented, answer the following questions:

1 How would you describe the sequencing of language skills covered in the course using the names given to syllabus types in Table 5.3?
2 Using the descriptions given in Table 5.4, what pattern of sequencing does the course use?
3 If you were to design a similar course, in what ways would you sequence the language skills differently (if any)? Give reasons for your answers.

Contentious issues in ESP: addressing the subject knowledge problem

In this section, I will return to an issue raised in Chapter 3 concerning the role of an ESP instructor in the classroom. If we consider that many ESP instructors lack specialist knowledge about the target disciplines their courses cover, how can they confidently define learning objectives for the classroom and explain to learners the *what*, *why*, and *how* of the target language setting?

The challenges facing ESP instructors when it comes to subject knowledge can be mitigated to some extent through careful planning. In the simplest case, they might be able to find a published ESP textbook that covers the target field and design their classes around that. However, as Anthony (1997) argues, this strategy is not really in line with the defining principles of ESP, as few published textbooks will exactly match the needs of the different stakeholders. Of course, the instructor might be able to modify or adjust the content of a published textbook to better match the different needs, but this returns us back to the original question: *what*, *why*, and *how* should the published material be modified?

An alternative solution to this problem is for ESP instructors to work in a team together with more experienced ESP administrators and subject specialists. Course syllabuses, lesson plans, classroom materials, and teaching methods can emerge out of this team effort, and any challenging language and concepts can be discussed within the team before the ESP instructor has to face learners. But, even in this case, ESP instructors are still likely to face subject-related questions from learners in the classroom that they are unable to answer. This topic was investigated by Wu and Badger (2009), who looked at the strategies that ESP instructors adopted when faced with such in-class subject knowledge dilemmas (ISKDs). What they found was that most instructors in their study adopted avoidance strategies rather than admit their ignorance of subject knowledge.

For ESP instructors working in isolation and those that face tough subject knowledge questions in the classroom, one effective way to address the problem is for them to embrace their own ignorance and use it to their advantage. If you want to follow this path, it is important to be honest with learners. In the first class, you should introduce yourself to learners by explaining your background, teaching experiences, and research interests. You can also say that you specialize in ESP and explain what that means. At this point, you can introduce the idea that the language of specialist subjects varies widely and that even subject specialists are often unaware of its characteristic features. You can then explain that rather than guessing the *what*, *why*, and *how* of target language settings, it is better to observe and analyze target language and then think about and discuss how and why it takes this form. You can also explain that not all the answers will emerge in the classroom, and that learners will need to take some questions back to their own departments, sections, supervisors, and managers. One important point to stress is that, as an ESP instructor, you have a vast knowledge about the ways in which language can vary across disciplines, and that one of your aims is to help learners to begin seeing language in the same way you do.

As a non-specialist working in a specialist field, you should also follow the advice you give to learners. Rather than making potentially incorrect statements about the target language setting based on your faulty assumptions and ignorance of the field, you should instead obtain target language examples, and then find out how and why the language takes this form. One way to do this is through reviews of specialist literature, Internet-based searches, and possibly discussions with subject specialists. However, you may find more useful and revealing information by actually conducting a text analysis yourself. As mentioned already in this book, free and easy-to-use text analysis tools such as *AntConc* (Anthony, 2017a) allow you to immediately identify the most frequent words and multi-word expressions that occur in target texts. As an example, Figure 5.2 shows an *AntConc* display of the most frequent keywords (characteristic words) appearing in the sample transcripts of the Air Traffic Control Complete Corpus (Godfrey, 1994).

Text analysis tools also allow you to see how words and multi-word expressions are used in context and the grammar constructions in which they are usually found. These tools can even reveal the location where particular words and expressions appear in texts, giving you insights into language use at the discourse level.

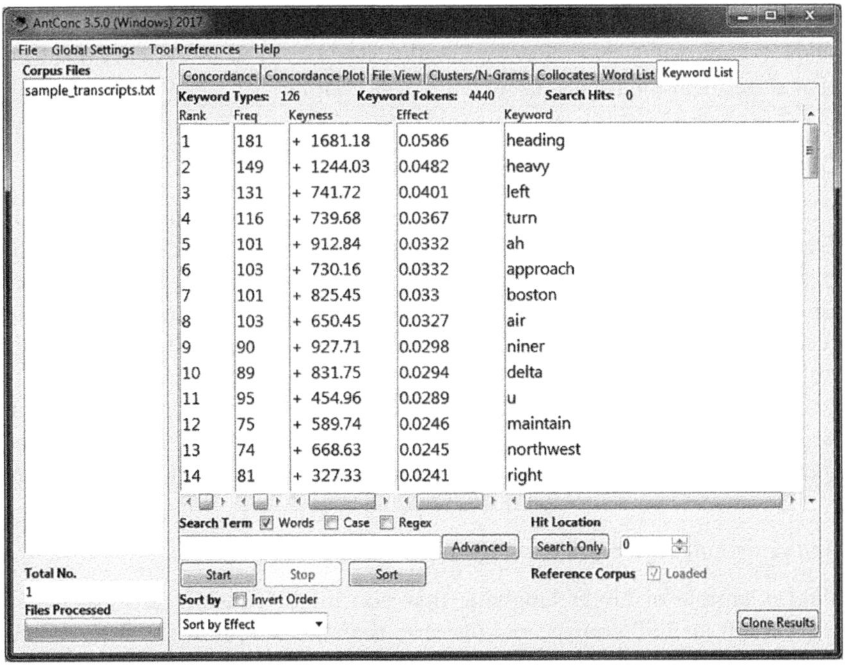

Figure 5.2 *AntConc* display of the most frequent keywords in the *Air Traffic Control Complete Corpus*.

The keywords here are generated by comparing word frequencies in the sample text against the AmE06 Corpus comprising one million words of general American English words (Potts & Baker, 2012). Note that all spoken numbers were removed from the transcript prior to the analysis.

Beyond language itself, you should also attempt to obtain objective data about the more general target language setting. For example, you can find out how many people in the target field use English, what their general English proficiency levels are expected to be, where and when they use the language, and what language issues they commonly experience. Again, this data might come from Internet searches and discussions with subject specialists, but you can also find relevant information from TV shows, newspaper reports, magazine articles, and other mainstream media sources. In short, the more you take an interest in the field, the more valuable your input will be to learners in the classroom.

Experience has shown that subject knowledge problems and in-class subject knowledge dilemmas (ISKDs) are rare when an ESP instructor explains from the outset what their role is in the classroom and how they can assist learners in meeting learning needs. The important thing to remember is that ESP instructors possess their own subject specialist knowledge, and this knowledge is extremely valuable to learners.

Research ideas

Here are some possible ideas for small-scale or large-scale research projects that stem from the topics discussed in this chapter.

Determining learning objectives for a new genre

Choose a genre that you might expect to teach in an ESP course or program. For the genre, obtain one or more samples of target language produced by members of the discourse community (e.g. research articles produced by chemists; executive reports produced by business managers). For each genre sample, identify characteristic features of vocabulary and grammar using a 'bottom-up' approach. Next, consider the text at a 'top-down' level, and attempt to understand its rhetorical structure and the reasons why it is constructed in this way for the target discourse community. Finally, consider what learning and metacognitive skills would be useful to master this genre. Report your findings.

Analyzing language outputs using corpus methods

Find a sample of target language that you might consider introducing to learners in an ESP course, making sure that the sample is in an electronic form (e.g. a web page, a Portable Document Format [PDF] file, or Microsoft Word document). If you can only find a paper-based sample, you will need to transcribe it or use optical character recognition (OCR) software to convert it into a digital form. Next, save the sample to a plain text (.txt) format using one of the options in the save menu of the software you use to view the file. Then, open the file in the *AntConc* text analysis software (Anthony, 2017a) and produce a list of all the words in the sample ordered by frequency using the word list tool option. Look through the word list and consider what it reveals about the vocabulary used in the sample. Report your findings. Finally, discuss how you might scale-up the study to gain a more complete understanding of vocabulary used in a target area of interest.

Critiquing syllabus and program design in ESP

Locate a description of an ESP course or program that you are involved in or would like to know more about. The description might appear as an internal document at an institution, on an Internet web page, or perhaps in a published journal article. Analyze the ESP course or program in terms of its stated learning objectives and its sequencing of those objectives. Summarize your findings and suggest how the ESP course or program might be improved.

Closing reflection

Now that you have come to the end of the chapter, you should have a good idea how to formulate learning objectives from the perspectives of register, rhetorical (discourse), genre, and metacognitive skills. You should also understand the different ways those objectives can be sequenced in an ESP course, and how ESP courses might combine together to form an entire program. Finally, you should have some ideas on how to deal with the subject knowledge problem that many ESP instructors experience.

Here are a few more questions to consider:

1 Which of the points covered in the chapter were new to you? Did you find them interesting and relevant in terms of your own learning goals? Were there any points that you found confusing or that you disagreed with?
2 What points from the chapter do you think you can immediately put to use in your own learning or teaching context?
3 Which of the different perspectives (register, rhetorical, genre, metacognitive) do you think are the most helpful in determining learning objectives for an ESP course? Why?
4 If you were free to choose how you sequenced the learning objectives for an ESP course, which syllabus type and sequencing pattern would you adopt? Give reasons.
5 If you were a learner in an ESP classroom and your instructor admitted to you that they were not an expert in your target discipline, how would you feel? What would they need to do to gain your trust and help you satisfy your learning requirements?

Further resources

Books

Hyon, S. (2018). *Introducing genre and English for specific purposes*. Abingdon, UK: Routledge.

Research articles

Estival, D., Farris, C., & Molesworth, B. (2016). *Aviation English. A lingua franca for pilots and air traffic controllers*. London: Routledge.

Corpora

Air Traffic Control Complete Corpus (Godfrey, 1994).
Philadelphia: Linguistic Data Consortium, 1994. Retrieved from https://catalog.ldc.upenn.edu/LDC94S14A

Software

Anthony, L. (2017). *AntConc* (Version 3.5.0) [Computer Software]. Tokyo, Japan: Waseda University. Retrieved from www.laurenceanthony.net/software/antconc/

Chapter 6

Deciding materials and methods in ESP

In Chapter 5, you learned how to formulate and sequence learning objectives for an ESP course or program, which form the second pillar of ESP. Ultimately, though, the success of any ESP course or program is determined by the classroom materials and methods that are chosen to operationalize these objectives. The decisions made here form the third pillar of ESP.

In some ESP settings, classroom materials are decided at the administrative level by ESP course and program designers. These might be adopted or adapted from existing sources, such as published textbooks, or they may be newly created based on authentic samples of language from the target setting. In other settings, the ESP instructor will have complete freedom to adopt, adapt, or create materials for their course. Each option has advantages and disadvantages, so it is important that you understand what these are. The choice of materials also directly impacts on the types of teaching and learning methods that can be used in class. So, as an ESP instructor, you need to understand how one impacts on the other and be able to adjust the materials and methods to your preferred teaching style and the needs of the learners.

In this chapter, I'll first discuss the role of materials in ESP and how best to evaluate them. Next, I'll explain how to adopt, adapt, or create effective materials for the ESP classroom based on the needs of different stakeholders and the limitations in terms of the resources and time available. Then, I'll explain how technologies such as corpus software tools can help to prepare suitable materials, even in highly subject-specific target settings. After that, I'll discuss how materials affect teaching methods. Here, I'll review a range of traditional and novel teaching methods that are particularly well-suited to EAP and EOP contexts where learner cohorts might be extremely homogenous groups with a narrow and clearly defined goal, or wide, extremely heterogeneous groups with broad, less well-defined goals. I'll also discuss how corpus software tools can facilitate teaching and learning in the ESP classroom. Finally, I'll discuss the topic of authenticity in materials and methods design. Here, I'll explain why authentic materials are often preferred but also how they can sometimes cause problems for both instructors and learners.

By the end of the chapter, you should be able to evaluate, adapt, and utilize published materials, create your own custom materials, and mesh published and custom-made materials together in a coherent fashion. You should also be able to use different teaching and learning methods to organize and present target materials, and help learners to engage with them. Most importantly, you should be in a good position to start teaching ESP classes.

Opening reflection

Think back to the different courses that you have taken as a student. Did the instructors use published textbooks, or did they use custom-made materials adapted from published sources and/or created uniquely? Which type of materials did you prefer? If you have experience of teaching, what types of materials do you prefer to use as an instructor? Why?

In the different courses that you have studied, could you predict what activities the instructor would use? Did they follow a set order (e.g. presentation – practice – discussion)? How did the activities help you engage with the materials? If you have experience of teaching, what activities do you tend to use in class? What purpose do they have? How do you decide the order in which they are presented?

Commentary

Many learners prefer instructors that adopt a published textbook and follow a consistent set of teaching and learning methods in their classes. Textbooks provide learners with a clear set of goals and a clear sequencing of materials designed to reach those goals. They also provide learners with a familiar reference source that they can use to prepare and review for the class. In addition, published textbooks are usually colorful and professional looking, sending a message to the learners that the course is also professionally developed and meaningful. What's more, if instructors use a well-constructed textbook in the classroom, their own class preparation time can be dramatically reduced, allowing them more time to perfect their delivery of the material and address individual learner issues. This final reason is no doubt one of the driving forces behind the very common practice of using textbooks in Asian EAP contexts, where contract and part-time instructors can be expected to teach 10 or more classes per week, with learners numbering 30 or more.

Custom materials, on the other hand, usually present only a fragmented picture of course goals. Also, as the materials are most commonly delivered on an as-need basis, the sequencing of goals will be less transparent.

Another disadvantage of custom materials is that they usually serve as a poor reference source, getting mixed up or lost between classes. They are also usually less professional looking, being printed in black and white on A4 paper, with occasional typos and misprints. Instructors can also be less predictable in the way they use custom materials, making it difficult for learners to know when or how the materials will be introduced, used, or referred to in class. They also take longer to prepare, reducing the instructor's time to focus on other aspects of class management. Of course, if the materials can be stored on a learning management system (LMS), they can be better organized and used again if the course is repeated. But, these systems also require time to learn and may not always be available.

I have presented the arguments here in a way that suggests all ESP instructors should be using published textbooks and teaching from them in a predictable way. But, this is not the case. As you will find in the following sections, textbooks have severe limitations in ESP contexts, making them sometimes the least preferable option. Also, ESP courses and programs are often set up in ways that make them highly unpredictable from the outset. The ability of an experienced ESP instructor to adapt to such an environment by quickly creating custom materials and using innovative teaching and learning methods sets them apart from other language instructors. You will see why and how they can do this later in this chapter.

Basic principles in ESP materials design

The roles of materials in ESP

One of the most difficult challenges that ESP administrators and instructors have is deciding what materials should be used in the classroom. Should they adopt a published textbook? Should they attempt to modify or adapt a published textbook in a way that reflects the nature of the target setting and is suited to the level, needs, and interests of the learners? Or, should they spend time to create a custom set of materials based on or adapted from real-world, authentic materials selected from the target setting?

To answer these questions, it is first important to understand the various roles that materials serve in the ESP classroom. Referring back to the learning objectives introduced in Chapter 5, we can list these in main and sub-category levels as follows:

- help learners to understand the what, why, and how of the target language setting
    - introduce and explain target language skills
    - expose learners to target language skills as used in real-world settings
    - provide relevant individual, pair, and group exercises

  - be complete and self-explanatory so as to serve as both an in-class or self-study learning resource
- help learners to build their language skills
  - present new language skills in clearly ordered steps and lessons
  - sequence steps and lessons to maximize learning
  - stretch learners with challenging but achievable exercises
- assist learners to use language skills actively
  - encourage learners to interact with others through pair and group exercises
  - encourage learners to reflect on the value and use of the target material in target language settings
  - encourage learners to monitor their progress
  - provide overviews, summaries, reviews, and evaluations of the target language skills
  - give clear indications of milestones reached
- encourage the incidental learning of target language skills
  - provide additional exercises, tasks, and readings
  - include a table of contents, an index, and a list of references
- help learners develop a positive emotional response to the target language skills
  - provide background information on the importance and usefulness of the language skills
  - introduce interesting and useful examples
  - use fun and humor where appropriate
  - match the materials to the target settings and interests of the learners
  - present the target language skills in a clear and professional way
- support non-specialist instructors
  - provide contextual information about the target setting
  - include supporting audio/video with transcripts
  - include an exercise answer key

Evaluating materials in ESP

Once you understand the role of materials in ESP, you are in a position to evaluate existing materials to determine if they can be used as is, or if they can be used after some modifications. At this point, if you find that existing materials cannot be used or adapted to fulfill the different roles required of ESP materials, you must then consider if it is possible to create custom materials that better fulfill the different roles.

Many researchers have presented lists of criteria on which to evaluate language materials. A useful summary of some of the early models of the 1980s and 1990s is provided by Jordan (1997), who notes that a two-stage process is often recommended. Charles and Pecoari (2016) follow this idea in their EAP materials evaluation, which is reminiscent of the more general model given by McDonough and Shaw (2013). In the first stage, they suggest quickly checking the introduction, table of contents, and publisher's description of the existing materials, with the aim of eliminating the least likely materials. Then, at the second stage, they suggest a more in-depth evaluation of at least two units of the materials before a final decision is made.

Following a similar two-stage approach here, if you want to assess the suitability of existing ESP materials in fulfilling the roles described previously, you could start by asking the initial review questions listed in Table 6.1.

Next, for any materials that score a high number of 'yes' answers at the initial review stage, you could proceed to ask the questions listed in Table 6.2 to probe candidate materials in more depth before making a final decision.

Table 6.1 Materials evaluation: stage one review questions

Role of materials	*Questions to consider*
help learners to understand the what, why, and how of the target language setting	• Are the materials relevant for the target language setting and learner group? • Are the materials up-to-date? • Can the materials be used with the target number of learners? • Do the materials provide a variety of exercises that address learner needs? • Is the cost of the materials acceptable to the learners and the institution?
help learners to build their language skills	• Does the level of the materials match that of the learners? • Are the units and exercises clearly and logically ordered? • Can the materials be covered within the timeframe of the course?
assist learners to use language skills actively	• Do the materials provide pair and group exercises (in addition to instructor-centered and individual exercises)?
encourage the incidental learning of target language skills	• Do the materials provide overviews, summaries, reviews, and additional exercises, tasks, and readings? • Do the materials include a table of contents, an index, and a list of references?

(Continued)

Table 6.1 (Continued)

Role of materials	*Questions to consider*
help learners develop a positive emotional response to the target language skills	• Do the materials introduce interesting and useful examples? • Are the materials presented in a clear and professional way?
support (non-specialist) instructors	• Do the materials include a teachers' book? • Do the materials including supporting audio/video, transcripts, and/or an answer key? • Do the materials require specialist knowledge? • Do the materials require space or resources that are unavailable?

Table 6.2 Materials evaluation: stage two in-depth review questions

Role of materials	*Questions to consider*
help learners to understand the what, why, and how of the target language setting	• Do the materials provide full coverage of target language skills? • Are authentic examples used? • Do exercises meet target language and learning objectives? • Can the materials be used in class and also outside of class as a learning resource?
help learners to build their language skills	• Can the materials be used with learners at a range of different levels? • Can the materials be conveniently divided up and presented within the designated lesson hours and the course timeframe? • Does the ordering of materials match instructor and learner preferences?
assist learners to use language skills actively	• Do the materials provide a suitable balance between different exercise types? • Do the materials include sample texts and model answers?
encourage the incidental learning of target language skills	• Do the materials provide clear and comprehensive overviews, summaries, reviews, and additional exercises, tasks, and readings that stretch the learners? • Does the table of contents, index, and list of references accurately reflect the content of the materials?

Role of materials	*Questions to consider*
help learners develop a positive emotional response to the target language skills	• Are the examples culturally or socially appropriate? • Are the examples timely? • Are the exercises sufficiently varied to avoid becoming repetitive? • Are the materials void of any major typos or production issues? • Is the layout clear and attractive? • Do the visuals help the explanations?
support (non-specialist) instructors	• Is the teacher's book suitably detailed? • Does the teacher's book match the quality of the main materials? • Are supporting materials of a high quality? • Are supporting materials correctly indexed and referenced in the main materials? • Are L1 explanations available (if necessary)?

TASK 6.1 Evaluating a published ESP textbook

Visit a local academic bookstore and quickly find several ESP-focused textbooks in a target discipline that interests you (e.g. academic writing, business, nursing). Now, imagine that you are an ESP instructor who has to select a textbook for a new course in this target area. The class is composed of 30 non-native speakers of English from a variety of countries with a beginner-level English ability. None of the students have experience of the target language setting.

Using the stage one review questions presented in Table 6.1, try to find a candidate textbook that scores a high number of 'yes' answers. If you are successful, proceed to the stage two in-depth review questions in Table 6.2 and decide if this textbook would work well in your imagined class.

If you already teach ESP courses, repeat the above for one of your courses and learner groups. If you already use a textbook in this course, would it pass the two review stages?

Adopting, adapting, and creating materials in ESP

Adopting published materials

In the "Commentary" section earlier in the chapter, I discussed various reasons why both learners and instructors might prefer to adopt published textbooks instead of using custom-made handouts and other materials. There is no doubt that textbooks are a convenience for both instructors and learners. They provide an overall structure for classes, reducing the instructor's need to plan for classes, and helping learners prepare for classes. They include explanations of activities and target language examples, which the instructor can use in place of explanations presented on the board, and learners can use as a permanent reference source. They also provide instructors with new ideas for introducing and explaining concepts, serving as an in-service training resource. And, they can help learners through familiar designs and sometimes novel explanations and activities. Assuming that a textbook can be found that fulfills some or most of the roles discussed earlier, the value of the textbook in terms of achieving learning objectives is also strengthened. This is especially true if the textbook has been created by an experienced ESP materials developer with a good knowledge of real-world teaching and a track record of producing quality ESP research.

In an ESP program setting, adopting a textbook also makes huge practical sense from an administrative standpoint. Textbooks are almost always the cheapest way to distribute materials because the cost of the materials is paid for directly by the learners. (In the case of custom materials in the form of printed handouts, the costs will almost always be paid for by the institution.) The tasks of managing the program, monitoring learner progress, diagnosing problems, and evaluating instructor performance are also much easier to do if instructors are using the same materials. If the ESP program is large enough, there is also the possibility to turn custom-made materials into a published textbook just for the target learners. In this case, many of the weaknesses of commercially created published textbooks can be minimized, including the need to market the materials to a broad audience to guarantee sales, and the need to follow a fixed format to reduce production costs and editorial work.

If you are an ESP instructor with the freedom to choose your course materials, the first step in materials design is certainly to consider the possibility of adopting a published textbook, especially if you lack experience in the target area. Using the evaluation criteria presented in Tables 6.1 and 6.2, you can review the possibilities, and even if you find no materials that completely fulfill the required roles, you can consider where and how those published materials might be adapted to more closely match the needs of the different stakeholders.

The reality for many ESP instructors, however, is that they actually have no choice in terms of the primary classroom materials they can use. ESP program administrators will decide on a published textbook or some in-house created materials (hopefully using a similar evaluation to that in Tables 6.1 and 6.2) and require instructors (and learners) to adopt them. If you find yourself in such a setting, it is important that you understand the administrators' rationale for choosing the materials and report back to them on how the materials are working in class. You should also feel able to suggest changes or improvements to the materials based on your in-class experiences. Administrators may have made the choice to use particular materials based on their perceived needs of the institution and those of learners and instructors. But, these perceived needs will almost always need adjustments after the materials are used 'in the wild' of real classrooms. You should also remember that instructors almost always have some flexibility in *how* adopted materials are used in class. For example, you might believe that some explanations and activities should be shortened, lengthened, or skipped altogether. Others might need to be replaced with your own custom explanations and activities. We will consider the topic of materials adaptation in the next section.

Adapting published materials

There are many reasons why published materials might need to be adapted before they can be used successfully in the ESP classroom. At the level of target learning objectives, the materials might present incorrect or outdated descriptions. In EAP settings, for example, citation formats might need to be updated to reflect the most recent specifications. Similarly, in EOP settings, new laws and treaties can require changes to the way information is presented in reports. The author of the materials may be unaware of these developments or the materials may have been published before the changes were initiated. Insights from corpus linguistics have also overturned some of the assumptions presented in both old and new materials (for examples, see Harwood, 2005). However, author and publisher circumstances may prevent published materials from being updated accordingly. The materials might also ignore important points or include irrelevant ones. Or, they may present points in an overly simplistic or overly complicated manner. They might even sequence the points in a confusing manner.

At the level of exercises, published materials will need to be adapted if they are aimed at a learner level that is too high or low for the in-class group. For example, reading passages may contain too many unknown words or be written in an overly restricted vocabulary set that does not challenge the learners in any way. Similarly, comprehension questions may be too easy or difficult. Another problem might be that the exercises do not provide enough practice of a particular learning skill (e.g. speaking or reading) or be suitably balanced to provide a range of meaning-focused input, meaning-focused output, target language, and fluency activities, following the *four-strands* concept of Nation and Macalister (2010) mentioned in Chapter 5.

The 'carrier content' in published materials might also need adapting. Dudley-Evans and St. John (1998) describe this as the content used to present the target language skills in a suitable context. For example, in an EAP academic listening course, the carrier content might be a recorded lecture on the birth of the Internet, or the discovery of the structure of the atom. In an EOP course on nursing, the carrier content might be a role-play involving a patient suffering from dementia. Sometimes, the carrier content will need updating to reflect contemporary practices. Or, it might need changing if it becomes socially or culturally inappropriate. This latter case happened in one academic listening course, where a model lecture in the textbook focused on the triumphs of the cyclist Lance Armstrong who won the Tour de France a record seven times. Later, he admitted to illegally doping and was stripped of all the titles (Beaubien, 2013).

Finally, there are often rather mundane reasons why published materials might need adapting. For example, they may require the use of audio and visual playback systems that are not available in the classroom. They might include activities that require learners to move around, even though the classroom prevents this. Or, they might include too few or too many units than the time allows.

To address those issues, you may need to *simplify*, *expand*, *delete*, *replace*, or *reorder* the materials and/or *add* new ones. For example, with a low-level class, you might want to *simplify* an explanation so that learners can grasp the main point. On the other hand, in a high-level class, you might want to *expand* the explanation, *replace* it with a more in-depth discussion, or perhaps simply *add* an interesting anecdote or example to deepen the learners' understanding of the concept. In other situations, you might want to *delete* certain exercises if you believe that the learners have already mastered the concept, *expand* a short exercise into a series of longer exercises if you believe that the learners need more scaffolding, or *reorder* the exercises to better fit the flow of the lesson. Finally, in the case of published materials containing too few or too many units, you might *reorder* the existing units, and then *add* or *delete* extra units as necessary.

Creating custom materials

Just as there are many ESP contexts where you will have to use published materials, there are others where creating materials will be the only option available. Perhaps the course is aimed at a niche target language setting where publishing companies see no market to produce a textbook. Or, perhaps the institution demands that all materials are created in-house in order to reduce the impact of outside influences on the overall management of the program and the running costs involved. This is particularly common in EOP settings. In other cases, you may believe that creating materials is preferable; for example, if existing materials contain critical flaws that prevent them from being adapted. Or, you may calculate that the time needed to evaluate a range of published materials and then adapt candidate materials for your own setting would be better spent creating uniquely tailored materials from the outset.

Five-step approach to custom materials creation

In cases where you are able to carefully plan for materials creation (e.g. when you are working in a team or if the course does not start for several months), you might consider using the following five-step approach.

STEP 1: REVIEW PREVIOUS WORK

There is no need to 'reinvent the wheel' when it comes to materials design. Many materials designers have proposed useful designs and exercise types that you can incorporate into your custom materials. First, you should make a list of useful ideas that have been reported in research articles and Internet articles, discussed at academic conferences, or said to you in face-to-face discussions. Also, you should review published materials in the same general area to see how they introduce, explain, and develop language skills.

STEP 2: CREATE A GENERAL PLAN

Once you have a strong knowledge base, you can create a general plan for what to target in the materials and how to sequence the items. The decisions regarding what to include should be based on the learning objectives of the course. It is important, here, to return to the concepts of register analysis, rhetorical (discourse) analysis, genre analysis, and learning and metacognitive skills development discussed in Chapter 5. To help you decide how the materials should be sequenced, again, you can return to the ideas about sequencing of learning objectives presented in Chapter 5.

STEP 3: SELECT 'CARRIER CONTENT'

Once a general plan has been formulated, the next step is to choose suitable 'carrier content' that will form the basis for explaining, exemplifying, and practicing different learning points. One option is to write this content yourself based on intuition or with reference to content already presented in published works. However, this is a risky proposition. The intuitions of experienced teachers (as well as administrators and researchers) have been proven incorrect numerous times (see, for example, Harwood, 2005). Also, if you are assigned to teach an ESP course for learners of an unfamiliar discipline, the chance of being wrong dramatically increases. Copying or adapting content presented in published works is also risky as it leads to questions concerning the originality and copyright of the materials.

In both EAP and EOP settings, perhaps a better option is to use 'authentic' language samples produced by members of the target discourse community or perhaps by colleagues who are experienced in the target field and who can serve as specialist informants. Authentic samples can be intrinsically interesting to the learners and help motivate them to reach a level where they can understand and generate similar samples themselves. On the other hand, these authentic samples may be at a level far beyond that of the learners, causing the learners to question their ability to reach the required level and demotivate them. If this is a worry, you might consider how the samples can be simplified for use early in the course, and gradually presented in their raw form later in the course. You also need to be careful that the samples you use are relevant in the immediate contexts of the learners or presented in a way that allows the learners to get insights on the target context and discourse community in which they were created. We will return to the topic of authenticity in materials design later in the chapter.

STEP 4: CREATE EXPLANATIONS AND EXERCISES

With useful, relevant, and hopefully interesting carrier content decided, you are now in a position to create explanations and exercises that allow learners to reach their learning objectives in the most efficient and effective way.

Explanations of learning points as well as exercise instructions should be written in a restricted (simplified) language to ensure that all learners, regardless of their level, can understand the main points and what they are supposed to do. In the next section, I will introduce several online and offline software tools that can help you identify which words or phrases in explanations and instructions might be problematic, but a general awareness of vocabulary levels will help you greatly (for an in-depth discussion, see Nation, 2001).

Exercises should be designed with a view to providing learners with a variety of learning opportunities. Nation and Macalister (2010) argue that exercises should be designed to allow for a balanced *four-strands* presentation of meaning-focused input, meaning-focused output, target language, and fluency development. You also need to ensure that they allow learners to interact with other members of the class in various ways. Some exercises may require learners to work independently of others, both inside and outside the classroom. These can include fact-finding missions, home experiments, vocabulary learning exercises, and various independent writing tasks. Other exercises may require learners to interact directly with the instructor or work with other learners in pairs or groups. There is a huge range of activities that you can adopt here, including reading comprehension exercises using true/false, multiple-choice, short, and long form questions, listening comprehension exercises followed by summary writing tasks, speaking fluency exercises utilizing rapid picture description tasks, and writing tasks to produce summaries, essays, and research reports. For all these exercises, you can encourage greater interaction between learners using various task designs, including information transfer, information gap, and jigsaw designs. You can also increase the variety of learning opportunities through the use of online and office resources that allow for the easy introduction of audio, video, images, graphics, and animation into the classroom.

When it comes to sequencing the exercises you design, you should first introduce simple, easy exercises that are largely supported by the instructor. Then, you can gradually introduce exercises that require more time, higher levels of proficiency and experience, and less instructor support. This design will allow you to more easily use the materials with a broad range of learners. With beginner and inexperienced learners, you can focus on the early exercises. With more advanced and experienced learners, you can quickly cover or skip the early exercises and allow them to focus on the more demanding ones.

Finally, you should pay careful attention to how the materials will be delivered to learners and what format you will use. For offline materials, you need to consider if they will be distributed as an electronic file, loose handouts, or perhaps stapled together in the form of a handbook. You may even consider binding them in a more professional way to appear like a published textbook. You also need to decide if the materials will be printed in black and white, or color. For online materials, you need to decide if they will be distributed within an institution's learning management system (LMS) or on a specially created website. And, for both offline and online materials, will you need to pay attention to the overall design and 'feel' of the materials, which will depend on the typefaces, styles, spacing, and visuals that you decide.

STEP 5: EVALUATE AND REVISE THE MATERIALS

The final step in the materials creation process takes us back to where we started. Here, you need to evaluate the created materials in terms of how well they fulfill the roles of materials described earlier in the chapter and decide if and where they might need to be revised (adapted) to better match the needs of the learners and other stakeholders. One effective way to do this is by piloting the materials with a small group of target learners. As the class proceeds, you can take mental notes on what 'carrier content' worked well, which instructions were easy for learners to follow, and which exercises seemed to generate the desired outcomes. You can also ask learners to complete after-class surveys on their impressions of the materials and where they think improvements can be made. For example, you can ask if they felt the materials were coherent and contained no missing gaps in terms of explanation and instructions. You can ask if the materials provided enough variety in terms medium of delivery, exercises types, and interactive learning opportunities. At a more basic level, you can also ask if the learners found the 'carrier content' interesting, and if they 'liked' or 'enjoyed' using the materials in general.

If you are in an administrative position, it is also important that you pilot new materials with a small group of target instructors. Again, you can use a survey or perhaps an interview to find out what they thought worked well in class and how the materials could be improved. You can also ask them to compare the materials to other materials they have used in the past. By asking these questions, you allow an important stakeholder group to have a more direct involvement in the creation of the materials. It also increases the likelihood that the instructors will form a positive attitude toward the materials once they are finalized.

'Just-in-time' custom materials creation

In some ESP contexts, you will not always have the time or resources to carefully plan and prepare materials using the five-stage process just described. For example, if you are working as a company consultant, you may suddenly receive a call to organize a workshop with just a few days' time to prepare. Or worse, you may need to create materials on the day of the course, after you have first met the learners, determined their needs, and established their immediate learning objectives. In these cases, the following 'just-in-time' materials creation process is worth knowing.

STEP 1: COLLECT TARGET LANGUAGE SAMPLES

For this step, ideally, you would already have a stock of target language samples in the form of written texts, audio files, transcripts, videos, and so on. If not, you could ask the course administrators to provide some, or you could instruct the learners to bring to the class some samples that they have encountered in the past. Another possibility is to ask the learners to produce their own target language samples in the first session of the course; for example, in a writing task or a role-play.

STEP 2: ANALYZE AND GROUP TARGET LANGUAGE SAMPLES

Once you have a set of target language samples, you can quickly analyze them and identify general areas to address and perhaps specific issues associated with individual learners. Then, you are in a position to group the samples into different focus areas, and pick prototypical examples that best model the language features you want to focus on in class.

STEP 3: PRESENT AND DISCUSS TARGET LANGUAGE SAMPLES

In the ESP classes, you can present the prototypical examples and then initiate a discussion with learners about why the particular examples were selected, what strengths and weaknesses they display, and how they can be improved. At this stage, if you are using learner-generated materials, you need to be careful to make sure that the examples are anonymized to avoid embarrassing individuals in the class.

TASK 6.2 Creating materials for ESP

Choose a set of language or learning objectives to meet a particular EAP or EOP learner need that you have some experience of (e.g. academic writing, conference presentation, hotel service encounter, doctor-patient interaction). Next, follow the five-step approach to custom materials creation discussed in this chapter and attempt to create one or more complete activities to meet these objectives. When you reach step 5, show the materials to another person you are studying or working with and get their opinions. Also, if possible, try out the materials with a group of learners.

How long did the task take to complete? If you followed the 'just-in-time' approach to materials creation, how would the materials differ? Do you think you could adopt or adapt published materials that would perform similarly, or even better?

Utilizing technology in the adaption and creation of ESP materials

In the earlier section on creating custom materials for ESP, I suggested that authentic language samples produced by members of the target discourse community can serve as useful carrier content for the classroom. The technology of the Internet now gives us access to a huge range of authentic samples of text, image, audio, and video that can be used in class, from academic journal papers written by top researchers in the field to video recordings of sales presentations given by world-leading business executives. If you want to find a sample of language from the target setting, the most productive first step is almost always to simply search for it on the Internet. It is important to note, also, that not only are these samples easy to find but they are usually released with information that allows you to judge their relevance and value. For example, journal papers will be listed with the number of times they have been cited and the impact factor of the journal. Newspaper articles, blogs, and videos will include information on the number of views, comments, and 'likes' they receive.

Corpus tools can also help you choose suitable samples for the classroom by identifying candidate samples that exhibit the characteristic features of language that you need to focus on in class. Tools like *AntConc* (Anthony, 2017a), for example, can be used to generate keywords from a target corpus of target texts that can then be used to identify good candidate texts for use as carrier content. The *ProtAnt* tool (Anthony & Baker, 2017) takes this idea one step further and automatically compares a set of candidate texts against a reference corpus of target language, ranking the texts in terms of their *prototypicality*. The highest ranked texts should serve not only as good carrier content samples, but also as useful samples to analyze when deciding the learning objectives for a course.

Earlier in this chapter, I recommended that target explanations and instructions in custom materials are written in a restricted (simplified) language. An easy way to do this is with an online lexical profile tool such as the one in *AntQuickTools* (Anthony, 2017c) or the one in the Compleat Lexical Tutor (Cobb, 2017). The text profiler in *AntQuickTools*, for example, allows you to copy and paste an explanation or instruction directly into a browser window, and the tool will immediately highlight words that are outside of the most frequent bands of English. This display gives you direct feedback on which words might be problematic for your learners. You might also consider using the tool to highlight problematic language in your carrier content and simplify it accordingly. There are also offline tools, such as *AntWordProfiler* (Anthony, 2014) that can be used to profile tens, hundreds, or even thousands of individual texts in one batch. The advantage of using an offline profiler is that it can be used with sensitive data, such as the content of examinations in an EAP setting or technical documentation in an EOP setting.

You should not forget that there are also many technologies that help you to easily distribute materials and allow learners to engage with the materials and other learners in an interactive way. These include webpages, email, messaging systems, blogs, and podcasts, as well as survey creation web tools and content management systems (CMSs). There are also a growing number of social media network platforms including Facebook, Twitter, and Instagram that allow learners to interact with each other and the instructor. In recent years, elements of all these technologies have come together in the form of massive open online courses (MOOCs), offered on for-profit platforms such as *Coursera* and *FutureLearn*, as well as a growing number of open platforms.

TASK 6.3 Embracing technology in language learning

Profiling vocabulary

Look at one of the explanations or instructions that you created for the materials you created in Task 6.2. Try to identify which words might cause problems for learners. Now, type or paste the text into an online text profiling tool (e.g. *AntQuickTools*) and note down which words are flagged as being potentially difficult. Do these words match what you predicted would cause the learners difficulties?

Joining a MOOC

Visit one of the popular for-profit or open platforms offering massive open online courses (MOOCs). Join a course that interests you which is offered freely or that you can join on a free trial. After completing the first few lessons or units, reflect on the experience by answering the following questions:

1. How successful was the MOOC in presenting an interactive learning environment?
2. What strategies did the MOOC developers employ to overcome the limitations of an online delivery system?
3. What strategies from the MOOC could you employ in your own classes to effectively meet target learning objectives and engage learners?

Basic principles in ESP methods selection

Using traditional teaching and learning methods

Many teaching and learning methods have been promoted in the field of English language teaching (ELT). These include the audio-lingual method, the grammar-translation method, the communicative language teaching (CLT) approach, task-based language teaching (TBLT), and more esoteric methods such as Suggestopedia, Total Physical Response (TPR), The Silent Way, The Natural Approach, and The Lexical Approach. For a review of these different methods, see Richards and Rodgers (2014).

Although all of these methods have value in some contexts, you will find that in an ESP classroom, the most successful teaching and learning methods are usually those that closely align with the materials that you adopt, adapt, or create, and the learning environment that you have to work in. As a result, it is not recommended that you try to force everything that happens in a classroom into a single, popular theory. Rather, you will find that an eclectic approach to ESP teaching and learning is usually more effective.

As an example, the audio-lingual method, which was popular in the 1960s, focuses on the drilling of learners in the separate skills of reading, writing, listening, and speaking using short dialogues and language items. In an ESP context, this behaviorist approach might prove to be very effective in the teaching and learning of opening statements and transition phrases in oral presentations. On the other hand, it will be of little use when helping learners manage the language required to understand and respond to questions in the Q&A session after a presentation. In this case, a communicative language approach is likely to prove more successful. Then again, the value of the communicative language approach is questionable if it is being applied in an intensive, one-day EOP course for restaurant waiters that have to master the language needed to explain the menu and take orders. In this context, perhaps the audio-lingual method will again prove effective.

Adjusting to the knowledge, experiences, and expectations of the target learners

In ESP, learners often bring specialist knowledge and experiences of the target language setting to the classroom that might not be available to the instructor. This unique situation can change the dynamics of the classroom and affect which teaching and learning methods are likely to be effective.

With beginners and intermediate-level learners, traditional teacher-centered approaches that follow a presentation-practice-perform (PPP) format might work well. But, they are likely to be problematic when dealing with advanced learners, as the instructor will be less confident about presenting the 'correct' way to use the target language. In these cases, a learner-centered approach can work well. For example, the learners might first produce examples of target language which are then critiqued and commented on by the instructor. Then, the learners can try producing the target language again, hopefully with improvements. This learner-centered approach works well in regularly scheduled courses, but it is particularly effective in short, intensive courses, where the instructor serves in the role of a language coach.

Teaching and learning methods that closely match those used in the target discipline are also more likely to be successful. As a result, in a business or law context, a case study approach to learning can work well, whereas in a scientific or engineering context, a more experimental, data-centric approach is likely to be successful. On the other hand, in medical fields and the hospitality industry, role-plays can be used as a useful teaching and learning method. In other fields, such as architecture, a task-based approach or a project-based approach is likely to prove successful.

Another factor that can affect the success of a teaching or learning method is the level of familiarly that learners have of it. Learners in an EAP setting in Asia, for example, will be very familiar with presentation-practice-perform (PPP) methods that are geared toward classes of 30, 50, or even 100 or more students. As a result, they are likely to respond more favorably to passive, teacher-centered approaches than learners in Europe or the USA who have generally studied in smaller classes and been exposed to task-based learning, problem solving, and other active learning methods from a young age. Of course, this is not to say that Asian students will respond poorly to active learning methods, or that learners in Europe or the USA will reject presentation-practice-perform (PPP) methods. What it does mean is that you need to be sensitive to these issues. If you are working in an Asian context and hope or need to introduce an active learning approach built around pair- and group work activities, you will probably first need to work with course and program administrators to reduce class sizes. Then, in the classroom, you will need to work with the learners, carefully explaining to them the advantages of an active learning approach and demonstrating ways in which they can interact to maximize their learning opportunities.

TASK 6.4 Selecting appropriate teaching and learning methods

A common problem found in non-native speaker English writing is the absence or misuse of articles (*a*, *an*, *the*). The following are samples of learner writing that reflect article-use issues.

Example 1: Osteoclasts play critical role in bone destruction.
Example 2: Microalgae are best candidate in biodiesel production systems.
Example 3: In this study, we propose the novel mechanism for genetic exchange.

Using these samples (and others) as 'carrier content', what teaching and learning methods would you use to help learners improve their writing in terms of article use.

Data-Driven Learning (DDL) in ESP

Earlier in the chapter, I discussed various ways in which corpus tools can support the development of effective ESP materials. You might have noticed that these tools can empower the instructor by providing them with insights into an unfamiliar target language setting. Following this line of argument, many corpus researchers have suggested that corpora and corpus tools should also be introduced to learners, empowering them to identify characteristic features of the target language (Flowerdew, 2002; Johns, 1991; Leech, 1997; Römer, 2010). This novel approach is usually referred to as Data-Driven Learning (DDL).

In the most popular form of DDL, learners will interact directly with a corpus of target language samples through inductive, self-directed exercises using an online tool such as *BNCweb* (Hoffmann & Evert, 2006) or an offline tool such as *AntConc* (Anthony, 2017a). Instructors play an important role in guiding learners through this inductive process, offering hints on ways to search the corpus effectively, demonstrating how to interpret the different results, and helping the learners to transfer the knowledge gained from a corpus analysis into their own language development.

Anthony (2016) discusses the many strengths of DDL including its use in EAP writing classes, where instructors may face a heterogeneous group of learners from a variety of highly specialized disciplines. Through DDL, each learner can address their unique discipline-specific language needs, and through discussion and collaboration with others working with different corpora, gain valuable knowledge of how language varies between disciplines. Anthony also discusses some of the challenges of DDL, the most commonly cited one being the difficulty faced by learners in obtaining a suitable corpus. Even here, though, progress has been made, and now there are tools such as *AntCorGen* (Anthony, 2017b) that allow learners to collect hundreds or thousands of specialist subject research articles for use in EAP writing classes at the click of a button.

To illustrate the DDL approach, Figure 6.1 shows a screenshot of *AntConc* during a search for phrases that include inflections of the verb *clear* in the

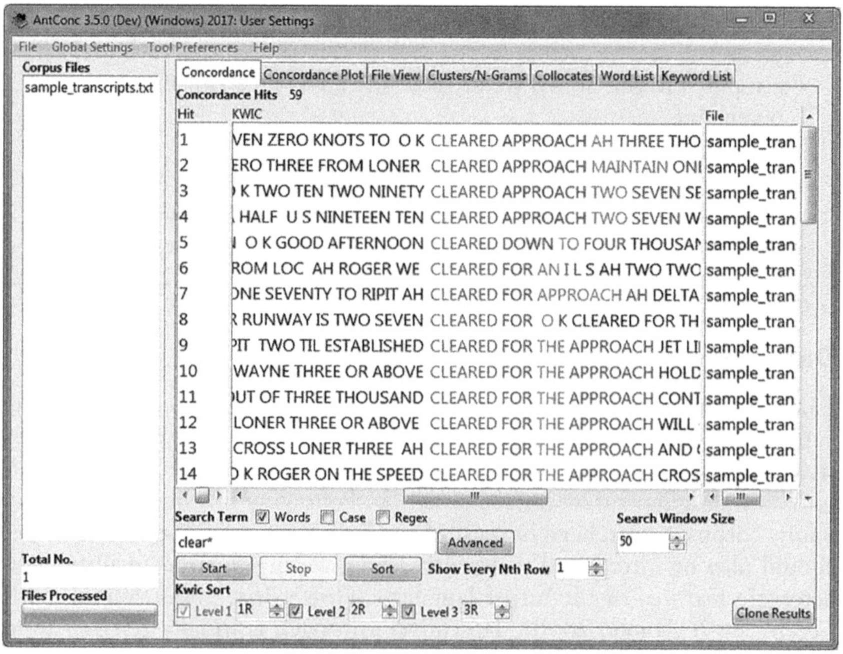

Figure 6.1 *AntConc* Key-Word-In-Context (KWIC) display showing phrases including the word "cleared" in the *Air Traffic Control Complete Sample Corpus.*

Air Traffic Control Complete Sample Corpus (Godfrey, 1994). The display immediately reveals to learners that *clear* can be used in the phrase 'cleared approach' or 'cleared for the approach', the difference in meaning of which can be rather subtle (U.S. Department of Transportation, 2011).

TASK 6.5 Experiencing Data-Driven Learning (DDL)

Download *AntConc* (Anthony, 2017a) and use the file menu options to load in a sample of your own writing (e.g. emails, essays, reports) saved in a plain text (.txt) format. Using the Concordancer tool of *AntConc*, search for common verbs or adjectives and try to identify common patterns of usage. Are the results what you would expect?

Next, load into *AntConc* a set of language samples produced in a language setting that you are not very familiar with (e.g. science lab reports, academic research articles, business executive reports, transcripts of service encounters). Again, search for common verbs or adjectives and try to identify frequent patterns. Are any of the patterns surprising to you?

Do you think learners could use this software to analyze language samples in their own fields? What could you do as an instructor to facilitate this type of learning?

Contentious issues in ESP: authenticity

The topic of 'authenticity' appears frequently in discussions on ESP materials and methods design. Strictly speaking, authentic materials refer to language samples that are created by members of a discourse community for use by other members of that community in order to achieve a recognizable communicative purpose. Many ESP administrators and instructors see authentic materials as an essential component of their courses and go to great lengths to identify and include language samples from the target language setting through research, field-work, and collaborations with specialist informants. Others, however, see authentic materials as just one option among many. Depending on the learning objectives of the course, they may also use completely artificial language samples or pseudo-authentic samples that are created artificially but are designed to reflect features in authentic texts. They may also use semi-authentic samples that are derived directly from authentic texts, but are simplified or adjusted in some way.

In reality, no target language sample can be truly 'authentic' if it is taken out of the context of the discourse community and used in a language learning classroom. It is perhaps useful, then, to consider different gradations or degrees of authenticity, as suggested by Jordan (1997). Some combinations of factors that will affect the degree of authenticity of materials are shown

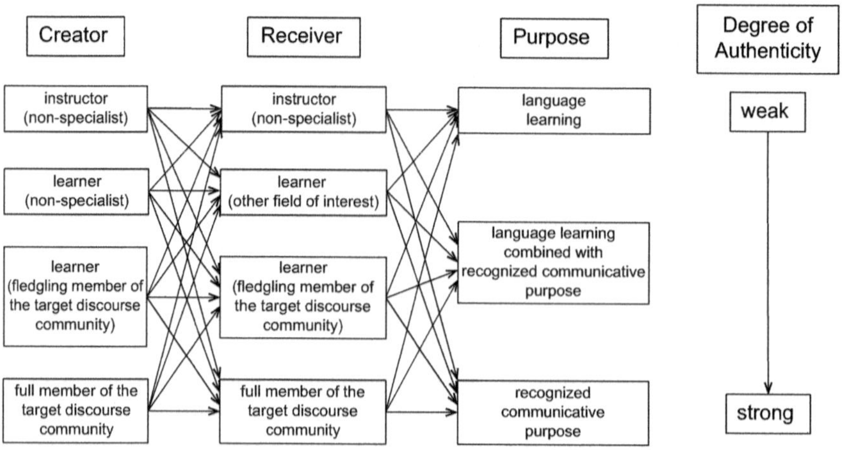

Figure 6.2 Factors affecting the degree of authenticity of materials.

in Figure 6.2. In the figure, you will see that materials created by a non-specialist ESP instructor will necessarily have a weak degree of authenticity. But, this can be strengthened if those materials are aimed at learners hoping to enter the target discourse community and used to develop the language skills needed to achieve a particular communicative purpose in the field. An even stronger degree of authenticity can be gained if those materials are created not by the instructor but by full members of the target discourse community.

There are many sound arguments for using materials with a high degree of authenticity in an ESP classroom. First, they are more likely to reflect the linguistic, pragmatic, and discoursal features that characterize the target language setting (Charles & Pecorari, 2016). Artificially created materials, on the other hand, might over- and under-represent features, misguiding both the instructor and learners. Second, the materials used in an ESP course might be the only sources of input that learners receive before they enter the target discourse community. If they don't get access to materials that closely match what they will encounter in a target language setting, they are likely to not succeed when it really matters. The same can be said for ESP instructors, whose exposure to the target language setting may derive solely from the materials available to them in the course. Without access to highly authentic materials, they are less likely to be able to help learners target their specific needs. Third, highly authentic materials can often be motivating to learners. They see not only how actual members of the discourse communities they hope to join communicate with each other, but also what they communicate about, and sometimes the impacts of those communications.

On the other hand, authentic materials can sometimes cause problems. One of the greatest challenges with using highly authentic materials is that they are often too difficult for learners at the level of language and concepts. To address this problem, you might choose to gradually introduce learners to such materials using artificial or simplified materials as a scaffold. Another problem with highly authentic materials is that they can sometimes be quite dry and boring. Rather than motivate learners, they can lead to learner apathy. A related issue is the fact that authentic materials may be taken from the target language context that is quite removed the context of the learners. If the learners were fully fledged members of the target discourse community, they might understand the importance and relevance of the materials. Without this contextual knowledge, the materials may simply baffle or confuse the learners unless the instructor works hard to provide the necessary background information. One further serious concern with using highly authentic materials is that by definition they are not created for the purpose of language learning. Although you may find ways to adapt and simplify these materials for use in the classroom, there will always be cases when materials designed specifically for the purpose of language learning will be more effective. The skill of an ESP instructor is to know when to use artificial materials and when to use materials at different degrees of authenticity.

Research ideas

Here are some possible ideas for small-scale or large-scale research projects that stem from the topics discussed in this chapter.

What do instructors do in the classroom?

If you are learning about ESP, analyze the materials and methods used by one of your instructors. Does the instructor adopt or adapt published materials, or do they use custom materials? What theories of language learning does the instructor incorporate in their classes? How do they integrate the materials into classroom activities? What degree of authenticity is reflected in the materials used in the class?

If you already teach an ESP course, reflect on your own choices of materials and methods using the questions above as a guide.

Which textbook should ESP instructors use (if any)?

In this chapter, it was mentioned that many researchers have proposed lists of criteria to evaluate published textbooks. Review the different models proposed in the literature, identify their strengths and weaknesses, and create a novel evaluation model that ESP instructors can use. If possible, test your model in a real learning context and report your findings.

How authentic are inauthentic materials?

Many English language textbooks contain samples of language that have a very low degree of authenticity in the sense that they have been written by instructors for use by learners in order to learn language. Collect samples of inauthentic language supposedly representing the language used in a particular target setting. Then, try to find authentic language samples from the same setting. Compare the two in terms of their grammar, vocabulary, and discourse features, perhaps using one or more of the corpus tools mentioned in the chapter. Investigate how authentic the inauthentic language is, and what the author might do to more closely represent the language features you discover in the authentic texts.

Closing reflection

Now that you have come to the end of the chapter, you should be confident in choosing effective materials and methods for use in an ESP classroom. You should also know the steps to take when creating custom materials in contexts where you have plenty of time to plan and others where the class might be starting in the next day. In addition, you should now understand how corpus tools and other technologies can assist you in preparing materials and helping learners achieve their learning objectives. Finally, you should be able to present a case for using materials at varying degrees of authenticity.

Here are a few more questions to consider:

1. Which of the points covered in the chapter were new to you? Did you find them interesting and relevant in terms of your own learning goals? Were there any points that you found confusing or that you disagreed with?
2. What points from the chapter do you think you can immediately put to use in your own learning or teaching context?
3. In view of all the arguments for and against adopting, adapting, and creating materials, which approach do you see yourself using most often? Why?
4. If you were required to use a Data-Driven Learning (DDL) approach as an ESP instructor, what would be your greatest worry? What could you do to address this?
5. What other arguments can you think of for using or not using authentic materials in the classroom?

Further resources

Research articles

Bremner, S. (2010). Collaborative writing: Bridging the gap between the textbook and the workplace. *English for Specific Purposes*, *29*(2), 121–132.
Candlin, C. N., Bhatia, V. K., & Jensen, C. H. (2002). Developing legal writing materials for English second language learners: Problems and perspectives. *English for Specific Purposes*, *21*(4), 299–320.
Chan, C. S. (2009). Forging a link between research and pedagogy: A holistic framework for evaluating business English materials. *English for Specific Purposes*, *28*(2), 125–136.
Chang, C. F., & Kuo, C. H. (2011). A corpus-based approach to online materials development for writing research articles. *English for Specific Purposes*, *30*(3), 222–234.
Jones, G. M. (1990). ESP textbooks: Do they really exist? *English for Specific Purposes*, *9*(1), 89–93.
Kuo, C. H. (1993). Problematic issues in EST materials development. *English for Specific Purposes*, *12*(2), 171–181.
Love, A. (1993). Lexico-grammatical features of geology textbooks: Process and product revisited. *English for Specific Purposes*, *12*(3), 197–218.
Stevens, V. (1991). Classroom concordancing: Vocabulary materials derived from relevant, authentic text. *English for Specific Purposes*, *10*(1), 35–46.
Swales, J. M. (1995). The role of the textbook in EAP writing research. *English for Specific Purposes*, *14*(1), 3–18.

Chapter 7

Evaluating learners, instructors, courses, and programs in ESP

This chapter looks at the fourth 'pillar' of ESP, which is evaluation. Although I present evaluation here as the final component of a successful ESP course or program, in reality, it is often the first and most important concern for many stakeholders. Learners in an EAP context might be taking an ESP course for an elective or required credit that allows them to proceed to the next stage of their studies, and ultimately graduation. Learners in an EOP context might need to successfully complete an ESP course in order to get a job, get an increase in salary, or get a promotion. Clearly, the results of the evaluation can have an immediate and real impact on learners' lives. The same is true for EAP and EOP instructors. Evaluation of their instruction can not only serve as a useful exercise in professional development, but it can often determine if their contract will be renewed. Administrators of ESP courses and programs are also concerned with evaluation because it allows them to determine if the learners are making progress and if the instructors are facilitating or hindering that progress. In the end, this evaluation might determine if an ESP course or program should be reduced or expanded in size, kept the same, or terminated altogether.

In the chapter, I'll first explain the close connection between evaluation and the related concepts of assessment and testing. Next, I'll describe four characteristic features of an effective evaluation measure and discuss how you can ensure that they are included in your own procedures. Then, I'll explain how you can apply these ideas in the evaluation of learners, instructors, courses, and programs, and discuss some of the challenges that are often faced when doing an evaluation. Finally, I'll discuss the problem of deception in evaluation, and how transparency, honesty, and trust between learners, instructors, and administrators can minimize its effects.

By the end of the chapter, you should understand the meaning, importance, and impact of evaluation at the learner, instructor, course, and program level. You should also be able to design effective evaluation procedures for different purposes and adopt useful strategies to address issues of cheating, plagiarism, and other forms of deception. Most importantly, by the end of the chapter you should know how to evaluate if your teaching is effective and if your learners are making progress toward their target learning goals.

Opening reflection

It is common for learners in both EAP and EOP settings to take some kind of formalized test at the end of the course. From a learner's perspective, what do you think is the primary aim of such a test? If you are a student, do you like such tests? Why or why not? From an instructor's perspective, what do you think is the primary aim of an end-of-course test? If you have experience teaching, do you like conducting these tests? Again, why or why not?

Based on your answers, how might the design of a test impact positively and/or negatively on the learners, instructors, and course as a whole?

Commentary

It is generally accepted that most learners don't like end-of-course tests. They often see these tests as a final, important, stressful obstacle that must be overcome before they can receive the awards of completing the course (e.g. a credit toward graduation, a certificate showing competence in an area, a license to carry out work) and move on to the next stage in their learning or career. The test is there to judge them. As a result, they often worry about the obstacle they face in terms of its nature, scope, and difficulty. They will also worry if they can perform at a level necessary to overcome the obstacle. They might also worry about if their performance will be evaluated accurately and fairly.

Most instructors don't like end-of-course tests, either. However, the reasons are quite different. Instructors are usually interested in knowing what aspects of their course help learners master the target learning objectives and what aspects of the course might hinder process. They are usually less interested in judging learners and assigning them pass or fail grades. Unfortunately, end-of-term tests provide instructors with little information about what works or doesn't work in class. They are more of an institutional burden to the instructor. Tests are often time-consuming to create, time-consuming to grade, and stressful to manage, especially if the results can have a dramatic impact on the learners' lives. Of course, it is nice to find that a learner has been able to pass a course. But, there is nothing worse than having to explain to a learner why they have failed to graduate, for example, due to a poor score on the final test of a one-credit course. So, testing can present instructors with a conflict of interest. On the one hand, they prefer tests that are quick and easy to create and grade. On the other hand, they need tests that accurately measure the performance of the learners.

In view of these different perspectives, you can probably see that end-of-course tests can have a huge impact on the way a course proceeds. They can affect what material is covered and how it is taught and learned in the course. Tests also affect the motivation and intensity that learners and instructors will devote to that material. Finally, the degree to which the tests are aligned with the needs, learning objectives, and course materials and methods will have a dramatic impact on the success of the learners, instructor, and the course as whole.

Understanding evaluation in ESP

Defining the terms test, assessment, *and* evaluation

In the literature on ESP and second language learning in general, you will often run into the terms *test*, *assessment*, and *evaluation*. In the context of language learning, a *test* can be defined simply as a performance measure. So, we can have a multiple-choice test to measure listening comprehension, a picture description test to measure speaking fluency, a timed reading test to measure reading speed, or an essay test to measure writing accuracy.

Assessment, on the other hand, is a more general term referring to the process of collecting, analyzing, and using data to gain an understanding of current performance for various purposes. Clearly, testing is one form of assessment, but there are others. For example, we might simply observe learners in the classroom and note down what they say and how they interact. We might also ask them to complete a survey or questionnaire.

Many test-based assessments are *objective* in that the results are not influenced by the feelings or opinions of the assessment grader. These include matching tests, true/false tests, correct/incorrect tests, multiple-choice tests, and completion tests. Most other tests and methods of assessment, however, are *subjective* in that the results depend on the feelings or opinions of the assessment grader. Subjective assessments include short and long answer comprehension tests, graded essay tests, interviews, questionnaires, surveys, reports, project portfolios, and classroom observations (Douglas, 2000).

Regardless of the type of assessment we use, the main purposes of assessment are:

- diagnostic: used to identify strengths, weaknesses, and gaps in the target area
- formative: used to measure the degree of progress and identify changes and/or improvements that can facilitate progress
- summative: used to judge the quality and/or adequacy of progress in the target area

Diagnostic assessment of learners is often used at the beginning of a course to determine learning objectives and assign learners to appropriate ability groups. It might involve learners taking a general English proficiency test, or having them complete a simple questionnaire asking about their experiences using English in the target language discipline. Formative assessment of learners is carried out throughout a course, perhaps using short in-class quizzes, homework reports, and other testing methods. It also involves instructors observing learners in class, seeing how they participate with others, and asking them informal questions about the course material and activities. Summative assessment, on the other hand, will often take the form of mid-term and end-of-course tests and/or the assessment of a project or portfolio of work. The results of this assessment usually determine if a learner passes or fails a course, and the grade they will receive.

Importantly, the term assessment is almost always applied *only* to learners. This is perhaps due to its strong association with the concept of testing. As a result, you will rarely see the term applied to instructors, administrators, course, and/or programs.

Evaluation is a synonym for *assessment* which can apply to learners but is also used more broadly, even in contexts where tests are not utilized. So, you will find some authors writing about summative and formative assessment of learners and others writing about summative and formative evaluation of learners. On the other hand, when it comes to instructors, administrators, courses, and/or programs, the usual practice is to talk about instructor/administrator and course/program evaluation. In the following sections, I will avoid confusion by using *evaluation* as an umbrella term that covers all forms of assessment of all target groups. So, we can evaluate learners with a formative assessment using a multiple-choice test, and also evaluate an ESP program with a summative assessment based on a survey. The relationships between the different terms is shown in Figure 7.1.

Interpreting results from evaluations

In both objective and subjective evaluations, one way to interpret the results of individuals is by comparing them against those of others in the group or those of some external normative group. This is usually done for the purpose of categorizing the individuals into levels or grade categories. This type of evaluation is called *norm-referenced* evaluation. As mentioned previously, you will often see *norm-referenced* evaluation used in ESP settings as a diagnostic tool in order to group learners into different course levels. Another way to interpret the results of individuals is by comparing them against criterion standards and determining the degree to which the results have reached those standards. This type of evaluation is called *criterion-referenced* evaluation (see Brown and Hudson (2002) for a detailed discussion on the topic). Again, you might use criterion-referenced evaluation in ESP settings as a diagnostic tool in order to group learners. However, as previously mentioned, you will also see it commonly used as a summative tool to determine the pass/fail grade of a learner. It is also used in many formal English proficiency examinations, such as the Test of English as a

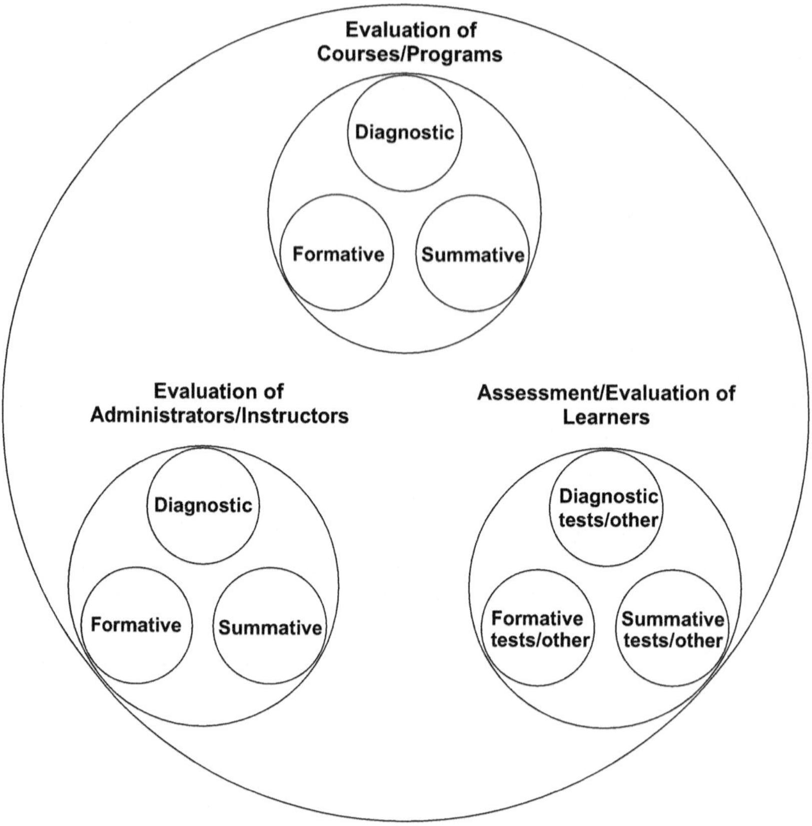

Figure 7.1 Relationships between *test, assessment,* and *evaluation.*

Foreign Language (TOEFL), the International English Language Testing System (IELTS), and the Pearson Test of English (PTS). Note, however, that a very popular English proficiency test used in the business world, the Test of English for International Communication (TOEIC), is a norm-referenced test (Wilson, 1989).

Understanding the three characteristics of effective evaluation

For an evaluation procedure to be successful, it should exhibit the same three characteristics that define a good needs analysis: *reliability*, *validity*, and *practicality* (Brown, 1989).

Reliability

As discussed in Chapter 4, an evaluation is reliable if it produces similar results when repeated (taking account of the effect of practice and change over time). There are many ways to increase the reliability of an evaluation, including the following:

- conduct equivalent evaluations under the same conditions (e.g. test duration, and the room environment)
- use a clear and unambiguous assessment format and layout
- give clear and explicit instructions
- identify assessment takers by number instead of name to avoid familiarity, gender, age, nationality, race, and other biases
- provide a clear and comprehensive grading rubric
- ensure that assessment takers are familiar with the assessment format, the types of questions and responses, and the grading rubric
- include multiple items that independently measure different aspects of the target area
- limit the freedom of assessment takers to interpret and respond to assessment items
- ensure that assessment takers understand the importance and value of the assessment and complete it in a serious manner
- process (mark, grade, evaluate) responses in a consistent way

As an example in an EAP setting, if you were evaluating the essay writing ability of learners in different sections of a course using a graded essay test, you would want to make sure that the test took place at the same point in the course. You would also want to make sure learners were given the same amount of time to complete the test, and the instructions were equivalent. You may not be able to use the same essay prompt in each class, but you would want to use prompts that produced writing of a similar level of complexity and depth. You would also need to make sure that the learners were familiar with the format, the types of questions asked, and the grading rubric, perhaps by showing the learners previous examples of graded learner essays at the different grade boundaries. In essence, you would want to make sure that the learners were not *surprised* by the evaluation and could perform to the best of their ability. After the test was run, ideally, the grading of each essay would be carried out by multiple graders using a double marking system. You would want to allow enough time so that the graders did not feel pressure to rapidly grade the essays in large blocks that could give rise to grading 'drift' (Leckie & Baird, 2011).

It is often much easier to achieve a high reliability in an EAP setting than it is in an EOP setting. EAP courses are usually repeated year after year with similar numbers of learners in similar or identical classrooms within a fixed curriculum and with the same instructors. Banks of previous tests grow over time and learners can easily check these and be prepared, especially as grading rubrics may remain identical from year to year. In an EOP setting, on the other hand, almost every aspect of the learning environment can change dramatically from one iteration of the course to the next. Changes might include the number, general proficiency, and needs of learners, the classroom environment, the time available for evaluation, and even the manner in which the evaluation can be conducted. Previous evaluation examples might also be unavailable due to privacy issues, non-disclosure agreements, or the simple fact that the evaluations were not test-based. For example, in a business training seminar on negotiation, the performance of a learner might be evaluated through observations of their interactions during a role-play. Unless this was video recorded, it would be impossible to use the evaluation as a model for later training sessions. In other settings, company requirements might result in the evaluation being comprised only of a participant survey asking them about their thoughts about the course.

Although it is not easy to maintain reliability in EOP environments, one thing you can do is work with the administration team to know ahead of time what variations might be encountered and prepare accordingly. You can also provide learners with as much information as possible about the ways in which they will be evaluated so they can prepare. Unfortunately, however well you and the learners prepare, wide variations in learner progress and evaluation performance are usually unavoidable. As a result, it is also important that you try to manage the expectations of the course administrators in terms of the overall effects of the course and the performance gains of learners.

Validity

An effective evaluation procedure must also be valid. This means the evaluation accurately measures what it is designed to measure. In the testing literature, this is often termed as *construct validity* (see, for example, Hughes, 2007), and it can be measured using a wide range of evidence.

One type of evidence for the validity of an evaluation is a measure of the extent to which the content of the evaluation sufficiently represents the components of the target of investigation. So, if you were designing a reading test, it would be more valid if the test included all the components of reading, such as skimming, scanning, close reading, and so on. You can also collect evidence of the degree to which the evaluation agrees with other evaluation conducted around the same time, and the degree to which it can predict future outcomes. So, in our reading test example, you might question the validity of the test if the results differed widely from those of a vocabulary test carried out at the same time, as reading ability and vocabulary knowledge are known to have a positive correlation (Ibrahim, Sarudin, & Muhamad, 2016). On the other hand, you could judge the test to have a stronger validity if previous iterations of the test were used to assign learners to different reading levels which then proved to be appropriate. Another type of evidence relates to the surface appearance of the evaluation. In essence, the evaluation should look like it will measure what it is designed for (especially from the perspective of those taking the evaluation). So, in the reading test example, learners will expect that they need to do some reading. You should note that in the testing literature, these different categories of validity evidence are sometimes discussed, respectively, using the terms *content*, *concurrent*, *predictive*, and *face* validity.

As we found in the discussion of reliability, it is often easier to design evaluations with a strong validity in an EAP setting than it is in an EOP setting. EAP knowledge and skills have been the focus of ESP research for decades. The components of academic reading, writing, lecture comprehension, presentation, and other academic skills are well understood. Also, identical courses and sections are often run in parallel and repeated yearly, which allows different assessment measures to be compared concurrently and reviewed in terms of their predictive power. What's more, it is relatively easy to design EAP evaluations that look like true EAP tasks. This is because they are conducted in the same institutional environment, and created and conducted by instructors who are academics in their own right.

The same is not true in many EOP settings. First, there is a relative lack of research on the needs of learners in many – if not most – EOP contexts. As a result, even the initial design of an evaluation procedure becomes problematic. Second, many EOP courses are run in isolation and each iteration of the course can be quite different. This makes it difficult to acquire evidence of how well the evaluation agrees with other evaluations. Also, there might be few opportunities to meet the participants after the course has finished, limiting the ability to gather evidence of the predictive power of the evaluation. But, perhaps the greatest challenge is creating an evaluation that looks valid. For example, if you are training pilots to communicate clearly and effectively with flight controllers, how do you create an environment for the evaluation that evenly closely matches the real experience the pilots will face? Again, there are no simple answers to this question. But, it is clearly important for non-specialist ESP instructors to work closely with course administrators in the design and running of evaluations. They also need to be constantly aware that learners might silently or openly question the validity of the evaluations, and so they should make efforts to explain the rationale, design, and limitations of the evaluations they use. We will return to the topic of 'authentic' evaluation in Chapter 8.

Practicality

The final characteristic of a successful evaluation procedure is its practicality. All evaluations need to be practical in terms of the space and financial costs involved, the human resources needed, the time required to conduct, analyze, and score the evaluation, and the training involved. This means that automated administration and scoring of evaluations are preferable to manual approaches. It also means that shorter, simpler evaluations are preferable to longer, more complex ones.

Of course, it is important to balance design decisions made for practical reasons against the impact they will have on the evaluation reliability and validity. For example, short tests tend to be less reliable than longer ones, and automatically graded tests are often less valid than tests that are subjectively graded by humans. However, it is also important to note that when the practical constraints of an ESP setting are ignored, what often happens is that shortcuts are taken that also affect the reliability and validity of the evaluation. For example, in an EAP setting, a course may be taken by 50–100 learners, making it impossible for instructors to follow a valid but highly elaborate evaluation method. In this case, the instructors might simply ignore the defined evaluation procedures and instead carry out their own intuitive evaluation, which lacks both validity and reliability. Similarly, in an EOP setting, learners may be too busy with their daily work to complete end-of-course evaluation surveys in a careful and thoughtful manner. Again, this would mean that the evaluation procedure had little reliability or validity, and perhaps should not be conducted at all.

TASK 7.1 Improving the reliability, validity, and practicality of test items

The questions below appear as a part of a tertiary-level EAP test of presentation English vocabulary. Read the instructions and attempt to answer the three questions. If this were the complete test, how could you redesign it in order to increase its reliability, validity, and practicality?

Instructions: circle the best options that fit in the blanks in the following sentences

1 Today, I'd like to ________ my research on the use of robots in the health care industry.

a explain you
b tell you
c discuss about
d talk about

2 In the slide here, the table ________ the conditions that we used.

a lists
b writes
c demonstrates
d prepares

3 The results here ________ that our theory was correct.

a may present
b might find
c describe
d suggest

Evaluating learners in ESP

To ensure that an ESP course or program is successful, learners need to be evaluated at various stages of their learning experience. By considering what information needs to be collected at each stage, we see that five different types of evaluation tools are needed:

- proficiency assessment
- placement assessment
- diagnostic assessment
- progress assessment
- achievement assessment

Let's look briefly at each of these in turn.

Proficiency assessment

Scores on general English proficiency assessments, such as the TOEFL, TOEIC, IELTS, and PVT tests mentioned earlier, are often used as an entry requirement to a language course or program, or used to determine if a learner can be exempted from a course. They are also used within a program to assign learners to suitable courses or group learners according to their ability levels. At the level of the institution, averaged proficiency scores of learners are sometimes used to determine the overall ability of the learner body when they enter and leave a course or program. These results then serve as a measure of program success. Institutions might also use averaged proficiency scores to compare their learner body with that of other institutions, providing them with data to support new educational initiatives.

Proficiency assessments are often high-stakes tests. In EAP settings, for example, the score on a general proficiency assessment may determine if somebody may enter the university of their choice. In EOP settings, the score might be a deciding factor in somebody getting an interview, getting a job, or getting a promotion. As a result, these assessments can exert a strong 'washback' effect on the motivations, efforts, and actions of different stakeholders in the learning process.

For example, if learners know that they have already reached the proficiency level to enter a course or program, they may lose motivation and make little effort to improve their ability any further. On the other hand, if they have not reached the required level, they may become strongly motivated and make every effort to succeed. Then again, this effort may manifest itself in the learner attempting to artificially raise their score through the study of test taking strategies to the detriment of other types of learning. Similarly, within a course, learners may feel strongly motivated if the instructors directly address issues on a high-stakes test that they must take later. However, if instructors know that they will be judged by both learners and the institution on their ability to raise the learners' scores on external proficiency tests, they are much more likely to teach to the test at the expense of addressing other learning objectives in the course.

Placement assessment

Many institutions run courses comprised of a heterogeneous group of learners of different ability levels and interests. For some, this is a design choice based on the belief that it will provide an exciting and beneficial environment for learners. For others, it is a design necessity resulting from a limited number of classrooms, experienced instructors, or a balanced number of learners. The alternative is for an institution to attempt to assign learners to similar groups and levels based on the results of a placement assessment.

From an institutional perspective, placement assessments are relatively low-stakes endeavors. This is especially true if learners have an option to move up or down or change their level based on their instructor's recommendation. However, placement assessments must be carried out before or at the very start of courses. This leads to the type of assessment, the duration of the assessment, and the time required to grade and analyze the results becoming critical factors.

One option that is common in EAP settings is to place learners based on their results on one or more previous assessments. These might comprise a profile of previously taken general proficiency tests, or the results from previously taken courses. Alternatively, an institution may run a custom-designed placement test that the learners take as an online test or a traditional paper-based test during an orientation session. Another option is to provide learners with a detailed description of the course levels and options and allow them to self-select the group or level they want to join. This is surprisingly common in EOP contexts, where various offline and online training programs and materials at different levels are offered to learners, who are expected to formulate their own learning program. In these cases, the institution may only be interested in the training time and the measurable outcomes of the training in terms of general proficiency score increases and improvements in work performance.

Diagnostic assessment

Diagnostic assessment is used to identify learners' strengths and weaknesses and serves as an important component of needs analysis. The results from a diagnostic assessment lead directly to the formulation of learning objectives for a course or program.

The results from general proficiency assessments and placement assessments are often used for diagnostic purposes, especially in EAP settings. The instructor may also ask learners to complete a short introductory task in the first lesson to assess their knowledge and skills in the target area. However, in an EOP context, useful information can also be gained through the design of a narrowly scoped assessment that reveals insights about the learners' language background, work context, and future aims. As an example, Figure 7.2 shows part of a diagnostic survey given to workers at a multinational company who are about to take a course on research writing and presentation skills. By conducting this assessment prior to the start of the course, the instructor can quickly establish the degree to which the learners prioritize this learning goal and their general experience and ability in the target areas.

1. **Over the past week, what percentage of your work was in the following areas?**

   Product Manufacturing: ___%   Research: ___%
   Administration: ___%   Other: ___%

2. **Estimate your research outputs over the past three years.**

   Number of research papers   1st language: ___ English: ___
   Number of research presentations   1st language: ___ English: ___

3. **Do you feel that you have enough time to conduct research? Circle your answer.**

   Strongly Agree   Agree   Neutral   Disagree   Strongly Disagree

Figure 7.2 Diagnostic survey given to learners at a multinational corporation.

Progress assessment

Progress assessments aim to establish if learners are understanding the course materials and methods and are making progress toward the learning objectives of the course. They can also be used to identify areas for change and improvement in the way the course is conducted.

Clearly, progress assessments are largely formative in nature, especially from the perspective of the instructor. However, the results of these assessments are often used also as part of a summative evaluation of the learners' overall performance in a course. They can also serve as a source of extrinsic motivation for the learners and provide them with useful feedback on their own learning progress.

Progress assessments may take the form of weekly in-class quizzes, homework assignments and mid-term tests. They can also be based on instructor observations of the learners' work, their interactions with others in the class, and their responses to instructor questions and comments. Another useful, albeit subjective, indication of learner progress and potential problems in class can be gained from an instructor's informal interactions with the learners before, during, and after lessons.

Regardless of which type of progress assessment is used, it is important that the assessment establishes the following points:

- Do the learners show an understanding of the learning objectives targeted by the particular materials and methods?
- Is there evidence that aspects of the materials and methods are redundant or confusing to learners?
- Does the performance of learners show evidence that the learning objectives are being met?
- Is there evidence that the learning objectives are too easy or too difficult to reach?
- Does the learning environment appear to promote learning?
- Is there evidence that the learning environment restricts, hinders, or prevents learning?

Achievement assessment

From an instructor's perspective, achievement assessment is often an extension of progress assessment in that it provides them with useful information about how well learners have made progress toward the learning objectives of the course. Achievement assessments can also provide instructors (and course administrators) with useful information about how well a course addresses the needs of learners and where adjustments and improvements can be made. Similarly, learners are likely to see achievement assessments as an extensive of progress assessments, except with a greater importance.

For them, the results of achievement assessment are summative in nature as they will determine how well the learners are judged to have successfully completed the course.

In most EAP settings, achievement assessments usually take the form of mid-term tests, end-of-term tests, reports, and project portfolios. These might comprise listening comprehension tests, response papers to reading assignments, argumentative essays, research report writing, spoken presentations, debates, and a host of other assessment types. It is also common to use learner surveys as part of achievement assessments in order to gain information about the effectiveness of the learning environment (classroom setting, resources, materials), the ability of the instructor (energy, enthusiasm, professionalism, organization skills, communication skills), and the value and interest of the course content (level, novelty, usefulness, timeliness).

In EOP settings, we also find these same forms of assessment being used. However, because the learners' target needs are usually more directly related to the learning objectives of the course, it is also common to use direct measures of how well the target need has been reached. As an example, the target need of a call-center operator might be to respond to a caller complaint in a quick, polite, and effective manner. To meet this need, they will require effective language skills. However, rather than assessing them using a fluency test and a test of politeness vocabulary, administrators might simply assess them in terms of how much more quickly on average they respond to learners and how many fewer complaints they receive after completing the course. Similarly, a working engineer who has taken an intensive course on report writing might be assessed simply by how many more articles they get accepted for publication.

TASK 7.2 Assessing learners in an English for business purposes setting

Imagine that you are assigned to teach a section of a course in English for business purposes that targets the language and skills of company internal project meetings. The course comprises three sections in total and 30 learners with non-English language backgrounds have enrolled. Even if you have no knowledge of business English, try to answer the following questions.

1 Would it be useful to know the general proficiency English scores of the learners? Why or why not?
2 What are the advantages of dividing the learners into three ability levels (based on a placement test) and assigning them to different sections? What would be the disadvantages of placing learners in different ability groups?

3 How could you quickly establish a set of learning objectives for your section of the course after meeting the learners for the first time?
4 What assessment measures could you use to track the progress of the learners?
5 What direct needs-related assessment measures could the administrators of the course use to evaluate individual learner progress?

Evaluating instructors in ESP

To ensure that an ESP course or program is successful, ESP administrators have as important a role in evaluating instructors as instructors do evaluating learners. However, the nature of the relationship between administrators and instructors necessitates a very different approach to that which occurs in the classroom, even though the components are essentially the same.

Before instructors are hired, ESP administrators are almost always going to review their resumes, interview them, and perhaps even review examples of their teaching materials and teaching methods. By following these procedures, the administrators can learn about their background experiences, assess their ability in English, and find out if they have any knowledge or an interest in a specialist discipline. In effect, they are conducting a proficiency assessment of the potential instructor. Also, if it is decided that the instructor will be hired, the administrators have valuable information that will help with placement of the instructor in the program as a whole.

Once an instructor becomes a part of a program, the administrators can work with them more closely to determine their strengths and weaknesses, and perhaps advise them on what they need to do to prepare for a target course. In effect, this serves as a diagnostic assessment of the instructor. Then, once the course is in operation, the administrators may arrange to do class observations or organize an informal meeting with the instructor to discuss how the course is progressing and what they might do to improve it. Again, this maps closely to the progress assessment that instructors normally carry out with learners.

Finally, at the end of the course, the ESP administrators are likely to review the results of learner achievement assessments and their responses on course surveys. If the results are surprisingly good and the survey responses overwhelmingly positive, the information may lead to the instructors being recommended for teaching awards and certainly a continuation of their contracts. On the other hand, if the results are poor or the survey responses are unusually negative, most administrators will feel the need to find out from the instructor what the causes were and what they might do to address the problems. You can see that these procedures are essentially an achievement assessment directed at the instructor.

TASK 7.3 Evaluating the suitability of instructors in an ESP program

Imagine that you have applied for a position in an ESP program that focuses mainly in the area of English for business purposes. What aspects of your resume would support your application in the eyes of the program administrators? What weaknesses might your resume reveal? How would you present your case if asked to come for an interview?

If you have experience teaching in an ESP program, in what ways (if any) did the administrators assess your proficiency to handle the course before you were hired? Do you believe that they made efforts to assign you to a suitable course? In what ways (if any) did they support your preparation and guide you as you taught the course for the first time? Did you receive any feedback from administrators on how well you addressed the learning objectives of the course?

Evaluating courses and programs in ESP

In order to conduct a successful course or program evaluation, it is essential that all stakeholders in the evaluation process have answers to the following two questions:

- Who is the evaluation for?
- Why is the evaluation being carried out?

Course evaluations may be carried out for use by individual instructors in order to improve their teaching materials and methods in a formative way. Or, they may be carried out for use by course administrators in a summative way to determine which instructors should be assigned to different levels and who should have their contracts renewed. Similarly, at the program level, evaluations might be carried out for use by senior management in a summative way to determine which courses should receive additional funding and resources, which courses should be expanded or reduced in size, and where, when, and how changes should be introduced.

Clearly, the implications of a formative evaluation are very different from those of a summative evaluation. So, a course or program-wide evaluation will only have value if it is designed for people who are in a position to take meaningful actions based on its results. However, the purpose of the evaluation will also have an important impact on the degree to which the people within the program support and contribute to the evaluation. Clearly, evaluation creates a power difference that you need to be aware of, whichever side of the evaluation you are on.

Once the answers to the prior two questions are determined, it is then necessary to consider the following three questions:

- Which stakeholders should be involved in the evaluation?
- What information needs to be collected?
- What resources (e.g. time, human resources, funding, technical support) are available?

Many simple course evaluations are designed by individual instructors to help them improve their own teaching materials and methods. In this case, the target learners might report on their views on the class through instructor-administered class surveys. The surveys might ask about them how well the instructor followed the syllabus, how well they explained the course material, and what noticeable learning gains (if any) they made during the course. These evaluations can be carried out very quickly at the end of the course, and require few resources or technical support. But, they might be unreliable, invalid, and prone to teacher and learner bias unless they are formalized as part of an institution's evaluation system. When they are, the design of the surveys can be carefully checked and the information collected anonymously through an Internet-based submission form or the use of automatically graded assessment cards. Then, the results can be relayed back to instructors through the institution's content management system (CMS). Clearly, this system requires more time and technical resources, but in theory would produce a more reliable and valid assessment (assuming the response rate was high). An example of an institutionally-administered learner survey is shown in Figure 7.3.

When it comes to evaluating the overall success of a course involving multiple instructors or the success of an entire ESP program, it is important to consider the needs of all the different stakeholders and determine how well they are addressed. A reliable, valid, and practical evaluation therefore requires input from not only from the target learners, but also instructors, administrators, institutional representatives, and perhaps even external stakeholders, such as potential future thesis supervisors and future employees in an EAP context, or clients and customers in an EOP context. It also follows that a triangulation of data collection methods should be employed to gain both objective and subjective measures of success. These can include the following:

- scores on general proficiency tests
- course grades
- learner-focused course evaluations
- data from interviews with learners
- data from interviews with instructors
- anonymous feedback reports from instructors

- observations of in-class learner behavior
- observations of instructor class management and teaching methods
- financial reports and profit statements

Advanced Technical Writing

Item	Example response					What was the best thing about the course (if anything)?
	[1]	[2]	[3]	[■]	[5]	
Attendance record	4 x	3 x	2 x	1 x	0 x	
1. Number of absences from the course	[1]	[2]	[3]	[4]	[5]	
Course design and content	strongly disagree←			→strongly agree		
2. Did you take the course seriously?	[1]	[2]	[3]	[4]	[5]	
3. Was the syllabus clearly written?	[1]	[2]	[3]	[4]	[5]	
4. Did the instructor follow the syllabus?	[1]	[2]	[3]	[4]	[5]	
5. Was the course content well organized?	[1]	[2]	[3]	[4]	[5]	
6. Were the course materials used effectively?	[1]	[2]	[3]	[4]	[5]	
7. Was an appropriate amount of homework given?	[1]	[2]	[3]	[4]	[5]	
8. Were the classroom facilities in working order?	[1]	[2]	[3]	[4]	[5]	
9. Was the class size appropriate?	[1]	[2]	[3]	[4]	[5]	
Course instruction	strongly disagree←			→strongly agree		If you could change one thing about the course, what would it be (if anything)?
10. Was the instructor enthusiastic?	[1]	[2]	[3]	[4]	[5]	
11. Were the explanations easy to understand?	[1]	[2]	[3]	[4]	[5]	
12. Did the instructor respond appropriately to questions?	[1]	[2]	[3]	[4]	[5]	
13. Were there plenty of opportunities for class interaction?	[1]	[2]	[3]	[4]	[5]	
14. Did the instructor motivate the learners?	[1]	[2]	[3]	[4]	[5]	
Course effectiveness	strongly disagree←			→strongly agree		
15. Did you develop your research article writing skill?	[1]	[2]	[3]	[4]	[5]	
16. Did you improve your technical vocabulary?	[1]	[2]	[3]	[4]	[5]	
17. Did you improve your general reading skills?	[1]	[2]	[3]	[4]	[5]	
18. Did you improve your general writing skills?	[1]	[2]	[3]	[4]	[5]	
19. Did you improve your general listening skills?	[1]	[2]	[3]	[4]	[5]	
20. Did you improve your general speaking skills?	[1]	[2]	[3]	[4]	[5]	
21. Did you gain an understanding of culture and society?	[1]	[2]	[3]	[4]	[5]	
22. Was this an important class?	[1]	[2]	[3]	[4]	[5]	
Overall impression	strongly disagree←			→strongly agree		
23. Was this a useful class?	[1]	[2]	[3]	[4]	[5]	
Other comments						

Figure 7.3 Institutional learner-focused course survey for use in a technical writing course.

Much of the data from all the different stakeholders can be collected by people within the institution. However, it is also useful to invite external evaluators to collect some of the data. For example, in EAP settings, potential thesis supervisors and prospective company employers can be invited to review course materials, interview learners and instructors, and observe classes. They can then be asked to create a formal written report on their views of the course or program, which may then serve as a valuable aid when defending the course or program to the senior management of an institution. In EOP settings, it is usually difficult if not impossible to invite potential clients and customers to evaluate the success of a course or program *directly*. However, as mentioned earlier, their actions and opinions can provide useful *indirect* data on success. For example, clients may agree to new contracts and customers may purchase more products.

TASK 7.4 Taking steps to evaluate a language course

Nation and Macalister (2010, p. 123) list the following nine steps in an effective course evaluation:

1 Find who the evaluation is for and what kind of information they need.
2 Find what the results of the evaluation will be used for.
3 Decide if the evaluation is necessary or if the needed information is already available.
4 Find out how much time and money are available to do the evaluation.
5 Decide what kind of information will be gathered.
6 Try to gain the support of the people involved in the evaluation
7 Decide how to gather the information and who will be involved in the gathering of information.
8 Decide how to present the findings.
9 Decide if a follow-up evaluation is planned to check the implementation of the findings.

Imagine that you worked in an administrative team that was tasked with evaluating an EAP program to see where costs might be reduced. Imagine also that the program was taught mainly by contract and part-time instructors.

What information (if any) would you want to obtain from instructors in step 5?

How would you attempt to gain the support of the instructors in step 6?

How would you go about collecting the data in step 7?

Contentious issues in ESP: addressing the problem of deception

Learner deception

At every level of assessment, there is always a danger that a stakeholder may resort to deception to achieve one or more of their aims. Deception is usually discussed in the context of learners, but we find that instructors and administrators can resort to deception, too. In this section, I will review some of the types of deception that different stakeholders may attempt to use, explain their rationale for doing this, and suggest ways that the deception can be identified and overcome – or better, prevented or reduced from the outset.

Learners may resort to deception at each stage of assessment. Here are a few examples that many experienced instructors and administrators will be familiar with:

- submitting an out-of-date general proficiency score or missing a placement test in order to be assigned to an easier or more difficult section of a course than their current ability would suggest
- not mentioning known language problems and learning difficulties during a diagnostic assessment interview to present a more positive image to the instructor
- missing a progress assessment or submitting it late to allow more time to complete it at a satisfactory level
- generating a false excuse for missing a progress assessment or submitting it late in order to avoid grade point reductions
- using machine translation in an end-of-term achievement assessment report to save time and artificially boost the grade
- plagiarizing content in an end-of-term achievement assessment report to save time and artificially boost the grade
- asking or paying somebody to write an end-of-term achievement assessment to artificially boost the grade
- cheating in a progress assessment or final assessment to artificially boost the grade

Instructors can prevent many of these types of deception through careful classroom management, the clear and explicit communication of assessment submission and grading guidelines to learners, and the use of institutional tools and procedures.

In particular, research has shown that the institutional environment is one of the most important factors that affect how learners perceive and resort to deception (McCabe & Trevino, 1993). In response to this, many academic institutions now have support tools and procedures to address these issues. For example, an institution may record all learners' scores and make these available to instructors. So, a review of previous results can provide instructors and administrators with useful information about learners that can be used to place them in the correct class and support them in their learning. Many academic institutions also use a content management system such as Moodle, Drupal, or Blackboard that make it very clear to learners what homework exercises, quizzes, and reports they need to submit and the deadlines for these. An increasing number of academic institutions have introduced strict rules regarding plagiarism and will process all student work through automated plagiarism detection systems, such as Turnitin. These systems are becoming increasingly sophisticated and are now starting to be able to detect uses of machine translations of plagiarized sources. Many academic institutions will also now require learners to complete a declaration of academic honesty that if broken can result in them being ejected from the institution.

It is important to remember that learners do not always intentionally try to deceive their instructors, despite it becoming increasingly easy to do as a result of advances in data access, searching tools, and online services. Erkaya (2009), Sutton and Taylor (2011), Yeo (2007) and many others, for example, have shown that learners may be uncertain or unaware of what is acceptable. Also, the research of McCabe, Butterfield, and Trevino (2006), Comas-Forgas and Sureda-Negre (2010) and others has suggested that some forms of deception such as plagiarism may be perceived differently depending on the target discipline of the learner. And, there is a large body or research (e.g. Abasi, Akbari, & Graves, 2006; Currie, 1998; Pecorari, 2010) that suggests that plagiarism can also result from learners simply not having sufficient language skills to correctly synthesize source material through paraphrasing, citation, quoting, and other methods. These results suggest that an effective way to address plagiarism and other forms of potential deception is to discuss them openly with learners and establish a level of trust with learners so that they feel able to explain how and why their actions might be perceived this way. Instructors are then in a good position to give the learners useful linguistic tools that they can use to avoid being perceived as deceptive. They can also introduce learners to various other tools and resources, such as machine translation systems, automated writing correction systems, and document services, and show them openly how to use these in a way that is academically, socially, and ethically appropriate.

Instructor and administrator deception

Instructors may resort to deception when they are being evaluated by both learners and administrators. Again, here are a few examples:

- limiting the time for learners to complete class evaluations in order to reduce the possibility of negative comments being recorded

- priming learners on the positive aspects of the course before they complete class evaluations to increase the possibility of positive comments
- removing negative student surveys from a collection before submitting them to administrators
- preparing model classes that they can give during peer-observations
- offering clues to learners about the content of upcoming assessments in an attempt to boost the class average grades
- inflating learner assessment grades in order to boost the class average grade and potentially improve class evaluations

Administrators, in contrast, may resort to deception in the following ways:

- indicating to instructors that course evaluations will not affect their teaching loads or course allocations when they will
- presenting changes to courses and programs as coming from above when they are actually initiated by the administrators themselves
- suggesting that a course has a stable future when known changes are about to occur

Instructors might choose to engage in deception when they do not agree with an institution's grading criteria or policies or they find them too time-consuming, complex, or confusing. In other cases, they may worry about how the evaluations of learners and their own performance will affect their future teaching opportunities. It is clear that the easiest and most effective way to deal with such issues is for administrators to create a meaningful, trusting, and open channel of communication with instructors. In this environment, the instructors will hopefully feel more able to question decisions related to grading criteria and policies, and also understand more clearly how the results of evaluations will affect their teaching loads and courses. On the other hand, if the instructors perceive or identify acts of deception at the level of administration, they are far more likely to conceal their own beliefs leading to an environment of fear and suspicion. Of course, it is not always possible or even appropriate for administrators to reveal all they know to instructors or for instructors to reveal all their true feelings to administrators. But, if both parties can maintain a high degree of trust and professionalism, it will allow them to navigate through the difficult discussions that will always arise at some point in the evolution of a course or program.

Research ideas

Here are some possible ideas for small-scale or large-scale research projects that stem from the topics discussed in this chapter.

How do commercial testing agencies ensure the reliability, validity, and practicality of their tests?

Review the descriptions of one or more commercial tests, such as the TOEFL, IELTS, PTS, TOEIC, or a commercial test that is used at your institution. Try to establish how the testing agency measures and ensures the reliability, validity, and practicality of the tests. Suggest ways in which these practices might inform and improve the quality of in-class quizzes created by instructors.

What tool can be used for the rapid assessment of in-class learner participation?

Review the research on in-class observation methods. Propose a new tool that can quickly and effectively measure the degree to which learners interact with the instructor and other learners in the class. Suggest ways in which the tool can be used as part of a professional development program.

Who to? What about? When?

Instructors often ask learners open and closed questions as part of classroom instruction. Review the ways in which instructors can monitor who they ask questions to, what they ask questions about, and when they ask questions. Propose an efficient monitoring method to help instructors more effectively use questioning in their classes.

What is discipline-specific plagiarism?

Earlier in the chapter it was mentioned that plagiarism is more common in some disciplines than others. Investigate the reasons why this might be the case, and suggest ways that the problem of discipline-specific plagiarism might be addressed.

Closing reflection

Now that you have come to the end of the chapter, you should understand how the concepts of tests, assessments, and evaluations are related and why it is important to unsure that evaluation procedures are reliable, valid, and practical. You should also have a better idea of how learners can be evaluated at different stages of a course, and also why it is important to evaluate instructors, courses, and programs. Finally, you should be able to understand why all stakeholders in an ESP program may resort at times to deception and know some steps that can be taken to create a more open and trusting learning environment.

Here are a few more questions to consider:

1. Which of the points covered in the chapter were new to you? Did you find them interesting and relevant in terms of your own learning goals? Were there any points that you found confusing or that you disagreed with?
2. What points from the chapter do you think you can immediately put to use in your own learning or teaching context?
3. If you were running a course for the first time, how would you prioritize proficiency, placement, diagnostic, progress, and achievement assessment in terms of the time you spent on each? How do you think your priorities would change if you were running the course for a second time?
4. Do you think learners should be given access to the plagiarism detection tools used by institutions to monitor their work? Why or why not?

Further resources

Book chapters

Douglas, D. (2013). ESP and assessment. In B. Paltridge & S. Starfield (Eds.), *The handbook of English for specific purposes* (pp. 367–383). Walden, MA: Wiley Blackwell.

Research articles

Feak, C. B., & Salehzadeh, J. (2001). Challenges and issues in developing an EAP video listening placement assessment: A view from one program. *English for Specific Purposes*, *20*, 477–493.

Giménez, J. C. (1996). Process assessment in ESP: Input, throughput and output. *English for Specific Purposes*, *15*(3), 233–241.

Paltridge, B. (1992). EAP placement testing: An integrated approach. *English for Specific Purposes*, *11*(3), 243–268.

Read, J. (1990). Providing relevant content in an EAP writing test. *English for specific purposes*, *9*(2), 109–121.

Stapleton, P., & Helms-Park, R. (2006). Evaluating Web sources in an EAP course: Introducing a multi-trait instrument for feedback and assessment. *English for Specific Purposes*, *25*(4), 438–455.

Tsou, W., & Chen, F. (2014). ESP program evaluation framework: Description and application to a Taiwanese university ESP program. *English for Specific Purposes*, *33*, 39–53.

Section 3

Applying ESP in real-world settings

Chapter 8

Implementing ESP in ideal, opportunistic, and 'just-in-time' settings

In any field, whether it is sport, entertainment, politics, business, or education, careful thought and planning usually leads to the greatest chance that target goals will be reached. This is also true of ESP course and program design. In an ideal setting, administrators and instructors can work together with other stakeholders to carefully build up the four pillars of ESP discussed in the previous four chapters. If they can do this, the likelihood of success is high. But, in practice, many ESP courses and programs are already in place, and unfortunately, they are built on more shaky foundations. In these settings, new instructors must learn to work with what they have and make improvements when the opportunity arises. There are also ESP settings where an ESP instructor might have to suddenly jump in and prepare materials 'just-in-time' for the first lesson, often without knowing the precise needs, learning objectives, or even target contexts of the learners.

In this chapter, I'll first discuss the characteristic features of ESP courses and programs developed within these three different settings, describing the strengths and weaknesses of each. Next, I'll explain how these settings can greatly affect the responsibilities of ESP instructors and the work they need to do. Then, I'll discuss the contentious issue of scope within ESP. Should an ESP course and/or program be set up to address the very specific, 'narrow-angled' needs of individual learners, or should it be designed to address the more general, shared, 'wide-angled' needs of a broad range of learners?

By the end of the chapter, you should understand how ESP administrators and instructors can work together or independently to build the four pillars of ESP. You should also understand how this work affects their roles in the building process, and how the learner setting affects the possible scope of an ESP course or program.

Opening reflection

If you were assigned to teach a new ESP course starting in a few months' time, would you want to be part of the team that investigated the needs of different stakeholders, established the different learning objectives, created a set of materials and methods for use in class, and decided the evaluation procedures? Or, would you prefer to receive the course description and materials after they were created by others, run the course in your own way, and then make improvements as you felt necessary? What reasons do you have for your preference? If you suddenly found that the new course was starting in just a few days' time, would your answer be different? Why?

Commentary

All three settings described in the opening reflection are seen in ESP. The first one is often presented in the literature on ESP. It describes a setting where all four pillars of ESP can be carefully designed and constructed before teaching begins. It is neat and clear, but also not so common. Rarely, in fact, do we have the opportunity to build a completely new ESP course from scratch, within a team or individually. The second setting is far more common. Most ESP instructors will be entering a program that is already running in some form. And, almost without question, there will be some aspects of that program that will need adjustments and others that cannot be changed, regardless of how negatively they affect the results. The third setting is one that no instructor wants to find themselves in. But, it can happen, especially in EOP settings. You may be assigned to a course or have to take over someone else's course with little or no time to prepare.

Let's look at the each of these settings in detail and consider how they affect the work of course administrators and instructors.

Implementing ESP in an ideal setting

Basic concept

An ideal setting for ESP is one in which a team of course administrators and instructors can work together to create a carefully planned, tested, and continually revised and updated set of ESP courses that integrate together to form an ESP program. In this setting, the team would start by building the first pillar of ESP through a careful needs analysis of the different stakeholders, including learners, instructors, and the administrators themselves. Next, they would build the second pillar of ESP through the creation of a set of learning objectives that address the various target needs. Then, they could work to build the third pillar of ESP by designing materials and in-class teaching and learning methods that mesh with those preferred by instructors and the target learners. Finally, they could construct the fourth pillar of

ESP through the design and implementation of placement tests, diagnostic assessments, regular in-class quizzes, final tests and reports, and other methods to evaluate what was achieved.

In this ideal setting, the design process would begin at the program level, with the long-term needs of learners (and other stakeholders) forming the foundations for the design of individual courses. This means that members of the design team would need to think carefully about how all the courses linked together to form a consistent whole. They would also need to think how the overall program could be evaluated and set up mechanisms to allow for it to be revised and improved over time.

You will rarely see large, integrated, team-designed ESP *programs* described in the ESP literature. But, there are exceptions such as Anthony's (2009) description of a English for Science and Technology (EST) program designed for tertiary learners in Japan, Bilici's (2016) description of an EAP program in China, and Tsou and Chen's (2014) description of a EAP program in Taiwan. There are also several reports of large-scale EAP and EOP programs described in Orr's (2002) edited collection of ESP case studies. On the other hand, you will find numerous descriptions of carefully planned and administered ESP *courses* described in the literature, sometimes under the title of an ESP 'program' (e.g. Yogman & Kaylani, 1996; Ching-ning, Wei, & Li-hua, 2008). Often these are developed by a team of ESP administrators and instructors, but you will also see examples where a single ESP expert has done the bulk of the work.

Strengths and weaknesses

There are many strengths to a large, integrated, team-designed ESP program. At the level of needs analysis, the team can make a coordinated effort to understand the immediate and longer-term *necessities*, *lacks*, and *wants* of different stakeholders both inside and outside the institution. This knowledge naturally leads to the creation of a comprehensive set of learning objectives, based ideally on the insights of not only ESP administrators and instructors but also those of specialist informants. In some cases, the target objectives might be addressed in a single, short-term ESP course. However, when the objectives become more complex and involved, a program framework allows more time to be given to the learning process. Also, when ESP courses are designed by a team, some members with strengths in ESP theory can work with others with strengths in ESP teaching and learning practices to develop theoretically sound but also practical and effective materials. A team-based approach to ESP design also allows for a wide range of evaluation procedures to be employed, including the running of standardized, institution-wide placement tests, end-of-course assessments and learner evaluation surveys, the use of instructor-based in-class quizzes, and the collection of informal instructor feedback through a team member assigned to the role of an instructor liaison. It should also be mentioned that large, integrated, team-designed ESP programs will more likely be sanctioned by the institution and be given the necessary funds and resources to make it a reality.

The major weaknesses of a large, integrated, team-designed ESP program are centered on the fact that it requires a common understanding among all the major stakeholders. At the institution level, funding, classrooms, time, equipment, and human resources need to be made available. At the design team level, the members need to have a good understanding of what ESP is and how the foundations of ESP courses should be built. They also need an ability to work together and with others in the institution, and dedicate lots of time to the initiative. At the classroom level, instructors need to be willing to learn to adapt to new materials and teaching methods, and be able to communicate to learners what they are doing and why. There also needs to be a level of trust between administrators and instructors so that administrators don't feel the need to micro-manage and constantly monitor instructors, and instructors can report honestly and accurately to administrators when things are not going according to the plan.

If you have ever worked in an academic institution, you will perhaps recognize that these weaknesses make creating a fully integrated EAP program extremely difficult. Institutions are often reluctant to introduce any sort of change, and when change occurs, it is often extremely slow. Also, the lack of interest by non-department institution officials and the stubbornness of even a single department faculty member can jeopardize such a project. In contrast, you will find many global companies integrate EOP programs smoothly into their training systems. In workplace environments, immediate changes can be initiated high up in the management chain, and as a result, workers are obliged to comply or they risk losing bonuses and opportunities for promotion. Also, much of the work that companies undertake is carried out in the form of team-based projects. So, perhaps the culture of workplaces is more suited to the development of a large-scale ESP program.

TASK 8.1 Forming an ESP course development team

Imagine that you have to design an EAP or EOP course targeting the language of a discipline that you are not very familiar with (e.g. mathematics, sports science, nursing). If you had the authority to form a team to create the course, what type of people would you include? What knowledge and experiences would you want them to have? How would you divide up the work? If you didn't have the support of a team, what could you do (on your own) to establish the needs, learning objectives, materials/methods, and evaluation procedures for the course?

If you have any direct experience of this sort of setting, what did you do and why? Were your actions successful? What would you do differently now?

Implementing ESP in an opportunistic setting

Basic concept

Most ESP instructors will find themselves working in a setting where they are assigned to an ESP course that has already been set up by others in the organization and run for several years. They may be given a short orientation session, an overview of the program as a whole (if it exists), a course syllabus, and perhaps a textbook and other materials used by previous instructors. They are then usually given flexibility to prepare in-class explanations and activities as appropriate before entering the class to teach.

If you find yourself in this 'do-what-you-can-when-you-can' setting (Nation & Macalister, 2010), it is essential that you start out by trying to establish what decisions have already been made and why. For example, if the course has a prescribed textbook, it implies that one or more administrators have considered the goals of the course and felt that this textbook matches them. If so, what are those goals? And, what are the learners' needs on which these goals are based? You might find the answers by speaking to the administrators directly, or you can perhaps extract the answers to these questions from the teachers' guide or the materials for the first lesson of the course. You also need to establish what learning objectives are suggested by the materials, and why those are deemed important in the field. This might lead you to read up about the target language setting and the discourse community that the learners will enter. Then, you can think about what teaching and learning methods you can employ in the classroom and what evaluation procedures you must employ and what flexibility in assessment you have.

Once you have started teaching, you can then observe the learners' reactions to the materials and classroom activities, monitor their progress, and make adjustments as necessary. Finally, you can report back to the administrators how the course progressed, describe how you improved on the original course design, and perhaps offer suggestions for integrating your changes into the course as a whole.

Strengths and weaknesses

The major strength of an opportunistic setting is that it invites a simple, time-efficient, and often effective way to create successful courses. Courses developed by a team over an extended time through multiple committee meetings often overlook characteristics of learners and classroom settings that individual instructors can immediately recognize and address. For example, prescribed materials may become overly rich or complicated, making it impossible to cover them in the time allocated. Individual instructors can decide what materials to simplify or cut altogether. Administrators may also underestimate the time needed to evaluate learners in class, proposing elaborate procedures that are impractical. Again, individual instructors can recognize this problem and replace the procedures with simpler ones. Changes that happen at the classroom level are also likely to be implemented more quickly because they do not need to go through a committee for approval. Also, one further strength of an opportunistic approach to ESP is that its effectiveness increases if instructors are given a chance to teach the course more than once. Problems that instructors might not notice or ignore the first time they teach the course are more likely to be addressed on the second iteration.

The major weakness of an opportunistic approach to implementing ESP is that it can lack coordination. Individual instructors may decide to make changes to a well-designed and carefully constructed course through a lack of experience of working in an ESP environment, a lack of understanding of stakeholder needs, a poor knowledge of the target learning objectives and discourse community, or simply their own personal reasons, e.g. lack of willingness to spend time preparing classes or evaluate learners. Another weakness is that perceived improvements made at one level may adversely affect the course or program at another level. For example, an instructor's choice to skip a textbook unit in the classroom may adversely affect the learners' performance on a standardized assessment carried out at the institutional level.

TASK 8.2 Teaching a ready-made ESP course

Imagine that you have joined the teaching staff in an EAP or EOP program where the courses have already been developed. In the first few classes, you find that things are not going well. Perhaps the learners look bored, or you believe that the materials are too difficult for them. What steps could you take to improve the situation?

If you have any direct experience of this setting, what did you do and why? Were your actions successful? What would you do differently now?

Implementing ESP in a 'just-in-time' setting

Basic concept

In some rare cases, you might find yourself having to prepare for an ESP course with only a few days to get ready. In EAP settings, another instructor might suddenly be taken ill or quit and you have to take over, or a scheduled course may suddenly become oversubscribed and require extra sections to be managed. In EOP settings, an employee might suddenly receive a work assignment that requires a specialized English skill and you are there to support them, or you might be working as a company training consultant and need to prepare a course but not know who will be on the course until just a few days before it starts.

If you find yourself in this situation but you are working within a well-established program, you can usually rely on the institution having a bank of ready-made materials and administrative support staff to help you prepare for the course. On the other hand, if you are on your own, one tried-and-tested strategy used by many instructors in all areas of English language teaching is simply to pick up a textbook and go. The assumption here is that the author of the textbook has followed good course design principles and written the book to match the learners' needs. You would also hope that the author has included a range of materials, activities, and assessment procedures that will ensure that learners meet their target learning objectives while keeping them motivated to complete the course.

Unfortunately, as you found in Chapter 6, it is often the case that a suitable textbook for a narrowly defined area of ESP simply doesn't exist (this is one area where ESP differs greatly from general English language teaching, which has an abundance of published materials). In this scenario, you need to adopt an alternative strategy. In Chapter 4, you learned how to do a 'just-in-time' needs analysis of target learners through the use of a quick pre-course or first-lesson survey. If you combine the results of this with a quick analysis of actual outputs from the target language setting, you can start to formulate learning objectives at the level of register rhetoric (discourse) and genre. Then, as discussed in Chapter 6, you can think how to employ some of the outputs from the target language setting as materials in a learner-centered classroom.

Although a truly 'just-in-time' approach to ESP course implementation is rare, it is important to remember that all classroom settings have a 'just-in-time' element to them. For example, it is impossible for an instructor to be fully prepared to explain all the materials they will cover. And, you may need to quickly adapt what you're doing if the learners suddenly reveal a lack of knowledge in an area you assumed they knew, or ask you challenging questions about an aspect of the target discipline that you are unfamiliar with. It is in these situations where a learner-centered, data-driven approach can be particularly effective.

Strengths and weaknesses

There are few obvious strengths of a 'just-in-time' approach to ESP over ideal and opportunistic approaches. As just mentioned, perhaps the only one is that it forces the instructor to place the learners at the center of the classroom experience. This, in turn, can create a more exciting, dynamic learning environment with greater opportunities for learner interaction.

On the other hand, the huge number of weaknesses means that you should make every effort to avoid 'just-in-time' ESP from happening. In particular, it significantly limits any kind of coordination between courses. It also limits the ability for good materials and practices to be utilized by others and improved, unless there is a platform for instructors to share their experiences. Perhaps the greatest weakness of this approach is that it assumes that either the instructor or the learners have a high degree of familiarity with the target language setting. If neither party has this, the chances of the learners meeting their needs become extremely low.

TASK 8.3 Working 'just-in-time' for the start of an ESP course

Imagine that you are working in an ESP program where another instructor has suddenly taken ill and you have to take over their teaching with just a few days to prepare. What would you do between now and your first class of the course?

If you have any direct experience of this setting, what did you do and why? Were your actions successful? What would you do differently now?

Responsibilities of ESP administrators and instructors

I have been careful throughout this book to distinguish between ESP administrators and instructors. ESP administrators are the people who manage the courses or program, whereas instructors are the people who actually teach the courses. Let's consider how the responsibilities of administrators and instructors vary depending on the ESP setting in which they have to work.

In an ideal ESP setting, the responsibilities of administrators and instructors are fairly easy to separate. Administrators establish the needs of the different stakeholders and determine the learning objectives for the courses. They also decide what materials and methods can or should be used in the classroom, and what procedures will be used to assess the learners, instructors, courses, and the program as a whole (the procedures used to evaluate the administrators will usually be decided at a higher level in the institution). Instructors, on the other hand, are responsible for carrying out the decisions made by the administrators and, ideally, contributing to the development of the program through constructive feedback to the administrators on the success and/or failure of those decisions.

This setup has distinct advantages over the other settings, because it allows for ESP experts to work together with subject specialists in the design of effective courses even when both groups may lack knowledge essential to the process. For example, the ESP experts may know little about the target language setting of the learners, but this knowledge can be provided by the subject specialists. Conversely, the subject specialists may know little about effective ESP teaching and learning methods, but this can be provided by the ESP experts. Unfortunately, as mentioned earlier, this ideal form of ESP is quite rare in practice.

Although most ESP settings are 'opportunistic' in nature, you will find that the degree of opportunity afforded to instructors varies considerably. This has a dramatic impact on the responsibilities of both the administrators and instructors. In very minimally opportunistic settings, administrators may be in total control of what happens in the classroom, forcing instructors to follow fixed materials and procedures, and having little say in how learners are evaluated. Naturally, in this setting, the motivation of instructors is likely to be low, and if the decisions made by the administrative staff are poor, the entire program is likely to fail. Unfortunately, most ESP settings are at the other end of the scale, being highly opportunistic in nature – which brings with it a different set of problems. Here, administrators play a very minimal role in determining what goes on in the classroom, providing perhaps just the name of a course and some very loose guidelines for what it should contain. They may not even have any detailed understanding of the learners' needs or how they should be evaluated. In this setting, you can perhaps see that the instructor must take on many of the responsibilities that an administrator would adopt in an ideal setting. This has led to ESP instructors being frequently described as ESP 'practitioners' in the literature (e.g. Charles & Pecorari, 2016; Dudley-Evans & St. John, 1998; Swales, 1985). In fact, as Dudley-Evans and St. John (1998, p. 13) describe, they need to take on at least six different roles:

- teacher
- course designer
- materials provider
- collaborator
- researcher
- evaluator

The main problem with such a setting is that it places great demands on the time, resources, and knowledge of instructors. If you are put into this setting and you are not familiar with the target needs of the learners or have experience of ESP teaching in general, creating a successful course can be a daunting proposition. We will return to the challenges of working in such an environment in Chapter 9.

In a 'just-in-time' ESP setting, administrators have a particularly important responsibility to provide instructors with the information they require to prepare and teach the course. If an instructor is not familiar with the target language setting or learner needs, ideally, the administrators would take on most of the responsibilities associated with course design and provide the instructors with a detailed and complete set of materials, methods, and evaluation procedures to run the course. Then, the instructor's responsibility would be minimized to implementing the course as best they could, adopting or adapting what they were given as necessary, and perhaps creating new materials once they became more familiar with the learners and the target setting. On the other hand, if the instructor is very familiar with the target language setting and learner needs, it would be unreasonable for the administrators to demand that they quickly master all the required materials and procedures established in the program and follow these in class. Rather, the administrators have a responsibility to step back a little and leave instructors with the responsibility to slowly incorporate the prescribed materials and procedures into their own existing approach.

TASK 8.4 Choosing a role in ESP

Dudley-Evans and St. John (1998) and others have described an ESP practitioner as being able to fulfill the roles of a teacher, course designer, materials provider, collaborator, researcher, and evaluator.

Q1 If you were to join an ESP course development team, what role (or roles) do you think you could most suitably fill? What reasons do you have?
Q2 If a subject specialist joined the team, what role or roles would you want them to fill? Again, what reasons do you have?

Contentious issues in ESP: deciding between narrow- and wide-angled ESP

Throughout the history of ESP, there have been several shifts toward and away from a focus on the unique features of specific subjects in ESP course teaching and learning. Now that you understand some of the different contexts in which ESP is conducted, let's look at this ongoing debate and see if some conclusions can be drawn.

In the early days of ESP in the 1960s and 1970s, many researchers focused on identifying the ways in which registers and rhetorical structures of specific disciplines, such as electrical engineering, differed from those in other disciplines, such as physics and biology, as well as general English. This work naturally led to a similar 'narrow-angled' focus on discipline-specific language in the ESP classroom. However, as the field moved through the 1980s and into the 1990s, an increasing number of researchers including Bloor and Bloor (1986), Blue (1988), Hutchinson and Waters (1987), Spack (1988) and others began noting that different disciplines had many overlaps and similarities and that the value of ESP was not in the discipline-specific products that emerged from ESP instruction but the learning processes that were involved. Again, this work started a new trend for ESP courses with a 'wide-angled' focus on the common, shared features of language across disciplines, as well as common, transferable skills and learning strategies.

As the field moved into the 2000s, the pendulum began to swing back toward a narrow-angled approach with the publication of several key articles by some prominent ESP researchers including Hyland (2002, 2004, 2008), Hyland and Bondi (2006), and later, Paltridge (2009). One of the main driving forces for this reassessment was the increased availability and ease of use of corpus tools that were highly suited to register and rhetorical analyses. Importantly, the results from these corpus-based ESP analyses strengthened earlier observations that the language of specific disciplines varied considerably, as illustrated in the works of Biber (1988, 1992).

Today, the debate over whether an ESP course or program should have a narrow-angled or wide-angled focus is still ongoing. Hyland (2017) and others continue to make a strong case for a narrow-angled approach, pointing to the fact that language features, discourse practices, and communicative skills differ considerably across disciplines. Anthony (2011), on the other hand, argues that this observation can be made not only across disciplines but also within them. As a result, it is more important for learners to understand the degree to which core elements of a language vary in and among disciplines rather than rules that distinguish one particular discipline from others. He also agrees with Huckin (2003), who makes the point that courses that target the language of narrowly defined disciplines are generally impractical. Dovey (2006) goes further, suggesting that the growing view within companies is that the most valuable skill that learners can gain in education is the ability to learn *how* to learn. This is a skill which they can later apply in a rapidly evolving and changing workplace environment. Again, the suggestion here is that a learner's ability to identify patterns of variation in core language concepts will be more useful than knowing and using a narrow set of language features associated with a specialist discipline. This point takes us back to the learning focus stressed by Hutchinson and Waters (1987).

It is clear that a case can be made for both a narrow- and a wide- angled approach to ESP. In fact, this is exactly what Basturkmen (2006) does when reviewing the debate. However, if we consider the different contexts in which ESP is usually implemented, it is also clear that a narrow-angled approach can only be introduced in certain contexts, whereas a wide-angled approach has a more general applicability. Let's look at which contexts match the different approaches.

In an ideal ESP setting where a team of course administrators can work together to carefully design and implement an ESP course, there is the scope to involve subject specialists at all levels of the creation process, allowing for the possibility of a narrow-angled approach. On the other hand, if that same team is required to develop an ESP *program* for a wide number of learners across a range of disciplines, the possibilities change. Now, the practical limitations of time and resources, the institution's usual preference to have standardized materials and evaluation procedures, and the many other institutional restrictions in place will make a narrow-angled approach far more difficult if not impossible to implement. Note, however, that both contexts match the conditions that would allow for a wide-angled approach to be used.

The possibility for using a narrow-angled approach is far greater in a highly opportunistic setting or a 'just-in-time' setting. In this case, an individual instructor has the freedom to introduce their own materials and methods and tailor these to exact needs of the learners in the classroom. However, even here, the opportunity will only be available to course instructors who have an extensive knowledge of a target discipline and a bank of materials that they have built up over time. It is highly unlikely that a non-specialist instructor would be able to develop an effective course on their own, especially if they had only a few days to do it. On the other hand, they might be able to cope if they were given the freedom to focus on the aspects of language and communication that are shared across disciplines as part of a wide-angled approach.

To conclude, it seems that there are some strong theoretical grounds for adopting a narrow-angled approach. But, there are also strong theoretical grounds for adopting a wide-angled approach, in addition to its broader, more practical strengths. Choosing which approach to adopt will depend on a range of factors, including the time constraints, the class size, the learners' and instructors' backgrounds and experiences, and of course, the needs of the different stakeholders. But, when in doubt, perhaps it is best to initially adopt a wide-angled approach and then narrow the focus as you learn more about the learners' needs.

Research ideas

Here are some possible ideas for small-scale or large-scale research projects that stem from the topics discussed in this chapter.

Who should develop an ESP program?

Conduct a case study on the development of a large, integrated ESP program focusing on who was part of the development team and what their contributions were. Based on what you find, make suggestions for improving the makeup of an ESP development team.

What are the perceived and desired responsibilities of subject specialists and ESP experts in ESP course and program design?

The relationship between ESP experts and target subject specialists is a complex one. In many institutions, subject specialists are in positions of power and have a belief that they know best what learners require in ESP courses. On the other hand, the design, implementation, and teaching of courses is usually the sole responsibility of ESP experts. Conduct a survey of subject specialists and ESP experts in different settings to find out what they perceive their responsibilities are and what responsibilities they believe they should take on during the development on an ESP course or program. What lessons can we learn about ESP course and program implementation from this study?

Which is better, a wide-angled or narrow-angled ESP approach?

Many arguments have been made to support or reject wide-angled and narrow-angled approaches to ESP. However, there are few empirical studies that investigate the different opinions of administrators, instructors, and learners on this topic. Choose one of these target groups and conduct a survey to find out which approach they prefer and why.

Closing reflection

Now that you have come to the end of the chapter, you should have a good understanding of the different settings in which the four pillars of ESP might need to be constructed. You should also understand how the setting in which ESP takes place directly affects the degree of planning possible, the responsibilities of administrators and instructors, and even the scope of ESP that can be covered in the classroom.

Here are a few more questions to consider:

1. Which of the points covered in the chapter were new to you? Did you find them interesting and relevant in terms of your own learning goals? Were there any points that you found confusing or that you disagreed with?
2. What points from the chapter do you think you can immediately put to use in your own learning or teaching context?
3. If you had complete control and unlimited resources to design and implement an EAP program at the tertiary level, what required and elective ESP courses would you include in your program? How would you involve subject specialists in the design and implementation of your program?

4 If you were working in the human resources section of a company and you were able to hire a new ESP expert to assist you in developing EOP courses and programs, would you prefer somebody with a deep knowledge of the company business but who lacked knowledge about ESP course and program design, or would you prefer somebody with an extensive knowledge of ESP course and program design but who had little experience of working in this business area. What reasons do you have for your decision?

Further resources

Books

Basturkmen, H. (2014). *Ideas and options in English for specific purposes.* Abingdon, UK: Routledge.

Belcher, D. D., Johns, A. M., & Paltridge, B. (Eds.). (2011). *New directions in English for specific purposes research.* Ann Arbor: University of Michigan Press.

Research articles

Belcher, D. D. (2006). English for specific purposes: Teaching to perceived needs and imagined futures in worlds of work, study, and everyday life. *TESOL Quarterly, 40*(1), 133–156.

Chapter 9

Dealing with challenges in ESP

Chapter 8 looked at implementing ESP in ideal, opportunistic, and 'just-in-time' settings. Each of these settings presents an ESP instructor with possibilities for and challenges to maximizing the effectiveness of teaching and learning practices. This chapter, in contrast, looks at some of the more general challenges that ESP instructors face in EAP or EOP settings. Knowing what these challenges are and how to address them will not only help you to become a better ESP instructor, but also give you important insights into the work faced by ESP administrators.

In the chapter, I'll first explain the challenges that affect needs analysis and the strategies that can help mitigate them. Then, in a similar way, I'll explain the challenges and mitigation strategies related to learning objectives, materials and methods, and evaluation procedures. At the end of the chapter, I'll discuss the contentious issue of managing change in ESP and how a program of change can lead to many of the challenges faced by ESP instructors being avoided from the outset.

By the end of the chapter, you should understand the challenges that ESP teachers and program designers face, know how to mitigate some of these challenges through before-class, in-class, and after-class actions, and understanding different ways to implement change in ESP at the course and program level. Most importantly, you should have made an important step to becoming not only a knowledgeable ESP instructor, but also an effective one.

Opening reflection

If you are still a student, imagine you were to be hired to teach an EAP course at the tertiary level. What concerns would you have about the work and your ability to serve as an effective instructor? Now, imagine that you were to be hired to teach an EOP course in a company. Which of your concerns would be the same? What other concerns would you have?

If you have experience of teaching in an EAP or EOP context, what challenges have you faced in your work? What strategies have you adopted to deal with those challenges? How successful have the strategies been?

Commentary

Novice ESP instructors who are hired to work in an EAP setting are often concerned about the nature of the learners (e.g. range of proficiency levels, number of department/faculty specializations, years of study, country of origin, class size), the details of the courses they will teach (e.g. syllabus details, course goals, learning objectives, textbook requirements, availability of online resources, use of a learning management systems, classroom resources, support staff), and the evaluation procedures (e.g. time allowed for creating, administrating, and grading in-class quizzes, the details and weighting of standardized tests, and the use of student surveys by instructors and administrators).

Novice instructors in EOP settings are likely to face similar concerns. However, they may also worry about the impact of evaluation of the learners' future possibilities as well as their own. For example, if the learners do not reach a certain performance level, will the course be cancelled? Will an individual learner lose their job (or not be hired), or will their contract be cancelled? The instructor might also be concerned about the environment in which they have to teach (e.g. Will there be a classroom with a whiteboard and projector? Will the learners be able to regularly attend? Will management be observing the classes?).

In the next few sections, let's try to address these concerns by understanding some of the main challenges faced by ESP instructors in the areas of needs, learning objectives, materials/methods, and evaluation. For each of the challenges discussed, I'll suggest some useful strategies that can help you.

Addressing challenges related to needs analysis and the motivations of stakeholders in ESP

Challenges to administrative needs

Identifying the *necessities*, *lacks*, and *wants* in a needs analysis is the first step in building a strong and stable ESP course or program. However, it can also be one of the most challenging steps. Administrators of ESP programs are often pressured to make decisions about course and program design based on limited or misinformed needs analyses. For example, in an EAP setting, they may themselves not be experts in the target disciplines and so have to rely on the input from specialist informants. However, it is rare that all specialist departments will take an active role in ESP course and program development (if any). If they do, there is still the problem of specialist informants knowing about the field but not knowing the target *language*, *genres*, and *skills* that a course necessitates. This leads to the danger of ESP administrators "believing all that they hear" Swales (1990, p. 29) even when it is not accurate or appropriate. Another problem is that the administrators may not be in a position to collect information from other stakeholders, such as those in industry. And, surprisingly, they may be quite divorced from actual teaching, so lack an awareness of the *necessities*, *lacks*, and *wants* of individual learners. Compounding the problem for instructors is the tendency for administrators to present some of their own *wants* for a course as another set of *necessities*. For example, administrators may dictate the days, the times, and the number of hours for a course. They may decide if it is to a have a required or elective status, and to whom it applies. They may also specify the goals of the course and prescribe the use of a published textbook

ESP instructors entering the classroom can quickly find that some administrator decisions are problematic. Perhaps the learners are not at the level or in the same specialist discipline as that suggested by the materials. Or, perhaps the course is not long enough to reach the intended goals. If you find yourself in this position, it is therefore essential that you communicate with the administrators to understand how they arrived at their decisions and learn which of their decisions are based truly on necessities, and which might be possible to modify or reject entirely. It will also be advantageous for you to learn more about the institution where you work, the way courses are created, the degree of flexibility that the department and institution finds acceptable, and, of course, the background and target setting of the learners you face. As you learn more about the educational setting, you will be in a better position to communicate with administrators about your own feelings and opinions of the course and your views on the *necessities*, *lacks*, and *wants* of learners.

Challenges to learner needs

One of the great challenges of understanding learner needs in an ESP context is that the learners themselves may not be fully aware of what their needs are. They may tell you they want to learn more technical vocabulary or develop their pronunciation. Depending on their country of origin, discipline background, and previous learning experiences, they may think that skills development is not as important as knowledge. They may also prefer that you lecture to them and not assign homework in each class.

Ideally, the learner *wants* will match their *necessities* and *lacks*, but when a mismatch occurs, the more you know about the target setting and discourse community that learners will enter, the more you will be able to motivate them and convince them that your classes will be valuable to them. This can include a course orientation where you review the global and local contexts, explain the importance of English in the target field, and review general and specific language problems. However, even if the learners' views are misplaced, it is still essential that you listen to what they are and communicate the views to the administrators.

Challenges to instructor needs

ESP instructors often come from very different backgrounds and will have their own *necessities*, *lacks*, and *wants* for an ESP course. Some may be experts in a target discipline but lack experience of language teaching, and others may be the exact opposite. Some may be native speakers with a strong command of general English but lack an understanding of specialist language. Others may be second language speakers with a strong knowledge of specialist language but weaker general English skills. Some, again, may require a textbook because they are inexperienced in the target context and have little time to prepare custom materials. Others may prefer to use their own materials and react negatively to administrators enforcing on them a prescribed course design and set of goals. Finally, almost every instructor has a different opinion on and approach to materials design, in class teaching, homework assignments, and testing. For example, some may expect to lecture to learners in the role of a discipline expert, whereas others may see themselves more as language coaches who guide learners toward their goals. Understanding who you are, what you know and believe, and what you need to know and understand are the keys to being able to seek appropriate advice and support in an ESP environment.

TASK 9.1 Recognizing challenges related to instructor needs

Look at the following candidates who have applied to teach a business English course in a university ESP program for international (non-native English) students. Answer the questions that follow.

Candidate A

Relevant Qualification: MA degree in Teaching English as a Foreign Language (with a specialization in ESP)
Language Ability: native English speaker
Work Experience: three years of experience as a Teaching Assistant (TA)

Candidate B

Relevant Qualification: BA degree in English Literature
Language Ability: native English speaker
Teaching Experience: twenty-five years of experience teaching EAP courses at universities in the Middle East

Candidate C

Relevant Qualification: Master of Business Administration (MBA)
Language Ability: native Spanish speaker; proficient in English
Work Experience: ten years of experience working in industry.

About the candidates

Based on the limited information given, which candidate would you choose? What challenges would you expect the chosen candidate to face as they prepare for the assigned course? What could the candidate do to address these challenges on their own?

About you

If you were selected for the position, what challenges would you expect to face as you prepared for the course? What could the administrators do to assist you?

Addressing challenges related to the specification of learning objectives in ESP

Challenges when the targeted learning objectives are wrong

Surprising as it may seem, ESP instructors sometimes find themselves working in an ESP course where some or all of the targeted learning objectives are simply wrong. In other words, there is a mismatch between the specified goals of the course and the actual needs of the different stakeholders. This situation can occur for various reasons, but perhaps the most common is that the course has been designed by administrators who are not familiar with the target setting. Rather than consulting with specialist informants and conducting a detailed needs analysis, they rely on their own experiences which might relate to a different field or are perhaps simply out of date. In other cases, decisions might be made out of convenience; for example, being based on a desire to use a particular (in-house) textbook, maintain the status quo, save time, or limit the need for additional resources.

If you find yourself teaching an ESP course in a context like this, you first need to establish who exactly is mistaken. It may be the case that you *think* the administrators have created objectives that are wrong, but there is also a good chance that you might be the one mistaken. Perhaps it is you who lacks familiarity or experience with the target setting. In short, you must always consult with administrators before taking actions that clearly go against the original design of a course. At this point, you can then start to assess the degree to which the course has an 'opportunistic' component. All courses have some degree of flexibility and by understanding what that is, you can start to introduce new goals, materials, and teaching methods based on the four pillars of ESP discussed in Section 2. Of course, you also need to align what you do to any coordinated evaluation system in place and ensure that the learners in your class do not get penalized in terms of their final grades for your inventiveness.

Challenges when the learning objectives are unspecified

Another problematic setting in which ESP instructors can find themselves is when an ESP course has few or no learning objectives. Again, you might be surprised that such a situation can exist, but the sad fact is that there are English courses around the world where this is the case.

One reason why the objectives might not be specified is a pedagogic one. Some administrators are happy to create 'empty course boxes' with generic titles that they expect experienced instructors to fill with their own objectives, materials, methods, and assessment procedures. Many general English programs in academia will include courses with names like "English I" or "Foundation English", "Academic English", "Technical English", or "English for Specific Purposes". It is left to the instructor to determine to what "I", "Foundation", "Academic", "Technical", and "Specific" should refer in terms of learning objectives. Even in programs deemed to have as ESP focus, you might find courses named "Nursing English", "Business English", or "English for Tourism" with little or no further specification. Again, it is left to the instructor to decide what aspects of nursing, business, tourism, and so on should be focused on in the classroom.

A more complex reason for not specifying course objectives is that they are unknown. Perhaps the administrators are not familiar with the target setting and do not have access to specialist informants or experienced ESP experts who can help them decide on the details of the course. In this case, they would be hiring you to fill that gap. Another reason is that the more specific an ESP course becomes, the less previous research exists that can inform course designers. As an example, Table 5.2 lists some of the commonly cited sub-skills of reading, writing, listening, and speaking. In a general English course, an instructor could decide to pay equal attention to all these features. In an ESP course, on the other hand, the importance of these different sub-skills will clearly vary depending on the target context. This means that their weighting in the specification of course objectives should also vary. In some high profile EAP contexts, such as tertiary-level academic reading and writing, much work has been done to identify the nature and importance of these sub-skills. The same can be said for some high profile EOP contexts, such as international business meetings, nurse-patient interactions, and call-center work. However, there is scant information about many – if not most – EAP and EOP language and learning skill requirements. Of course, ESP researchers can choose to look at these requirements in ever narrower disciplines and contexts. But, not only is it a reality that this work has yet to be done, there is also the question of if it should be done. This returns us to the debate about wide-angled and narrow-angled ESP discussed in Chapter 8.

If you find yourself teaching in an ESP setting where the learning objectives are lacking or unspecified, you will find you have a lesser challenge than that faced by instructors who are given incorrect objectives to follow. Here, you don't have to fight against the system or work to introduce changes in policy. You also don't have to worry that your decisions will negatively affect learner grades. One further advantage is that you are likely to recognize the challenge much earlier. In the previous case, you may only realize that the objectives are mistaken on the first day you enter the classroom. However, the setting here still requires that you design your own course. This means that you will first need to determine the needs of the learners (on your own). Then, you can decide if you are going to adopt a wide- or narrow-angled approach. Finally, you can create a set of objectives, and design materials, methods, and evaluation procedures. Again, the ideas discussed in Section 2 should help you.

Challenges when the targeted learning objectives are known

In a surprisingly rare number of cases, an ESP course is built on a clear and detailed set of learning objectives. Even here, though, instructors can face significant challenges implementing the course as it is designed.

At the most mundane level, the course may require facilities, resources, class sizes, and time allowances that the institution, instructors, and learners cannot or will not provide. As a simple example, an EAP writing course design may be built on the assumption that learners will receive detailed individual feedback after each weekly assignment. However, if the class size is more than 50 and instructors only have one hour to review all homework assignments for the class, the course will clearly fail. In short, these courses are unrealistic.

Sometimes, the course objectives require instructors with a high level of experience, training, and/or understanding of a specialist discipline. This introduces the challenge of hiring the right people. But, it also raises the question of what to do if the currently employed instructors do not fill these requirements. Should their contracts be terminated, should they be encouraged or required to take training courses, or should the course objectives be modified to adjust to the reality of the setting? In practice, we find all three strategies are being employed in ESP courses and programs around the world.

If you find yourself teaching in an ESP setting where the learning objectives seem unrealistic or you lack the knowledge necessary to address them in class, perhaps the key skills you need to develop are negotiation and collaboration. If the course design appears unrealistic, you will need to negotiate with an administrative team to decide what components of the course can be adjusted, simplified, or removed entirely. Perhaps the removal of a unit of the course materials or a simplification of the grading procedure can resolve your greatest concerns.

If you are concerned about your lack of knowledge of the field, you can collaborate with the team of other instructors in the program (if it exists) to address your weaknesses. You can also seek knowledge from people working in the field, giving you more insights on the target discourse community and the relative importance of different language skills. Perhaps the most important group of informants that you can collaborate with are the learners themselves. Depending on their own experience in the field, they can bring to the classroom a huge knowledge base and skill set. Remember that learner needs comprise *necessities*, *lacks*, and *wants*. Even though the *necessities* of the target setting might be highly complex, it is unlikely that the learner will *lack* all of these. One important skill of a good ESP instructor is knowing what not to focus on in the classroom.

TASK 9.2 Recognizing challenges related to learning objectives

Imagine that you applied for a job as an EAP writing instructor at a university that offers a six-week preparatory writing course for incoming international graduate students. In the interview, you find that students meet once a week for a 60-minute lesson and instructors are free to design weekly activities as they see fit. The only requirement is that they follow the short syllabus statement below. The post will start in three months.

Course Title: Introduction to Academic Writing

Course description: This course helps students to improve their writing skills. The course focuses on developing a general academic vocabulary, writing research articles following an IMRD model, adopting the APA citation and reference standard, and using coherence, cohesion, and hedging in writing.

What questions could you ask of the interview panel to help you decide if you are qualified for this position?

What questions could you ask the interview panel to help you prepare for any issues or challenges related to the stated objectives?

Addressing challenges related to materials and methods in ESP

Challenges locating suitable materials

In Chapter 6, we looked at ways to evaluate, adopt, and adapt readily available materials for the ESP classroom. We also looked at how you might develop custom materials centered on suitable 'carrier content'. The challenge that faces many novice ESP instructors is locating potentially useful materials and carrier content before the materials evaluation stage begins. Fortunately, the Internet has helped significantly in this respect. Now, all major publishers will list their ESP-related textbooks on their websites and provide relatively easy search functions to locate them. Some publishers also add a preview feature to a textbook listing, allowing you to look at the front material and perhaps review a sample chapter. If the publisher does not offer this preview feature, you might still be able to find it as a service offered by companies like Amazon (www.amazon.com). Of course, you can also visit a traditional bookstore or contact the publisher directly.

The Internet has also dramatically improved the chances of finding authentic language samples produced by members of the target discourse community. In EAP settings, conference proceedings and journal articles are available for download (often at a cost) through global information analytics businesses, such as Elsevier (www.elsevier.com), international organizations such as the IEEE (www.ieee.org), and national digital archives, such as PubMed (www.ncbi.nlm.nih.gov/pubmed). Fortunately, there is a growing trend for institutions to release final drafts of conference proceedings and research articles through their own portals free of charge, and there is also growing support for free, open-access journals. In a recent trend, student theses and other unpublished writings are being increasingly made available for download at research-oriented social networking sites such as ResearchGate (www.researchgate.net) and Academia.edu (www.academia.

edu), and regional repositories, such as Trove (trove.nla.gov.au). What's more, through the endeavors of corpus researchers, it is now much easier to find publicly available collections of other academic written and spoken academic genres, such as student papers, course lectures, tutorials, and even on-campus service encounters. Some of these are listed in the resources section at the end of the chapter.

It is generally much more difficult to find readily available *collections* of authentic language produced in EOP settings. However, there are some notable exceptions in the area of air traffic control, business, and law. Again, some of these resources are listed at the end of the chapter. On the other hand, the Internet can provide us with instant access to a surprisingly wide array of individual samples of EOP language. As a result, one of the mantras you should follow is "Internet search engines are your friend". In particular, sites like Creative Commons (creativecommons.org) offer access to a huge variety of audio and visual materials that can provide you with insights on the target language and also be used directly or after some editing in the classroom. There are also video upload sites like YouTube (www.youtube.com) and Youku (www.youku.com) that can be very helpful. One caution to note, however, is that some of these video samples are clips from professional training materials, raising the question of authenticity. There is also the issue of copyright, so you should read the disclaimers that accompany video materials on these sites carefully before you use them in your own classroom.

TASK 9.3 Finding authentic source materials

Imagine you are teaching an EOP course in medical English but you have little experience in the target discipline beyond your own experiences of visiting a doctor. As you prepare for the classes, you need some examples of doctor-patient interactions. Go to your favorite Internet video upload site and type the following:

"doctors speaking with patients"

Review some of the results that you find. Could you use any of the examples in the class? Why or why not?

Challenges dealing with specialist vocabulary and subject knowledge

When English language teachers think of taking on an ESP course, the first worry that often comes to mind is what to do about specialist vocabulary and subject knowledge. Figure 9.1 shows a research article abstract in the field of bioscience. You can see here that the abstract contains a great many technical words with which you are likely to be unfamiliar. You are also unlikely to be able to judge the merits of the research content. If a

Prediction of mRNA N6-Methyladenosine (m6A) in the Mammalian Genome with Improved Sensitivity
Yiqian Zhang
Graduate School of Advanced Science and Engineering, Waseda University

Abstract— N6-Methyladenosine (m6A) is a common RNA modification which plays an important role in diverse RNA activities such as alternative splicing, interplay with microRNA, and translation efficiency. However, predicting precise mRNA m6A sites in the mammalian genome is difficult due to the absence of intron sequences. In this research, we utilized Support Vector Machine (SVM) to develop a predictor by combining efficient genomic features. Our predictor achieved comparable accuracy and higher sensitivity than existing tools.

Figure 9.1 Research article abstract in the field of bioscience.

learner wanted to write in a similar way, how could you help them? Are you expected to provide them with a glossary of all the technical vocabulary in the writing? Should you attempt to explain the concepts that the author of the writing describes?

In Chapter 5, we discussed some of the ways that you can deal with vocabulary and in-class subject knowledge dilemmas (ISKDs). The important point to remember, though, is that learners rarely need their ESP instructor to provide them with technical vocabulary and content instruction. They have dictionaries, specialist course books, and content instructors for that. You should also remember that there is often a strong one-to-one relationship between an L2 technical word and its L1 translation. In many languages, the word might even be an L1 cognate or loan word, simplifying the learning process more. Machine translation tools also greatly help when it comes to knowing the meaning of technical words in the target language. Huge advancements in machine translation technology have made the task of understanding highly technical language (and also creating the same language) a significantly easier task than it was just a few years ago.

What learners most often lack is an ability to recognize *how* technical vocabulary and content knowledge are used in appropriate ways that follow the genre conventions of the field. Here, as an ESP instructor, you have an important role to play. In Figure 9.1, for example, you can help learners to understand the rhetorical structure by dividing up the text and labeling the parts. You can then help them to understand how general and academic language is used to signal that structure and link complex ideas together by replacing the numerous subject-specific noun phrases with A, B, C, and so on. The resulting simplified texts, shown in Figure 9.2, can serve both as a

[**Title**] Prediction of mRNA N6-Methyladenosine (m6A) in the Mammalian Genome with Improved Sensitivity

[**Background**] N6-Methyladenosine (m6A) is a common RNA modification which plays an important role in diverse RNA activities such as alternative splicing, interplay with microRNA and translation efficiency. [**Problem**] However, predicting precise mRNA m6A sites in the mammalian genome is difficult due to the absence of intron sequences. [**Aim**] In this research, we utilized Support Vector Machine (SVM) to develop a predictor by combining efficient genomic features. [**Results**] Our predictor achieved comparable accuracy and higher sensitivity than existing tools.

[**Title**] A of B in C with D
[**Background**] A is a common B which plays an important role in diverse C such as D, E with F, and G. [**Problem**] However, predicting precise H in the I is difficult due to the absence of J. [**Aim**] In this research, we utilized K to develop L by combining efficient M. [**Results**] Our L achieved comparable accuracy and higher sensitivity than existing tools.

Figure 9.2 Simplified research article abstract in the field of bioscience.

useful teaching aid and also as a useful template for the learners when they write similar texts in the future.

The different presentations of the abstract in Figure 9.2 naturally lead to a discussion of logical connectors and the use of academic vocabulary. As a result, you might choose to explain how to use other logical connectors and provide learners with a list of common academic vocabulary items to study and memorize, such as that proposed by Coxhead (2000). Learners can be further empowered if they create a discipline-specific corpus of target text and then use the Data-Driven Learning (DDL) methods explained in Chapter 6 to investigate how technical vocabulary is used in context.

Challenges working in a team with subject specialists

In previous chapters, we have looked at how you might work with subject specialists in the design and creation of an ESP course or program. In some cases, you might also find yourself working with subject specialists in the actual teaching of an ESP course.

One of the great challenges of team-teaching with a subject specialist is knowing (and respecting) the role of the other member of the team. Who decides what materials are used? Who will provide the in-class explanations?

Who will evaluate the learners? Who has ultimate responsibility for the success of the course? Without answers to these questions at the start of the project, there is a danger that the subject specialist will immediately assume the leadership role and start dictating what materials should be used, how they should be taught in class, and the how learners should be tested on the course material. This can easily happen when the course is being run in the subject specialist's own department and the ESP instructor has been hired from outside. However, it may also be the case that the ESP instructor is expected to take ultimate responsibility for the success of the course, with failure leading to a termination of their contract and the course itself. Clearly, it is not in their interest for the course to be dictated by the specialist informant, especially if they can predict or directly see that the resulting course is not working.

A related problem is that a power difference can emerge in team-taught ESP courses when the ESP instructor feels inadequate due to their lack of specialist subject knowledge. This leads to the suggestions and opinions of the subject specialist taking precedence over those of the ESP instructor, regardless of how knowledgeable about language teaching the specialist is. It is a regrettable fact that subject specialists are often overly confident about the truth of their assertions about what language should be taught, and how.

If you find yourself involved in a ESP team-teaching project, it is important that the whole team has an open and frank discussion about the way the course should be implemented. Also, it is important that you make clear to the rest of the members what contributions you can make and their importance. In simple terms, you must communicate to the others that you are also a specialist – a specialist in English for specific purposes. If you can provide them with clear evidence for this (for example, in terms of your insightful observations about learner challenges and creative ways to introduce and utilize specialist subject materials), you can gain their respect and play an equal – if not more important – role in the team.

Challenges working in a learner-centered classroom

One of most challenging aspects of ESP faced by traditional English instructors is adjusting to a learner-centered classroom environment. In traditional general English teaching, the instructor is assumed to be the expert. They provide information on grammar rules, present new vocabulary items with definitions or L1 translations, and introduce various productive and receptive exercises in which learners can apply and master that knowledge. In ESP teaching, things are not so simple. The instructor may not know at the outset which grammar rules are relevant, what the vocabulary of the field even means, and how people in the discourse community use language to complete their studies or work. And, the more advanced and narrowly focused the ESP course becomes, the more challenging these issues become. So, the obvious solution is to give up on the idea of being an expert in the target discipline and hand at least some of the authority and control in the classroom to the learners.

Depending on the culture and background of both the instructor and learners, a learner-centered classroom may be quite unfamiliar. It is therefore necessary that you explain from the outset why this format is being adopted and the advantages it offers. In particular, it is important that you don't create an impression with learners that you are unsure what you're doing. In a similar way to handling the challenges of working in a team with subject specialist informants, you need to provide the learners with clear evidence that even though you are not an expert in their target field, you are an expert in the field of ESP. This means providing them with convincing explanations why their contributions in class are important. It also means demonstrating to them that you can provide useful observations, guidance, insights, and knowledge that can help them achieve their learning objectives.

At a practical level, in class, you should resist the temptation to always select source materials to show as examples. Sometimes, let the learners pick the materials. Also, you shouldn't feel that you always need to explain everything. Let the learners offer their own explanations and insights on their own work and that of others. And, when it comes to identifying errors and correcting a learner's performance, try letting the learners do some of this work. In an EAP writing class, for example, perhaps you can simply underline questionable grammar, vocabulary, and style uses, and let them find out if and how to correct the points. Similarly, in an EOP business presentation class, perhaps video record the learners' presentations, give the recordings to the individual learners, and let them watch, critique, and improve their performances.

TASK 9.4 Working with authentic source materials

The following text is an authentic conference proceedings abstract from the field of mechanical engineering. Review the abstract, highlight the rhetorical structure, and then simplify the abstract by replacing any unfamiliar technical noun phrases with A, B, C, and so on in a similar way to the example shown in Figure 9.2. If you were teaching a technical writing course, would you be confident in using this example? How could you present this source material in a learner-centered way in order to capitalize on the learners' own knowledge of mechanical engineering?

Chip formation mechanism of pure Niobium plates in superconducting accelerator cavities
T. Kaneeda[1], M. Yamada[1], Laurence Anthony[2]

[1]Okayama University of Science, Japan

[2]Waseda University, Japan

Abstract

This paper investigates the chip formation mechanism of pure niobium, a material used in the construction of superconducting accelerator cavities. Cutting experiments were conducted in order to clarify the chip formation mechanism using NC precision cutting apparatus. The cutting forces and machined surface roughness were determined under various cutting conditions. In addition, the effects of depth of cut, depth of cut in last-precutting, and cutting speeds on the chip formation were examined.

Addressing challenges related to learner, instructor, and course/program evaluation

Challenges in the design of authentic evaluation procedures

As you learned in Chapter 7, authentic materials are language samples that are created by members of a discourse community for use by other members of that community. In a similar way, when it comes to evaluation in ESP, we can consider developing authentic tests and other evaluation procedures. However, this is where the challenge comes. In both EAP and EOP settings, even though you may be working in the same institution, except in special cases, you will not be considered to be a member of the learner's target discourse community. So, any test or evaluation procedure you implement will not necessarily produce a learner performance that matches what they can achieve in an authentic setting. As an example, a learner in an EOP business English course might be able to produce a relaxed, confident, and effective presentation in an end-of-course assessment setting, but collapse under the weight of nerves when delivering the same presentation in front of actual customers.

ESP course designers and instructors have devised various ways to increase the authenticity of their evaluation procedures. Douglas (2000) describes various national and international ESP tests, such as the Occupational English Test (OET) (www.occupationalenglishtest.org) that require learners to recreate the tasks that members of the discourse community undertake through the use of role-plays. We see the same approach undertaken at a more local level in business English courses, such as those described by Planken and Nickerson (2008), and tourism courses, such as that described by Cheng (2013). Raising the level of authenticity higher, ESP training programs have been designed in which the target performance of learners is assessed in the real-world target setting. Friginal (2013), for example, describes how the oral performance of call-center workers is assessed as they perform their daily duties using an innovative criterion-based assessment tool that also includes the results of customer satisfaction surveys. At a more basic level, many EOP courses that cannot be documented due to non-disclosure agreements use quantitative measures of learner performance gains, such as the increased number of customers they are able to invite, and the increased number of paper and presentation acceptances, and award nominations they gain.

Again, you will see that collaboration is a useful skill to have if you want to introduce authentic evaluation procedures into an ESP classroom. In some cases, you might need the assistance of specialist informants to review your testing materials to determine if the questions are relevant and important. At other times, you might want them to participate directly in the assessment perhaps serving as a role-play partner for learners (e.g. acting in the role of a customer), or as a direct assessor of their performance.

TASK 9.5 Increasing the authenticity of a writing assessment

In Task 9.4, you adapted and simplified a research article abstract from the field of mechanical engineering. If you were teaching a graduate-level ESP writing course for learners in this field and their final assessment was to write a report, what could you do to make this assessment more authentic for them? Here are some initial suggestions.

1 Ask the learners to write a report on their own research.
2 Have the learners imagine they are writing the report for submission to a target journal in their field.
3 . . .

Challenges integrating standardized tests into an ESP course/program

Dudley-Evans and St. John (1998), Douglas (2000) and others describe numerous standardized tests that have been or can be used in ESP courses and programs. Each can be placed on a continuum of specificity that ranges from very general to highly specific. Also, each has different strengths and weaknesses in terms of cost, authenticity, ease of use, and external value, reputation, and acceptance. A challenge for ESP course designers creating a completely new course, therefore, is deciding which of these tests, if any, should be adopted. Perhaps a more common challenge, on the other hand, is what to do as an ESP instructor when one of these tests is already adopted by the institution, but it does not mesh well with the stated learning objectives of the course. We find many of the latter cases in EAP settings where students are required to achieve a certain score on a general English proficiency test in order to graduate or proceed to the next level of their studies, but they still have to take a variety of EAP courses each week.

If you are working as an ESP instructor in complete isolation, it is rare that you will experience the first challenge of needing to choose a suitable standardized test to introduce to your learners. In fact, the learners will probably already know what tests they need to take. Also, the costs and administrative overload will limit your ability to make such a proposal to them. However, if you are part of a team of administrators, the team as a whole might certainly need to make such a decision. Here, the obvious strategy is to carefully review all the available tests, consult with specialist informants about their relative merits and value, and then consult with senior administrators in the institution about the logistics of running the tests in terms cost, time, and space, test management, and so on.

Addressing the second challenge is something that many ESP instructors have to deal with. In Japan, for example, a huge number of universities require students to take the Test of English for International Communication (TOEIC) and use it for placement testing, as a pre-condition for course exceptions, and entering graduate school (Weaver, 2016). Companies in Japan also use the results of this test as a filter at the hiring stage and use it to determine who qualifies for a promotion (Nakamura, 2014). The washback from such a test cannot be ignored in the classroom. One useful strategy you can adopt is to explain to the learners at the outset that their results on a standardized test, while important, are just one component of their learning experience and that their ESP training will also help them to graduate, find a job, seek promotion, and so on. You can also try to find an overlap between the content of the standardized test and the knowledge and skills addressed in the ESP course and then highlight the similarities where possible. Another strategy is to collect quantitative data on learner performances on the standardized test and their performances in the ESP class and show the degree to which the scores are correlated. While correlation does not imply causation (Aldrich, 1995), it is still a useful observation that can motivate learners to take their ESP studies seriously.

Contentious issues in ESP: introducing change in ESP course and program design

One of the most contentious issues in any human system is the introduction of change. Needless to say, the same is true of change in language teaching, where changes might be introduced at the course and program level. Some of these are listed in Table 9.1.

Table 9.1 Possible changes at the ESP course and program level

Classroom level changes

- moving rooms (e.g. from a small to a large classroom)
- changing the seating arrangement (e.g. from rows to a circle)
- changing learner pairings (e.g. from pairs to groups)
- using additional materials (e.g. adding a reference book)
- introducing new activities (e.g. introducing new speaking exercises)
- introducing new teaching methods (e.g. making the class more learner-centered)
- using new presentation technologies (e.g. moving from a whiteboard to presentation slides)

Course/Program level changes

- changing the course textbook (e.g. updating the current book)
- changing class sizes (e.g. making the classes smaller or larger)
- introducing ability grouping (e.g. placing high-level learners in a special advanced class)
- changing hiring policies (e.g. recruiting instructors with a knowledge of the specialist field)
- changing class loads and times (e.g. assigning instructors more classes at the beginning of the week)
- introducing a standardized assessment procedure (e.g. TOEIC)

Change often implies more work for the people implementing the change and also more work for those that the change affects. So, why bother? Those who advocate for change usually make the argument that the change will save time, save resources, and produce better results. But, in reality, we all have experienced changes that do the exact opposite and waste time and resources and leave a system in a worse position. Also, those who advocate for change may perceive the system differently to those working in it. For example, in an ESP context, administrators may want to introduce changes to save money by reducing the number of teachers and increasing the size of classes. But, the problem of costs is unlikely to be felt by the instructors and learners in the classroom, nor will the cost savings be felt as an advantage to them. Rather, the instructors are likely to see the changes as negatively affecting their working conditions, and the learners are likely to see the changes as a policy that reduces the quality of their education.

At the ground level, we can also find mismatches in the perceptions of change. An instructor might want to introduce new materials that better match the learners' needs. The learners, on the other hand, may be happy to use the current materials because they can be purchased second-hand at a local bookstore. Similarly, the instructor might want to introduce a new assessment format that better measures the learners' performance. However, the learners may be happier with the current test, because they are familiar with the format and can prepare for it better through careful study and revision of past tests.

Nation and Macalister (2010, p. 173) propose implementing a successful change policy in five steps:

Step 1: make sure that the change is really needed
Step 2: plan the type of change so that is not too great and not too small
Step 3: make sure that enough people see that the kind of change is possible
Step 4: use a wide range of change strategies
Step 5: be prepared for the change to take a long time

The first step is fairly obvious. But, again, it is important to stress that change is not always seen by everyone as beneficial. The more people that agree that change is necessary, the more likely it will be successful. The second step relates to work done by Stoller (1994, p. 314), who describes a "zone of innovation" that motivates individuals to accept change. The results show that successful innovation should not introduce "too little" or "too much" change along the six axes of explicitness, complexity/difficulty, compatibility, visibility, flexibility, and originality. The third step relates back to the first but emphasizes the importance that those who perceive the need for change and are responsible for implementing it (often the instructors) believe that the change is realistic and achievable.

The fourth step in Nation and Macalister's list is perhaps the most contentious aspect of change. How should it be done? Here, they cite Chin and Benne (1969) who describe three strategies: 1) power-coercive strategies, 2) rational-empirical strategies, and 3) normative-re-educative strategies. Power-coercive strategies introduce change through direct or indirect force. In a classroom setting, for example, an instructor may simply instruct learners to sit in a new position, assign them to a new pairing, or switch to using a different type of presentation format. The power difference that usually exists between instructors and learners would prevent the learners from raising any objections. Rational-empirical strategies are based on the premise that change can be introduced and adopted if evidence demonstrating the benefits of the change are shown to those whom it will affect. Using the same scenarios again, an instructor may first explain to learners why rotating seating positions, mixing with other learners, and using a variety of presentation formats will help them reach their target learning objectives, before initiating the changes. You can probably see, though, that there is still an element of power-coercion here. In contrast, normative-re-educative strategies are based on the premise that people's actions are strongly connected with the values and attitudes that they learn as members of a society or culture. Within this paradigm, introducing change requires a deep understanding of those values and attitudes. This knowledge can also be usefully applied when predicting which changes are likely to be quickly accepted and which will be initially resisted by the target group. As an example, Japan has a relatively well-defined social hierarchy, in which teachers are seen as authority figures. Asking learners to recite passages, complete dictations, and work in pairs and groups to complete a task is likely to meet little resistance. On the other hand, asking learners to challenge the instructors with questions, comments, and suggestions for improving a course might well be met with silence and confusion. This last point leads to the final step in introducing change. Depending on what you hope to change, you may need to be patient, take things slowly, and work hard to capture both the minds and hearts of those who will be affected.

One final point to note is that people can agree to change and even go through the motions of carrying out a change, but still reject it. In an ESP program, for example, a new course book might be introduced that instructors (reluctantly) agree to use. However, in the confines of their own classrooms, they may proceed to sabotage the change by pointing out the textbook's limitations to the learners and justifying to them why alternative materials should be used. This reality emphasizes the weakness of a power-coercive strategy and suggests that long-term successful innovation and change can only be achieved through a weighted combination of all three strategies.

Research ideas

Here are some possible ideas for small-scale or large-scale research projects that stem from the topics discussed in this chapter.

What do instructors fear when it comes to adopting an ESP approach?

This chapter has introduced a number of challenges that face instructors who hope to implement an ESP approach. Some of these overlap with the challenges faced by any EFL teacher, and other are unique to ESP. Conduct a survey of instructors with and without experience of ESP to find out what they fear are ESP's greatest challenges. Compare the opinions of both groups to find similarities and differences. Based on the findings, make suggestions for how to include the results in future ESP teacher training courses.

How is successful change achieved in ESP?

Relatively few ESP experts have documented in the literature the steps they had to take to initiate, design, develop, and maintain a successful ESP course or program. Locate an ESP course or program that has received either internal or external recognition, and carry out a case study on its growth. Next, try to identify the challenges that the designers had to overcome and some of the keys to its success. Finally, provide some lessons for others who might be undertaking a similar project.

Closing reflection

Now that you have come to the end of the chapter, you should understand some of the main challenges that administrators and instructors face when it comes to developing and running ESP courses and programs. You should also have some ideas for meeting and overcoming these challenges if and when you enter the world of ESP. Finally, you should be able to understand and maybe even follow the steps that ESP administrators and instructors take in order to introduce innovative changes to a teaching and learning environment.

Here are a few more questions to consider:

1 Which of the points covered in the chapter were new to you? Did you find them interesting and relevant in terms of your own learning goals? Were there any points that you found confusing or that you disagreed with?
2 What points from the chapter do you think you can immediately put to use in your own learning or teaching context?
3 Which of the three strategies for initiating change discussed in the chapter do you see most commonly adopted in educational settings?
4 If you were an administrator of an ESP course or program, how would you attempt to ensure that instructors were correctly adopting a new policy that you introduced?

Further resources

Research articles

Nesi, H. (2013). ESP and corpus studies. In B. Paltridge & S. Starfield (Eds.), *The handbook of English for specific purposes* (pp. 407–421). Walden, MA: Wiley Blackwell.

Useful corpora

Air Traffic Control Complete Corpus (Godfrey, 1994). Philadelphia: Linguistic Data Consortium, 1994. Retrieved from https://catalog.ldc. upenn.edu/LDC94S14A

British Academic Spoken English (BASE) Corpus. Retrieved from https://www2.warwick.ac.uk/fac/soc/al/research/collections/base

British Academic Written English (BAWE) Corpus. Retrieved from http://www2.warwick.ac.uk/fac/soc/al/research/collections/bawe

Business Letter Corpus. Retrieved from www.someya-net.com/concordancer/

Enron Email Dataset. Retrieved from www.cs.cmu.edu/~./enron/

Michigan Corpus of Academic Spoken English. Retrieved from https://quod.lib.umich.edu/cgi/c/corpus/corpus?c=micase
Michigan Corpus of Upper-Level Student Papers (MICUSP). Retrieved from http://micusp.elicorpora.info/
PERC Corpus ("Corpus of Professional English"). Retrieved from https://scn.jkn21.com/~percinfo/
PolyU Business Corpora. Retrieved from http://langbank.engl.polyu.edu.hk/corpus/polyu_business.html
SRI American Express travel agent dialogue corpus. Retrieved from www.ai.sri.com/~communic/amex/amex.html
The Twitter Political Corpus. Retrieved from www.usna.edu/Users/cs/nchamber/data/twitter/

Chapter 10

Moving forward in ESP

If you have read through all the previous chapters of this book, you should now have a good understanding of the history of ESP, its place in the world, its core principles, how people implement ESP in the real world, and some ways to deal with the challenges of using an ESP approach. In this final chapter, we will shift perspective and look briefly to the future of ESP. Knowing where the field is heading and what the future might bring can help you to notice opportunities and foresee possible problems, and allow you to prepare accordingly.

In this final chapter, I'll describe the future of ESP from four different perspectives: context, curriculum design, classroom practices, and research in ESP. Then, I'll discuss the contentious issue of how learners should best position themselves within their discourse communities and the role that ESP should have in empowering learners to close the gap between their current skills/knowledge and the skills/knowledge that the discipline community might want and accept.

By the end of the chapter, you should have a good idea about where ESP is heading, and understand what is meant by critical ESP. Most importantly, you should have built a strong foundation of knowledge and practice in ESP that will serve you well as you begin your own journey into the world of ESP.

Opening reflection

From what you have read about ESP in the previous chapters, where do you see ESP heading from now? Do you think ESP will be more or less relevant and/or important in the future compared to now? Why? What factors do you think will affect the future of ESP?

Commentary

Throughout this book, ESP has been used as an acronym for *English for Specific Purposes*. But, you may know that among the general public, ESP is more commonly associated with the completely different concept of *Extra Sensory Perception*: mind reading, fortune telling, and so on. During the writing of this book, I have in some way been using my own *Extra Sensory Perception* skills to try to read your mind and predict what questions and concerns you might have about ESP. Depending on how successful I have been, I hope you have got at least some of the answers you wanted. This reflection exercise turns the tables and gives you an opportunity to use your own *Extra Sensory Perception* skills to see into the future of ESP. Of course, the only way to really do this is to think carefully about the past and the present trends in ESP and then make good predictions based on what you know. There is no harm in trying to predict the future. In fact, it allows you to anticipate problems and notice opportunities. But, you should always remember that the future is inherently unpredictable. We can always be wrong.

The future of globalization and ESP

In recent years, we have seen huge political changes across the world that have been motivated, in part, by one of the driving forces of ESP: globalization. Globalization has enabled people to travel and meet people more easily. It has led to the rapid development of new technologies. It has also provided people and even countries with new opportunities. However, it is also abundantly clear that globalization is not always a good thing. Globalization has been blamed for the demise of local economies, the destruction of the environment, the growing instability in world financial markets, and the rise in terrorism. We see in countries such as the United Kingdom (UK) and the United States of America (USA) a growing support for political stances that emphasize domestic interests, the effects of which are still largely unknown.

What is clear is that the policies adopted by some of the world biggest economies, such as China, the European Union, the USA, India, Japan, and Germany, will have a continued and perhaps an even greater impact on the future needs of people to work in and with English-speaking communities. It follows that these policies will also have a major impact on ESP. Even so, it is difficult to imagine that the importance of ESP will be diminished anytime soon. In the case of the UK, for example, a vote in 2016 to leave the European Union was quickly followed by a government push to strengthen and form new political, business, and educational relationships with countries around the world. Clearly, English serves as an important lingua franca in the discussions and any future partnerships that emerge from these initiatives.

It is important to remember that many of the reasons for the growth of English in industry and academia are largely unaffected by recent events in the world. Companies continue to target international markets in their drive for greater profitability, and universities continue to target international students to stabilize and/or grow their student bodies. These trends mean that there are likely to be more opportunities for people who are knowledgeable about ESP and can develop effective language programs and courses that address the needs of a diverse group of learners in industry and academia.

The future of ESP curriculum design

In almost every major industry in the world, the trend toward 'bigger is better' appears unstoppable. In the information technology (IT) world, we see the growth of massive tech companies like Apple, Amazon, Google, and Facebook. In the pharmaceutical industry, we see more and more company mergers and acquisitions leading to companies like GlaxoSmithKline, AstraZeneca, and Gilead. In the finance industry, we see a similar trend of mergers and acquisitions leading to growth of 'mega' banks like the Industrial and Commercial Bank of China, HSBC Holdings, JPMorgan Chase & Co., BNP Paribas, and Mitsubishi UFJ Financial Group. The same 'bigger is better' policy can be seen in the industries of agriculture, energy, food, manufacturing, media, retail, real estate, transport, and many others.

One industry that has remained relatively isolated from this trend is the education industry. Schools and universities continue to operate largely independently, and we see few mergers and acquisitions. However, we can predict that in the future this will change. In fact, we are already seeing signs of a 'bigger is better' movement beginning to develop in education. One example is the growth of satellite campuses of high-ranked universities in countries with rapidly growing economies, such as those in Africa (Oguntoyinbo, 2015) and Asia (Neumark, 2013). Carnegie Mellon University, for example, has created a new campus in Kigali, Rwanda; Yale University has created a new campus in Singapore; and New York University has created one in Abu Dhabi (one of many campuses throughout the world). We can also see a rapid rise in the creation of Massive Open Online Courses (MOOCs) that give an institution exposure to thousands if not millions of online learners using platforms such as *Coursera* (www.coursera.org) and *FutureLearn* (www.futurelearn.com), which were discussed in Chapter 6.

If the 'bigger is better' trend in academia continues to grow, this is likely to have a profound effect on ESP curriculum design. First, institutions will have a greater imperative to create ESP courses and programs that address the needs of their international learners. It is also likely that these courses and programs will require some sort of centralized coordination. In this scenario, no longer will ESP 'practitioners' need to or be able to design their own courses. Instead, teams of ESP course experts and subject specialists can be contracted to work together to create effective courses and programs that address a wide range of learners not only in different disciplines, but also with different native languages and cultural backgrounds. It follows that at the program level, a wide-angled approach to ESP is perhaps the most manageable. But, it also follows that very narrow-angled ESP courses can be usefully (and profitably) developed for large but widely dispersed groups of learners. Problems related to the creation of materials, the hiring of local staff, the management of multiple small-sized classrooms, and so on, are avoided through an online delivery system. We see this already in the creation of very narrow-focused MOOC courses on topics such as persuasive writing, intercultural communication, data visualization, and others too numerous to mention. In short, the wide-angled and narrow-angled approaches to ESP each look to have an important role to play.

In addition, a 'bigger is better' growth in academia will almost certainly lead to the increasing importance of English-Medium Instruction (EMI). Again, evidence for this already exists in the fact that the number of English-mediated MOOC courses massively outweighs the number of MOOCs in any other language. This raises an interesting possibility. Large, prestigious, high-ranked international education institutions can offer English-mediated specialist subject courses developed by some of the world's leading researchers, some perhaps with Nobel prizes. These courses can be managed centrally, accessed by people across the world, and provide a very high level and quality of content. If an institution in a non-English speaking country adopts one or more of these courses, not only do they save time and money developing their own courses, but they also have less need to hire local subject specialists. On the other hand, it is clear that they would have an important need for ESP instructors to provide learners with language support. Perhaps the future of ESP is brighter than any current ESP instructor can imagine.

The future of ESP classroom materials and methods

In their seminal work on ESP, Dudley-Evans and St. John (1998) discussed the future of materials design by explaining that there was a need for more flexibility, explanations, practice items, and reference resources. They also suggested a need for more modular-based courses, more sociological framing of materials, and a better foundation of knowledge in terms of what language is used, when, and with what effect. Since 1998, ESP materials development has advanced in various ways, but there is still a tendency, especially in Asia and the Middle East, for instructors to rely on rather fixed, linear, decontextualized, generic, textbook-based materials.

In order to realize some of the predictions made by Dudley-Evans and St. John (1998), ESP instructors almost certainly need to embrace the use of new materials. Perhaps the most important of these is the discipline-specific corpus. As explained in Chapter 6, discipline-specific corpora are now much easier to find or create than ever before. They empower instructors and learners by giving them direct access to the language of the target discourse community. They circumvent the need to always consult with a subject specialist by revealing the insights of specialists through searches and results inspection. And, they offer new possibilities for in-class teaching and learning by providing flexibility in content delivery, providing learners with plenty of examples and practice items, and serving as a unique language resource for learners.

Data and analysis tools have had a huge and extremely valuable impact in almost all fields of study. From this perspective, it seems clear that large, well-designed corpora that can be accessed through powerful and easy-to-use corpus analysis software will have an equally huge and valuable impact on future ESP materials and methods development. We can also imagine the emergence of other new technologies that can assist learners in understanding their field, and help them to experience and interact in the world of their target discourse community. One obvious example is the technology of virtual reality (VR). Already this is being used in medical training; for example, to help dental students to learn and practice drilling, cavity preparation, and so on (Tse, Harwin, Barrow, Quinn, & Cox, 2010). There are also VR applications that help people to overcome their nerves when giving academic presentations and interacting in business meetings (Zakrzewski, 2016). We can anticipate that the next generation of learners will be quite comfortable with such technology. The challenge for ESP instructors will be how to familiarize themselves with these new resources.

The future of ESP research

In a study of research methods used in the journals *English for Specific Purposes* and the *Journal of English for Academic Purposes* between 2003 and 2012, Gollin-Kies (2014) found a strong preference for qualitative studies on written discourse that were based on a manual or computer-based analysis of a corpus. She also found that when qualitative studies were not focused on discourse, there was growing tendency to use ethnographic and mixed methods. As Dressen-Hammouda (2013) explains, these methods provide us with rich insights into the sociocultural setting in which ESP exists.

We can predict that future ESP research will continue in the same manner as it has in the past, with a strong focus on the qualitative analysis of linguistic and rhetorical features of written texts. We can also expect that corpora will continue to be the primary source of data, although the data obtained from ethnographic and mixed methods approaches will also contribute greatly to our understanding of how those texts are situated in the discourse community. Importantly, the growing availability of spoken corpora and multi-modal corpora suggests that we might also see ESP researchers moving away from written genres and begin looking at the many other genres that are used in target language settings.

It is also easy to imagine a future in which ESP research becomes increasingly dominated by quantitative analyses of corpora and other language data. Advanced statistical and quantitative approaches are being used increasingly in many areas of educational research, notably testing. We also see their use in language data mapping and social media studies. As statistics packages and data analysis toolkits become cheaper and easier to use, their use and impact in the field of ESP can only grow. This leads to another area of ESP research that seems likely to grow in importance: the creation and application of hardware and software tools that facilitate communication within and between specialist disciplines. The technology of virtual reality (VR) has already been mentioned in this chapter. But, at a more mundane level, we can see the rapid development of software writing aids, plagiarism detection systems, automatic simultaneous translation systems, and an almost never-ending list of new technologies emerging from research in artificial intelligence (AI). The potential disruptive influences that these innovations can have on ESP research, teaching and learning are difficult to predict, but they certainly cannot be discounted.

TASK 10.1 Creating a proposal for the future of ESP

Review the discussions of the future of ESP from the perspectives of globalization, curriculum design, classroom materials and methods, and research. Choose one of the perspectives and try to support the positions presented in the chapter with further evidence from your own experience and studies. Now, try to locate evidence from your experience and studies that contradicts the positions presented. Consider all the data you have collected and form your own opinion about the future of ESP from the perspective you investigated.

Contentious issues in ESP: critical ESP

Throughout this book, ESP has been presented as a force of good in English language education. ESP is built on the principle of needs, with those of all stakeholders taken into consideration. The underlying assumption we make is that addressing needs leads to a better world for the stakeholders concerned. The challenge, of course, is balancing those needs. For example, learners may *have to* develop their speaking fluency to achieve their goal of being successful presenters, but *lack* that skill, and for whatever reason, they may *want* to study reading. ESP instructors, on the other hand, usually *have to* administer the classes, but might *lack* adequate preparation time, and *want* to teach the learners about grammar and vocabulary, because that is their research interest. Similarly, an ESP administrator of the program might *have to* manage it, but *lack* the skills, and *want* to work for a minimal time on the project.

Presented in this way, the main challenges in ESP seem to be deciding what the needs are, prioritizing them in some way, and then finding a way to balance them all. Indeed, the answers to these questions have been the focus of all the chapters in this book. But, one question that we have not considered is: "how do we know that the needs analysis is correct?" What if the needs analysis is biased, or shortsighted, or simply wrong? Is it possible that the mission of ESP could be ultimately restricting the opportunities of learners?

For much of its history, ESP has been seen as a pragmatic approach that prioritizes the immediate or near-future needs of learners. From this perspective, the aim of ESP is to help learners to address their needs, allowing them to be able to actively participate within the discourse community of a target language setting. While it is known that the needs of learners can vary dramatically depending on the setting and that the setting itself will change depending on the community that it forms from, the goal of being accepted into the community has largely gone unchallenged. In the words of Basturkmen (2006, p. 140), the conventional role of ESP has been "to close the gap between the students' present state of skills and knowledge and the level required by members of the target environment".

Critical ESP is a branch of research that questions this premise. Perhaps ESP should not be encouraging learners to adopt or adapt to the norms and practices of the target discourse community, especially when those norms and practices serve as a barrier to entry. Instead, maybe ESP instructors should be providing learners with the knowledge and skills to actively challenge how the discourse community operates. For example, in EAP settings, instructors might help learners to understand the roles played by editors and reviewers as gatekeepers in the research article submission process. They can also raise questions in the minds of learners about the need for their work to be checked (and approved) by 'native speakers' prior to submission. In EOP settings, ESP instructors might help learners understand how the cultures of English-speaking countries can affect and shape international business practices, and help them reflect on what might be lost as a result.

A large body of research has emerged out of the critical ESP movement, including the frequently cited works of Benesch (2001), Chun (2009), and Pennycook (1997). There have also been challenges to this position and defenses of a more pragmatic approach from scholars such as Allison (1996, 1998), who argues for "functional efficiency" (1998, p. 314) in ESP teaching. It is interesting to note that recent innovations in ESP classroom practices have addressed some of the concerns of critical ESP. Data-Driven Learning (DDL) methods, for example, expose learners to the huge variation and quality in writing that exists in published research articles. Once learners have seen for themselves that high-impact and widely cited published articles can contain a 'non-standard' English expressions and clear errors in grammar and vocabulary use, they can start to see their own developing language abilities from a more balanced perspective.

If you are interested in reading more about critical ESP, you can find critiques of both sides of the debate in the works of Basturkmen (2006) and

Morgan (2009). A more comprehensive and in-depth review of the different positions is presented by Starfield (2013a).

Research ideas

Here are some possible ideas for small-scale or large-scale research projects that stem from the topics discussed in this chapter.

What can technology do for ESP?

Review recent technological innovations that have a potential impact on language education. Focus on one of the technologies you identify and discuss its relative merits and disadvantages from an ESP perspective. If possible, experiment with the technology in a real ESP classroom and report your findings.

What barriers exist on the road to publication?

Choose a specialist research journal with an English-only submission policy in a field that interests you. Review the journal's article submission procedures and consider which of them might be biased in favor of native speakers of English (regardless of their knowledge and expertise in the target field). Try to locate one or more non-native speakers of English who regularly submits or hopes to submit articles to that journal. Conduct a case study to find out what steps they need to take in order to get their work published.

Closing reflection

Now that you have come to the end of the chapter, you should have some ideas about how ESP might develop in the future. Hopefully, some of these directions interest you to the extent that you will pursue them as part of your own ESP learning and development. You should also understand why some people critique the principles on which ESP is based and question its overall mission. If you read more about the debate on critical ESP and then tie that in with what you have learned about ESP in this book, you should be in a good position to defend ESP and explain to others why ESP has grown to become one of the most important and influential areas of English language teaching today. ESP most certainly has a bright future. Hopefully you can play an important part in that future.

Here are a few more questions to consider:

1 Which of the points covered in the chapter were new to you? Did you find them interesting and relevant in terms of your own

learning goals? Were there any points that you found confusing or that you disagreed with?

2 What points from the chapter do you think you can immediately put to use in your own learning or teaching context?

3 On which side of the critical ESP debate do you stand? Do you think ESP instructors should employ 'functional efficiency' in their teaching? Or, do you think a critical perspective should be an essential component of every lesson?

Further resources

Book chapters

Belcher, D. (2009). What ESP is and can be: An introduction. In D. Belcher (Ed.), *English for specific purposes in theory and practice* (pp. 1–20). Ann Arbor, MI: University of Michigan Press.

Belcher, D. (2013). The future of ESP research: Resources for access and choice. In B. Paltridge & S. Starfield (Eds.), *Handbook of English for specific purposes* (pp. 535–551). New York: Wiley-Blackwell.

Research articles

Bloch, J. (2013). Technology and ESP. In B. Paltridge & S. Starfield (Eds.), *The handbook of English for specific purposes* (pp. 385–402). Walden, MA: Wiley Blackwell.

Brunton, M. (2009). An account of ESP – with possible future directions. *English for Specific Purposes*, *3*(24), 1–15.

Carrell, P. L. (1987). ESP in applied linguistics: Refining research agenda implications and future directions of research on second language reading. *English for Specific Purposes*, 6(3), 233–244.

Massive Open Online Courses (MOOCs)

Coursera Retrieved from www.coursera.org/
FutureLearn Retrieved from www.futurelearn.com/

References

Abasi, A. R., Akbari, N., & Graves, B. (2006). Discourse appropriation, construction of identities, and the complex issue of plagiarism: ESL students writing in graduate school. *Journal of Second Language Writing*, *15*(2), 102–117.

Aldrich, J. (1995). Correlations genuine and spurious in Pearson and Yule. *Statistical Science*, *10*(4), 364–376. doi:10.1214/ss/1177009870. Retrieved from https://projecteuclid.org/euclid.ss/1177009870.

Allison, D. (1996). Pragmatist discourse and English for academic purposes. *English for Specific Purposes*, *15*(2), 85–103.

Allison, D. (1998). Response to Pennycook: Whether, why and how. *English for Specific Purposes*, *17*(3), 313–316.

Anthony, L. (1997). English for specific purposes: What does it mean? Why is it different? *On-CUE*, *5*(3), 9–10.

Anthony, L. (2009). ESP at the center of program design. In K. Fukui, J. Noguchi, & N. Watanabe (Eds.), *Towards ESP bilingualism* (pp. 18–35). Osaka, Japan: Osaka University Press. Retrieved from www.laurenceanthony.net/research/20090402_esp_bilingualism_chap/anthony_esp_bilinguaism_chp.pdf.

Anthony, L. (2011). Products, processes and practitioners: A critical look at the importance of specificity in ESP. *Taiwan International ESP Journal*, *3*(2), 19–50.

Anthony, L. (2014). *AntWordProfiler* [Computer Software]. Tokyo, Japan: Waseda University. Retrieved from www.laurenceanthony.net/software/antwordprofiler/.

Anthony, L. (2016). Introducing corpora and corpus tools into the technical writing classroom through Data-Driven Learning (DDL). In J. Flowerdew & T. Costley (Eds.), *Discipline specific writing* (pp. 162–180). Abingdon, UK: Routledge.

Anthony, L. (2017a). *AntConc* (Version 3.5.0) [Computer Software]. Tokyo, Japan: Waseda University. Retrieved from www.laurenceanthony.net/software/antconc/.

Anthony, L. (2017b). *AntCorGen* (Version 1.1.0) [Computer Software]. Tokyo, Japan: Waseda University. Retrieved from www.laurenceanthony.net/software/antcorgen/.

Anthony, L. (2017c). *AntQuickTools* [Computer Software]. Tokyo, Japan: Waseda University. Retrieved from www.laurenceanthony.net/software/antquicktools/.

Anthony, L., & Baker, P. (2017). *ProtAnt* (Version 1.2.1) [Computer Software]. Tokyo, Japan: Waseda University. Retrieved from www.laurenceanthony.net/software/protant/.

Anthony, L., & Bowen, M. (2013). The language of mathematics: A corpus-based analysis of research article writing in a neglected field. *Asian ESP Journal*, *9*(2), 5–25.

Arnó-Macià, E., & Mancho-Barés, G. (2015). The role of content and language in Content and Language Integrated Learning (CLIL) at university: Challenges and implications for ESP. *English for Specific Purposes*, *37*, 63–73.

Artemeva, N., & Freedman, A. (Eds.). (2008). *Rhetorical genre studies and beyond*. Winnipeg: Inkshed Publications.

Ausubel, D. P. (1968). *Educational psychology: A cognitive view*. New York, US: Holt, Rinehart and Winston.

Barber, C. L. (1962). Some measurable characteristics of modern scientific prose. *Contributions to English Syntax and Philology*, 21–43.

Bargiela-Chiappini, F., & Zhang, Z. (2013). Business English. In B. Paltridge & S. Starfield (Eds.), *The handbook of English for specific purposes* (pp. 193–212). Walden, MA: Wiley Blackwell.

Barron, C. (1992). Cultural syntonicity: Co-operative relationships between the ESP unit and other departments. *Hong Kong Papers in Linguistics and Language Teaching*, *15*, 1–14.

Basturkmen, H. (2006). *Ideas and options in English for specific purposes*. Abingdon, UK: Routledge.

Bawarshi, A. S., & Reiff, M. J. (2010). *Genre: An introduction to history, theory, research, and pedagogy*. West Lafayette, IN: Parlor Press.

Beaubien, G. (2013). Disgraced by doping, can Lance Armstrong redeem himself? *Public Relations Tactics*, *20*(2), 6.

Belcher, D. (2009). What ESP is and can be: An introduction. In D. Belcher (Ed.), *English for specific purposes in theory and practice* (pp. 1–20). Ann Arbor, MI: University of Michigan Press.

Belcher, D. (2013). The future of ESP research: Resources for access and choice. In B. Paltridge & S. Starfield (Eds.), *Handbook of English for specific purposes* (pp. 535–551). New York: Wiley-Blackwell.

Benesch, S. (2001). *Critical English for academic purposes*. Mahwah, NJ: Lawrence Erlbaum.

Bhatia, V. K. (2008). Genre analysis, ESP and professional practice. *English for Specific Purposes*, *27*, 161–174.

Biber, D. (1988). *Variation across speech and writing*. Cambridge, UK: Cambridge University Press.

Biber, D. (1992). On the complexity of discourse complexity: A multidimensional analysis. *Discourse Processes*, *15*, 133–163.

Bilici, H. B. (2016). The effectiveness of year 1 international studies strand of an ESP program in year 2: Student perceptions. *Asian EFL Journal*, *91*, 90–106.

Bloch, J. (2013). Technology and ESP. In B. Paltridge & S. Starfield (Eds.), *The handbook of English for specific purposes* (pp. 385–402). Walden, MA: Wiley Blackwell.

Bloor, M., & Bloor, T. (1986). Languages for specific purposes: Practice and theory. *Occasional Paper-Centre for Language and Communication Studies*, *19*, 1–35. Retrieved from http://files.eric.ed.gov/fulltext/ED280285.pdf.

Blue, G. M. (1988). Individualising academic writing tuition. In P. C. Robinson (Ed.), *Academic writing: Process and product*. ELT Document 129. London, UK: Modern English Publications.

Blue, G. M., & Harun, M. (2003). Hospitality language as a professional skill. *English for Specific Purposes*, *22*(1), 73–91.

Bolton, K., & Graddol, D. (2012). English in China today. *English Today*, *28*(3), 3–9.

Bordons, M., & Gómez, I. (2004). Towards a single language in science? A Spanish view. *Serials*, *17*(2), 189–195.

Bosher, S. (2013). English for nursing. In B. Paltridge & S. Starfield (Eds.), *The handbook of English for specific purposes* (pp. 263–282). Walden, MA: Wiley Blackwell.

Boulton, A., Carter-Thomas, S., & Rowley-Jolivet, E. (Eds.). (2012). *Corpus-informed research and learning in ESP: Issues and applications* (Vol. 52). Amsterdam: John Benjamins Publishing.

Bremner, S. (2010). Collaborative writing: Bridging the gap between the textbook and the workplace. *English for Specific Purposes*, *29*(2), 121–132.

Brenn-White, M., & Faethe, E. (2013). English-taught Master's programs in Europe: A 2013 update. *Institute of International Education*. Retrieved from www.iie.org/mobility.

Brinton, D., Snow, M. A., & Wesche, M. B. (2003). *Content-based second language instruction*. Ann Arbor, MI: University of Michigan Press.

Brown, J. D. (1989). Language program evaluation: A synthesis of existing possibilities. In K. Johnson (Ed.), *The second language curriculum* (pp. 222–241). Cambridge, UK: Cambridge University Press.

Brown, J. D. (2016). *Introducing needs analysis and English specific purposes*. Abingdon, UK: Routledge.

Brown, J. D., & Hudson, T. (2002). *Criterion-referenced language testing*. Cambridge, UK: Cambridge University Press.

Brunton, M. (2009). An account of ESP – With possible future directions. *English for Specific Purposes*, *3*(24), 1–15.

Candlin, C. N., Bhatia, V. K., & Jensen, C. H. (2002). Developing legal writing materials for English second language learners: Problems and perspectives. *English for Specific Purposes*, *21*(4), 299–320.

Carrell, P. L. (1987). ESP in applied linguistics: Refining research agenda implications and future directions of research on second language reading. *English for Specific Purposes*, *6*(3), 233–244.

Chan, C. S. (2009). Forging a link between research and pedagogy: A holistic framework for evaluating business English materials. *English for Specific Purposes*, *28*(2), 125–136.

Chang, C. F., & Kuo, C. H. (2011). A corpus-based approach to online materials development for writing research articles. *English for Specific Purposes*, *30*(3), 222–234.

Charles, M. (2013). English for academic purposes. In B. Paltridge & S. Starfield (Eds.), *The handbook of English for specific purposes* (pp. 137–154). Walden, MA: Wiley Blackwell.

Charles, M., & Pecorari, D. (2016). *Introducing English for academic purposes*. Abingdon, UK: Routledge.

Cheng, S. (2013). Rethinking authenticity: On the implementation and practice of an English for tourism class. In W. Tsou & S. Kao (Eds.), *Towards a new paradigm for English teaching and learning in higher education in Taiwan* (pp. 155–176). Taipei, Taiwan: Bookman Books.

Chin, R., & Benne, K. D. (1969). *General strategies for effecting changes in human systems*. In W. G. Bennis, K. D. Benne, & R. Chin (Eds.), The planning of change (pp. 32–59). New York: Holt, Rinehart & Winston.

Ching-ning, C., Wei, L., & Li-hua, K. (2008). Collaborative teaching in an ESP program. *Asian EFL Journal*, *10*(4), 114–133.
Choi, L. L. S. (2005). Literature review: Issues surrounding education of English-as-a-Second Language (ESL) nursing students. *Journal of Transcultural Nursing*, *16*(3), 263–268.
Chomsky, N. (1957). *Syntactic structures*. Berlin, Germany: Mouton de Gruyter.
Chun, C. W. (2009). Contesting neoliberal discourses in EAP: Critical praxis in an IEP classroom. *Journal of English for Academic Purposes*, *8*(2), 111–120.
Cobb, T. (2017). *Compleat Lexical Tutor* [Computer Software]. Retrieved from https://www.lextutor.ca.
Comas-Forgas, R., & Sureda-Negre, J. (2010). Academic plagiarism: Explanatory factors from students' perspective. *Journal of Academic Ethics*, *8*(3), 217–232.
Coxhead, A. (2000). A new academic word list. *TESOL Quarterly*, *34*(2), 213–238.
Cromer, D. E. (1992). English: The lingua franca of international scientific communication. *Science & Technology Libraries*, *12*(1), 21–34.
Currie, P. (1998). Staying out of trouble: Apparent plagiarism and academic survival. *Journal of Second Language Writing*, *7*(1), 1–18.
Ding, A., & Campion, G. (2016). EAP teacher development. In K. Hyland & P. Shaw (Eds.), *The Routledge handbook of English for academic purposes*. Abingdon, UK: Routledge.
Douglas, D. (2000). *Assessing languages for specific purposes*. Cambridge, UK: Cambridge University Press.
Dovey, T. (2006). What purposes, specifically? Re-thinking purposes and specificity in the context of the 'new vocationalism'. *English for specific purposes*, *25*(4), 387–402.
Dressen-Hammouda, D. (2013). Ethnographic approaches to ESP research. In B. Paltridge & S. Starfield (Eds.), *The handbook of English for specific purposes* (pp. 501–517). Walden, MA: Wiley Blackwell.
Dubin, F., & Olshtain, E. (1986). *Course design: Developing programs and materials for language learning*. Cambridge, UK: Cambridge University Press.
Dudley-Evans, T., & St. John, M. J. (1998). *Developments in English for specific purposes: A multi-disciplinary approach*. Cambridge, UK: Cambridge University Press.
Ellis, R. (2003). *Task-based language learning and teaching*. Oxford, UK: Oxford University Press.
Emery, H., & Roberts, A. (2008). *Aviation English*. Basingstoke, UK: Macmillan Publishers.
Erkaya, O. R. (2009). Plagiarism by Turkish students: Causes and solutions. Asian. *EFL Journal*, *11*(2), 86–103.
Ertmer, P. A., & Newby, T. J. (1993). Behaviorism, cognitivism, constructivism: Comparing critical features from an instructional design perspective. *Performance Improvement Quarterly*, *6*(4), 50–72.
Estrada, R., & Bruggeman, P. (2014). *2014 Application trends survey report*. Graduate Management Admission Council. Retrieved from www.gmac.com/market-intelligence-and-research/research-library/admissions-and-application-trends/2014-app-trends-report.aspx.
Farris, C., Trofimovich, P., Segalowitz, N., & Gatbonton, E. (2008). Air traffic communication in a second language: Implications of cognitive factors for training and assessment. *TESOL Quarterly*, *42*(3), 397–410.

Feak, C. B., & Salehzadeh, J. (2001). Challenges and issues in developing an EAP video listening placement assessment: A view from one program. *English for Specific Purposes, 20*, 477–493.

Ferguson, G. (2013). English for medical purposes. In B. Paltridge & S. Starfield (Eds.), *The handbook of English for specific purposes* (pp. 243–262). Walden, MA: Wiley Blackwell.

Finch, A. (2014). Caring in English: ESP for nurses. *International Journal of English Language Teaching, 1*(1), 1–10.

Flowerdew, J. (2013). English for research publication purposes. In B. Paltridge & S. Starfield (Eds.), *The handbook of English for specific purposes* (pp. 301–322). Walden, MA: Wiley Blackwell.

Flowerdew, L. (2002). Corpus-based analyses in EAP. In J. Flowerdew (Ed.), *Academic discourse* (pp. 95–114). London, UK: Longman.

Flowerdew, L. (2013). Needs analysis and curriculum development in ESP. In B. Paltridge & S. Starfield (Eds.), *The handbook of English for specific purposes* (pp. 325–346). Walden, MA: Wiley Blackwell.

Flowerdew, J., & Peacock, M. (2001). The EAP curriculum: Issues, methods, and challenges. In J. Flowerdew & M. Peacock (Eds.), *Research perspectives on English for academic purposes* (pp. 177–194). Cambridge, UK: Cambridge University Press.

Fortanet-Gómez, I., & Räisänen, C. (Eds.). (2008). *ESP in European higher education: Integrating language and content* (Vol. 4). Amsterdam: John Benjamins Publishing.

Freedman, A., & Medway, P. (Eds.). (1994). *Genre and the new rhetoric*. London, UK: Taylor & Francis.

Friedman, T. (2005). *The world is flat: A brief history of the globalized world in the 21st century*. London, UK: Allen Lane.

Friginal, E. (2007). Outsourced call centers and English in the Philippines. *World Englishes, 26*(3), 331–345.

Friginal, E. (2013). Assessment of Oral Performance in Outsourced Call Centers. *English for Specific Purposes, 32*, 25–35.

Giménez, J. C. (1996). Process assessment in ESP: Input, throughput and output. *English for Specific Purposes, 15*(3), 233–241.

Godfrey, J. (1994). *Air traffic control complete LDC94S14A*. Philadelphia: Linguistic Data Consortium. Retrieved from https://catalog.ldc.upenn.edu/LDC94S14A.

Gollin-Kies, S. (2014). Methods reported in ESP research articles: A comparative survey of two leading journals. *English for Specific Purposes*, 27–34.

Graddol, D. (1997). *The future of English?: A guide to forecasting the popularity of the English language in the 21st century*. London, UK: British Council.

Green, A., Fangqing, W., Cochrane, P., Dyson, J., & Paun, C. (2012). English spreads as teaching language in universities worldwide. *University World News, 229*. Retrieved from www.universityworldnews.com/article.php?story=20120621131543827.

Gregory Dawes, B. S. (2001). Communicating nursing care and crossing language barriers. *Aorn Journal, 73*(5), 892, 894.

Halliday, M. A. K. (1978). *Language as a social semiotic: Social interpretation of language and meaning*. London, UK: Edward Arnold.

Halliday, M. A. K. (1989). Register variation. In M. A. K. Halliday & R. Hasan (Eds.), *Language, context, and text: Aspects of language in a social-semiotic perspective* (pp. 29–43). Oxford: Oxford University Press.

Harwood, N. (2005). What do we want EAP teaching materials for? *Journal of English for Academic Purposes*, *4*(2), 149–161.

Henter, R. (2014). Affective factors involved in learning a foreign language. *Procedia-Social and Behavioral Sciences*, *127*, 373–378.

Hoffmann, S., & Evert, S. (2006). BNCweb (CQP-edition): The marriage of two corpus tools. *Corpus Technology and Language Pedagogy: New Resources, New Tools, New Methods*, *3*, 177–195. Retrieved from http://corpora.lancs.ac.uk/BNCweb/Hoffmann-Evert.pdf.

Holme, R. (1996). *ESP ideas: Recipes for teaching professional and academic English*. London, UK: Longman.

Huckin, T. (2003). Specificity in LSP. *Ibérica*, *5*, 3–17. Retrieved from www.redalyc.org/html/2870/287026293001/.

Hughes, A. (2007). *Testing for language teachers*. Cambridge, UK: Cambridge University Press.

Hutchinson, T., & Waters, A. (1987). *English for specific purposes*. Cambridge, UK: Cambridge University Press.

Hyland, K. (2002). Specificity revisited: How far should we go now? *English for Specific Purposes*, *21*(4), 385–395.

Hyland, K. (2004). *Disciplinary discourses: Social interactions in academic writing*. Ann Arbor, MI: University of Michigan Press.

Hyland, K. (2008). As can be seen: Lexical bundles and disciplinary variation. *English for Specific Purposes*, *27*(1), 4–21.

Hyland, K. (2017). English in the disciplines: Arguments for specificity. *ESP Today*, *5*(1), 5–23.

Hyland, K., & Bondi, M. (Eds.). (2006). *Academic discourse across disciplines*. Bern, Switzerland: Peter Lang.

Ibrahim, E. H. E., Sarudin, I., & Muhamad, A. J. (2016). The relationship between vocabulary size and reading comprehension of ESL learners. *English Language Teaching*, *9*(2), 116.

ICEF Monitor. (2013). *Hong Kong's allure underscores strengthening Asian education hubs*. Retrieved from http://monitor.icef.com/2013/09/hong-kongs-allure-underscores-strengthening-asian-education-hubs/.

ICEF Monitor. (2014). *Foreign applications to Hong Kong universities up sharply this year*. Retrieved from http://monitor.icef.com/2012/07/foreign-applications-to-hong-kong-universities-up-sharply-this-year/.

Invernizzi, E. (2010). *Which English should we use? From local Englishes to English as a Lingua Franca*. Euprera. Retrieved from www.euprera.org/?p=89.

Johns, T. (1991). Should you be persuaded: Two examples of data-driven learning. *ELR Journal*, *4*, 1–16.

Jones, G. M. (1990). ESP textbooks: Do they really exist? *English for Specific Purposes*, *9*(1), 89–93.

Jordan, R. R. (1997). *English for academic purposes: A guide and resource book for teachers*. Cambridge, UK: Cambridge University Press.

Kang, H. (2012). English-only instruction at Korean universities: Help or hindrance to higher learning? *English Today*, *28*(1), 29–34.

Koike, I., Takada, T., Matsui, J., & Terauchi, H. (2010). *Kigyo ga motomeru eigoryoku* (in Japanese) [English skills: What do companies really need?]. Tokyo, Japan: Asahi Press.

Kuo, C. H. (1993). Problematic issues in EST materials development. *English for Specific Purposes*, *12*(2), 171–181.

Lackstrom, J., Selinker, L., & Trimble, L. (1973). Technical rhetorical principles and grammatical choice. *TESOL Quarterly*, 127–136.

Larsen, P. O., & von Ins, M. (2010). The rate of growth in scientific publication and the decline in coverage provided by Science Citation Index. *Scientometrics*, *84*(3), 575–603.

Larsen-Freeman, D., & Anderson, M. (2013). *Techniques and principles in language teaching*, 3rd ed. Oxford, UK: Oxford University Press.

Leckie, G., & Baird, J. (2011). Rater effects on essay scoring: A multilevel analysis of severity drift, central tendency, and rater experience. *Journal of Educational Measurement*, *48*(4), 399–418.

Leech, G. (1997). Teaching and language corpora: A convergence. In A. Wichmann, S. Fligelstone, T. McEnery & G. Knowles (Eds.), *Teaching and language corpora* (pp. 1–23). New York: Addison Wesley Longman.

Lillis, T., & Curry, M. J. (2010). *Academic writing in a global context*. London, UK: Routledge.

Lockwood, J. (2012). Developing an English for specific purpose curriculum for Asian call centres: How theory can inform practice. *English for Specific Purposes*, *31*(1), 14–24.

Louhiala-Salminen, L., Charles, M., & Kankaanranta, A. (2005). English as a lingua franca in Nordic corporate mergers: Two case companies. *English for Specific Purposes*, *24*(4), 401–421.

Love, A. (1993). Lexico-grammatical features of geology textbooks: Process and product revisited. *English for Specific Purposes*, *12*(3), 197–218.

Madeleine, B. L. L. (2007). Lost in translation. *Nature*, *445*, 454–455.

Magkilat, B. (2014). Strong call center growth continues. *Manila Bulletin*. Retrieved from www.mb.com.ph/strong-call-center-growth-continues/.

Marra, M. (2013). English in the workplace. In B. Paltridge & S. Starfield (Eds.), *The handbook of English for specific purposes* (pp. 175–192). Walden, MA: Wiley Blackwell.

Maslen, G. (2014). Mass movement of the world's students. *University World News*, *305*. Retrieved from www.universityworldnews.com/article.php?story=20140129200018337.

McCabe, D. L., Butterfield, K. D., & Trevino, L. K. (2006). Academic dishonesty in graduate business programs: Prevalence, causes, and proposed action. *Academy of Management Learning & Education*, *5*(3), 294–305.

McCabe, D. L., & Trevino, L. K. (1993). Academic dishonesty: Honor codes and other contextual influences. *The Journal of Higher Education*, *64*(5), 522–538.

McDonough, J., & Shaw, C. (2013). *Materials and Methods in ELT*. Oxford, UK: John Wiley & Sons.

McGerr, P., & Allum, V. (2010). *Cambridge English for nursing*. Cambridge, UK: Cambridge University Press.

Miller, C. R. (1984). Genre as social action. *Quarterly Journal of Speech*, *70*, 151–167.

Moder, C. L. (2013). Aviation English. In B. Paltridge & S. Starfield (Eds.), *The handbook of English for specific purposes* (pp. 227–242). Walden, MA: Wiley Blackwell.

Morgan, B. (2009). Fostering transformative practitioners for critical EAP: Possibilities and challenges. *Journal of English for Academic Purposes, 8*(2), 86–99.

Munby, J. (1978). *Communicative syllabus design: A sociolinguistic model for designing the content of purpose-specific language programmes*. Cambridge, UK: Cambridge University Press.

Nakamura, J. (2014). Workplace English language needs of Japanese business undergraduates. *OnCUE Journal, 7*(3), 151–167.

Nation, I. S. P. (2001). *Learning vocabulary in another language*. Cambridge, UK: Cambridge University Press.

Nation, I. S. P., & Macalister, J. (2010). *Language curriculum design*. Abingdon, UK: Routledge.

Neeley, T. (2011). Language and globalization: 'Englishnization' at Rakuten. *Harvard Business School Organizational Behavior Unit Case*, 412–002. Retrieved from www.hbs.edu/faculty/Pages/item.aspx?num=40849.

Neeley, T. (2012). Global business speaks English. *Harvard Business Review*. Retrieved from https://hbr.org/2012/05/global-business-speaks-english.

Neumark, V. (2013). Branch campuses: The lay of the land. *The Guardian*. Retrieved from www.theguardian.com/higher-education-network/2013/jan/16/branch-campuses-hong-kong-asia.

Nickerson, C. (2013). English for specific purposes and English as a lingua franca. In B. Paltridge & S. Starfield (Eds.), *The handbook of English for specific purposes* (pp. 445–460). Walden, MA: Wiley Blackwell.

Nickerson, C., & Planken, B. (2016). *Introducing business English*. Abingdon, UK: Routledge.

OECD. (2014). *Education at a glance 2014: OECD indicators*. OECD Publishing. Retrieved from http://dx.doi.org/10.1787/eag-2014-en.

Oguntoyinbo, L. (2015). *American colleges expanding campuses to Africa: Diverse issues in higher education*. Retrieved from http://diverseeducation.com/article/69164/.

Orr, T. (Ed.). (2002). *English for specific purposes*. Alexandria, VA: TESOL.

Paltridge, B. (1992). EAP placement testing: An integrated approach. *English for Specific Purposes, 11*(3), 243–268.

Paltridge, B. (2009). Afterword: Where have we come from and where are we now? In D. Belcher (Ed.), *English for specific purposes in theory and practice* (pp. 289–296). Ann Arbor, MI: University of Michigan Press.

Paltridge, B. (2013). Genre and English for specific purposes. In B. Paltridge & S. Starfield (Eds.), *The handbook of English for specific purposes* (pp. 347–366). Malden, MA: Wiley-Blackwell.

Pavlov, I. P. (1897). *Lectures on the work of the principal digestive glands*. St. Petersburg: Kushnereff.

Peachey, N. (2004). *Content-based instruction*. Retrieved from www.teachingenglish.org.uk/article/content-based-instruction.

Pecorari, D. (2010). *Academic writing and plagiarism: A linguistic analysis*. London, UK: Continuum.

Pennycook, A. (1997). Vulgar pragmatism, critical pragmatism, and EAP. *English for Specific Purposes, 16*(4), 253–269.

Pienemann, M., & Kessler, J. U. (2012). Processability theory. In S. M. Gass & A. Mackey (Eds.), *The Routledge handbook of second language acquisition* (pp. 228–247). Abingdon, UK: Routledge.

Planken, B., & Nickerson, C. (2008). Business English and the Bologna declaration in the Netherlands. In I. Fortanet-Gómez & C. Räisänen (Eds.), *ESP in European higher education: Integrating language and content* (pp. 165–179). Amsterdam: John Benjamins Publishing.

Potts, A., & Baker, P. (2012). Does semantic tagging identify cultural change in British and American English? *International Journal of Corpus Linguistics*, *17*(3), 295–324.

Prabhu, N. S. (1987). *Second language pedagogy*. Oxford: Oxford University Press.

Read, J. (1990). Providing relevant content in an EAP writing test. *English for Specific Purposes*, *9*(2), 109–121.

Richards, J. C. (2001). *Curriculum development in language teaching*. Cambridge, UK: Cambridge University Press.

Richards, J. C., & Rodgers, T. S. (2014). *Approaches and methods in language teaching*, 3rd ed. Cambridge, UK: Cambridge University Press.

Römer, U. (2010). Using general and specialized corpora in English language teaching: Past, present and future. In M. C. Campoy-Cubillo, B. Belles-Fortuño & M. L. Gea-Valor (Eds.), *Corpus-based approaches to English language teaching* (pp. 18–35). London: Continuum.

Ruiz-Garrido, M. F., & Palmer-Silveira, J. C. (2008). Content learning in business communication. In I. Fortanet-Gómez & C. Räisänen (Eds.), *ESP in European higher education: Integrating language and content* (pp. 147–164). Amsterdam: John Benjamins Publishing.

Serafini, E. J., Lake, J. B., & Long, M. H. (2015). Needs analysis for specialized learner populations: Essential methodological improvements. *English for Specific Purposes*, *40*, 11–26.

Shoshany, B. (2014). *What is the working language at CERN?* Retrieved from www.quora.com/What-is-the-working-language-at-CERN.

Skinner, B. F. (1957). The science of learning and the art of teaching. *Harvard Educational Review*, *24*(2), 86–97.

Spack, R. (1988). Initiating ESL students into the academic discourse community: How far should we go? *TESOL Quarterly*, *22*(1), 29–51.

Spence, P., & Liu, G. Z. (2013). Engineering English and the high-tech industry: A case study of an English needs analysis of process integration engineers at a semiconductor manufacturing company in Taiwan. *English for Specific Purposes*, *32*(2), 97–109.

Staples, S. (2015). Examining the linguistic needs of internationally educated nurses: A corpus-based study of lexico-grammatical features in nurse – Patient interactions. *English for Specific Purposes*, *37*, 122–136.

Stapleton, P., & Helms-Park, R. (2006). Evaluating Web sources in an EAP course: Introducing a multi-trait instrument for feedback and assessment. *English for Specific Purposes*, *25*(4), 438–455.

Starfield, S. (2013a). Critical perspectives on ESP. In B. Paltridge & S. Starfield (Eds.), *The handbook of English for specific purposes* (pp. 461–479). Walden, MA: Wiley Blackwell.

Starfield, S. (2013b). Historical development of language for specific purposes. In C. A. Chapelle (Ed.), *The encyclopedia of applied linguistics* (10 Volume Set, Original, pp. 1–6). Hoboken, NJ: Blackwell Publishing.

Statista. (2017). *The most spoken languages worldwide (speakers and native speakers in millions)*. Retrieved from www.statista.com/statistics/266808/the-most-spoken-languages-worldwide/t.

Stevens, V. (1991). Classroom concordancing: Vocabulary materials derived from relevant, authentic text. *English for Specific Purposes*, *10*(1), 35–46.

Stoller, F. L. (1994). The diffusion of innovations in intensive ESL programs. *Applied Linguistics*, *15*(3), 300–327.

Strevens, P. (1988). ESP after twenty years: A re-appraisal. *ESP: State of the Art*, 1–13.

Strutt, P. (2015). *English for international tourism*. Harlow, UK: Pearson Education Limited.

Sutton, A., & Taylor, D. (2011). Confusion about collusion: Working together and academic integrity. *Assessment & Evaluation in Higher Education*, *36*(7), 831–841.

Swales, J. M. (1985). *Episodes in ESP*. Oxford, UK: Pergamon Press.

Swales, J. M. (1990). *Genre analysis: English in academic research settings*. Cambridge, UK: Cambridge University Press.

Swales, J. M. (1995). The role of the textbook in EAP writing research. *English for Specific Purposes*, *14*(1), 3–18.

Thorndike, E. L. (1898). Animal intelligence: An experimental study of the associative processes in animals. *The Psychological Review: Monograph Supplements*, 2(4). Retrieved from https://archive.org/details/animalintelligen00thoruoft.

Tse, B., Harwin, W., Barrow, A., Quinn, B., & Cox, M. (2010). Design and development of a haptic dental training system-hapTEL. In *International Conference on Human Haptic Sensing and Touch Enabled Computer Applications* (pp. 101–108). Berlin and Heidelberg: Springer.

Tsou, W., & Chen, F. (2014). ESP program evaluation framework: Description and application to a Taiwanese university ESP program. *English for Specific Purposes*, *33*, 39–53.

Tuschman, R. (2012). English-only policies in the workplace: Are they legal? Are they smart? *Forbes*. Retrieved from www.forbes.com/sites/richardtuschman/2012/11/15/english-only-policies-in-the-workplace-are-they-legal-are-they-smart/#4785df826876.

U.S. Department of Transportation. (2011). *Section 8: Approach clearance procedures*. Retrieved from http://tfmlearning.faa.gov/Publications/ATpubs/ATC/atc0408.html.

Watson, J. B. (1913). Psychology as the behaviorist views it. *Psychological Review*, *20*(2), 158.

Weaver, C. (2016). The TOEIC IP Test as a placement test: Its potential formative value. *JALT Journal*, *38*(1), 5–25.

Weijen, D. (2012). The language of (future) scientific communication. *Research Trends*, *31*(12). Retrieved from www.researchtrends.com/issue-31-november-2012/the-language-of-future-scientific-communication/.

West, R. (1997). Needs analysis: State of the art. In R. Howard & G. Brown (Eds.), *Teacher education for LSP* (pp. 68–79). Clevedon, UK: Multilingual Matters.

Wilkinson, R. (2008). Locating the ESP space in problem-based learning. In I. Fortanet-Gómez & C. Räisänen (Eds.), *ESP in European higher education: Integrating language and content* (pp. 55–73). Chicago: John Benjamins Publishing.

Willis, J. (1996). A flexible framework for task-based learning. In J. Willis & D. Willis, (Eds.), *Challenge and change in language teaching* (pp. 52–62). Macmillan Education Australia. Retrieved from www.academia.edu/download/50948055/PDF_A_flexible_framework_for_Task-based_Learning__Jane_Willis.pdf.

Wilson, K. M. (1989). Enhancing the interpretation of a norm-referenced second-language test through criterion-referencing: A research assessment of experience in the TOEIC testing context. *ETS Research Report Series*, *1989*(2). Retrieved from www.ets.org/research/policy_research_reports/publications/report/1989/hwwb.

Woodrow, L. (2018). *Introducing course design in English for specific purposes*. Abingdon, UK: Routledge.

Wozniak, S. (2010). Language needs analysis from a perspective of international professional mobility: The case of French mountain guides. *English for Specific Purposes*, *29*(4), 243–252.

Wu, H., & Badger, R. G. (2009). In a strange and uncharted land: ESP teachers' strategies for dealing with unpredicted problems in subject knowledge during class. *English for Specific Purposes*, *28*(1), 19–32.

Yeo, S. (2007). First-year university science and engineering students' understanding of plagiarism. *High Education Research & Development*, *26*(2), 199–216.

Yogman, J., & Kaylani, C. T. (1996). ESP program design for mixed level students. *English for Specific Purposes*, *15*(4), 311–324.

Zakrzewski, C. (2016). Virtual reality takes on the videoconference. *The Wall Street Journal*. Retrieved from www.wsj.com/articles/virtual-reality-takes-on-the-videoconference-1474250761.

Index